CUBAN
Ballet

CUBAN
Ballet

Octavio Roca

Forewords by
Alicia Alonso &
Mikhail Baryshnikov

GIBBS SMITH
TO ENRICH AND INSPIRE HUMANKIND

First Edition
14 13 12 11 10   5 4 3 2 1

Text © 2010 Octavio Roca
Photograph copyrights noted throughout

Published by
Gibbs Smith
P.O. Box 667
Layton, Utah 84041

1.800.835.4993 orders
www.gibbs-smith.com

Interior design by Kurt Wahlner
Printed and bound in China
Gibbs Smith books are printed on either recycled, 100% post-consumer waste,
FSC-certified papers or on paper produced from a 100% certified sustainable
forest/controlled wood source.

Library of Congress Cataloging-in-Publication Data

Roca, Octavio, 1949-
  Cuban ballet / Octavio Roca; forewords by Alicia Alonso & Mikhail
Baryshnikov. — 1st ed.
     p. cm.
  Includes bibliographical references.
  ISBN-13: 978-1-4236-0758-8
  ISBN-10: 1-4236-0758-9
  1. Ballet—Cuba—History. 2. Ballet Nacional de Cuba—History. 3. Ballet
dancers—Cuba. 4. Alonso, Alicia, 1921- I. Title.
  GV1632.C9R64 2010
  792.8097291—dc22
                    2010012658

PREVIOUS SPREAD: Lorena Feijóo and Joan Boada
in *Don Quixote*. Courtesy of R. J. Muna.

OPPOSITE: Lorena Feijóo preparing to go on stage.
Courtesy of David Martínez.

For Luis Palomares

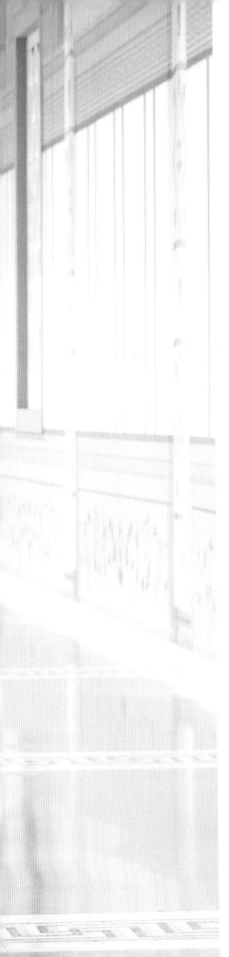

Contents

Lorena and Lorna Feijóo having fun at a photo shoot.
Courtesy of Robb Aaron Gordon.

Foreword

I am often asked what makes our ballet Cuban, but definitions and descriptions are not easy. When it comes to the Cuban School of Ballet, the task before me is always both challenging and complex, for here is movement as a pure form of expression, and it is difficult to put into words what is in practice a phenomenon expressed precisely in the movements, gestures, dynamics, shadings, and accents of dance itself. We are of course speaking of a school in the

Alicia Alonso. Courtesy of the Ballet Nacional de Cuba, photo by Frank Alvarez.

sense of a particular way of dancing, of expressing ourselves, and using classical technique in a particular way. We are also speaking of style, of aesthetics, of taste, and of other factors that over several generations have emerged as belonging to a particular place. We should be clear that there are not many such schools. There are countries that have good dancers, many ballet companies, and fine centers for the artistic formation of dancers, yet they do not have a recognizable school. Today we can admire the presence of a few great national schools, and we also cannot fail to notice some whose full splendor lies in the past but have

devolved or declined as a result of historical circumstances. There once was a Russian School, which later developed into the Soviet School—which is not the same—that incorporated over half a century of new technical, cultural, and stylistic elements. There is the Danish School, usually identified with August Bournonville, the great ballet master and choreographer who systematized it and gave it a distinctive physiognomy. There are the French and English schools, this last of more recent origins. There is some discussion of the existence of an American school, difficult to delineate because the great dance figures in the United States—its dancers, ballet masters, and choreographers—themselves come from various schools, but doubtless there is an American school. And there is a Cuban School of Ballet, recognized by critics over several decades, but also the youngest among schools in the world today.

A ballet school has its foundation, first of all, in a country's national culture and in the talent unique to a people to express itself in dance. Classical technique is layered on this foundation. Academic ballet is, frankly, the same all over the world. When that classical technique is assumed in a country with its own distinctive culture, and when within that technique are assimilated a people's national culture, the labors of its ballet masters and its dancers, that technique begins acquiring unique shadings. This is not to say that the principles of a dancer's academic training are changed or that historical styles and traditional choreographies are adulterated. It means rather that these dancers begin dancing everything they dance with a different accent.

There is no clear recipe for this, no written set of rules. Such a definition would be impossible for any of the schools of ballet. Common qualities emerge collectively, however, and they are unmistakable. There are, of course, differences in the methodologies of ballet training, in the way to use steps, in the order of exercises, the combinations, and the dynamics. And each individual dancer is herself a world of peculiarities. But the matter is more complex than that. Today, for example, the Royal Ballet, Covent Garden is the maximum expression of the English School of Ballet. But to analyze that school it is not enough to notice whether or not British dancers execute steps one way or another, but also to consider their own way of interpreting their repertory, mainly the classics.

To speak of the Cuban School of Ballet, we first take note of its roots. I can do this only briefly here, but I will mention that Cuba's theatrical dance tradition goes back to the eighteenth century, with a string of Spanish and other European companies that regularly visited the country and helped create a dance public. In the nineteenth century we had the privilege of hosting several seasons with the great Austrian Romantic ballerina Fanny Elsser, and in the twentieth Havana saw the mythical Anna Pavlova. Havana, due to its geographical location, was a logical stop for the many artists and companies touring the New World in the nineteenth and early twentieth centuries, and this helped immensely in creating an awareness and a love of dance in Cuba.

Professional Cuban ballet emerged decisively in 1931 with the creation of the Escuela de Ballet de Pro-Arte Musical de La Habana, directed by the Russian ballet master Nikolai Yavorsky, my first teacher. It was with Yavorsky that those of us responsible for spearheading ballet in Cuba studied. We soon left to study in the United States, where, it must be said, there was no single homogeneous school but rather

there were several brilliant ballet masters teaching in their own distinctive ways. I did not dance with anything like an "Alonso style" at the time, but I did choose what I thought served my dancing best from the many great teachers and choreographers with whom I worked. As my career grew, I did not limit myself to having an international presence. Together with Fernando Alonso, then my husband, and with my brother-in-law, Alberto Alonso, we founded the Ballet Alicia Alonso in 1948. This

was the company that became the Ballet Nacional de Cuba. It was in the 1940s that the three of us began thinking seriously about the matter of teaching, to analyze the details of the methodology of ballet class. At first we established a simple system taken from many schools but mainly from our own experience in the School of American Ballet. It was from this base that we set off on our own, and Fernando and I helped Alberto Alonso in developing a pedagogical system, when he was appointed to run the Escuela de Pro-Arte Musical.

In my long career I have worked directly with great choreographers such as Fokine, Balanchine,

Escuela Nacional de Ballet students between classes, Havana. Courtesy of Illume productions/Candela, photo by Christina Thompson.

Nijinska, Massine, Tudor, Loring, Agnes de Mille, Robbins, and others. They and others helped and enriched the Ballet Nacional de Cuba. But they helped only as tempered by our own traditions, our roots, and our idiosyncrasies.

When I danced in the Soviet Union in 1957 and 1958, I returned to Havana to share my experiences from Moscow, Leningrad, and Riga with our dancers and ballet masters. But we always remained vigilant, wary of mimetism; we used our criteria to determine what worked and what did not in our own dancers' bodies, what helped us best aim for our own concept of beauty, of elegance, and of grace. We noticed there were certain accents that appeared more frequently on our dancers, in Cuban or other Hispanic American dancers, certain virtues, a certain facility. We integrated these, all along studying how to teach them. We also noted with pleasure our own absence of racial prejudice, our assurance in that matter. We came to the opinion that there are no unsalvageable ethnic

characteristics in ballet. You can feel this conviction today in our Ballet Nacional de Cuba. To take one example, in Act Two of our *Giselle* one can see girls of many different ethnic types, yet this is the romantic ballet that has been singled out more than once by critics for the perfection of its corps, for its exactitude, its stylistic homogeneity, and for the atmosphere it creates. Other companies have very strict selection procedures for these roles, mistakenly believing that ethnic homogeneity is necessary for artistic homogeneity. I remember one critic, who had not seen the Ballet Nacional de Cuba in performance, first seeing us in class and becoming alarmed at seeing all the colors and sizes present in the studio. He asked me, "How can they dance *Giselle*?" Then he saw our company's *Giselle*, and he admitted he had never seen a more homogeneous corps de ballet, which means that when a dancer is well prepared, what matters is the interpretation, not other factors that retain mythical authority in some companies. That, too, has

been an element of the Cuban School of Ballet,
its integration of all races.

Cubans are a dancing people. Dance matters to us, and it matters deeply. As for further
describing the Cuban School of Ballet in words
rather than dance, I leave that to the critics. One
of them, the British critic Arnold Haskell, was the
first to identify the Cuban School of Ballet and
describe some of its characteristics. My old friend,
the American critic Walter Terry, also wrote about
it memorably. Now comes Octavio Roca, whom
I have known for decades and who has known
us his whole life, and he has seen our dancers
at home and abroad as well as on tour and with
other companies. As a guest of the International
Ballet Festival in Havana, Octavio Roca was able
to observe the Cuban dance movement in its own
environment and to witness the Cuban School of
Ballet in all its richness. For me, his critical writing
on dance carries a unique sensitivity to an art he
clearly loves. The rest I leave to the future.

Foreword

I was twelve years old when I first saw them. It was 1960, right after the Cuban Revolution, when Alicia Alonso brought her entire company to Riga, Latvia, for the first time. What stood out to me then were *Apollo* and *Coppélia*. I'll never forget; the Muses were Loipa Araújo, Josefina Méndez and Mirta Plá, with Rodolfo Rodríguez as Apollo. That was the first Balanchine ballet I had ever seen and the Cubans danced the original version complete with the prologue. I thought I was going to pass out from excitement. Those girls! All three were absolutely phenomenal; beautiful long legs, sumptuous lines, and exotic looks. It was at that tender age that I confirmed my suspicions that I liked girls.

As for *Coppélia*, Alicia Alonso's delicious Swanilda, along with, of course, the great José Pares as Dr. Coppélius, made the ballet come alive for me. Alicia was in great shape—

Alicia Alonso, in her version of *Coppélia*, as the mischievous Swanilda who "had everybody in stitches," when the twelve-year-old Baryshnikov first saw her in 1960. Courtesy of the Alicia Alonso Collection.

even with all the problems with her vision—and very funny. I know she is known to the world as a great romantic tragedienne, but I have to tell you, in my view, she was a wonderful comedienne. She had everybody in stitches. When she played the doll she was exactly like a doll and when she came alive, she was luminous and girlish. We all fell in love with her. These are vivid childhood memories for me.

Later on in my own career, I came to know some Cuban dancers personally and continued to be impressed with them professionally. Loipa Araújo and Mirta Plá became my close friends.

And Lázaro Carreño, my schoolmate in Russia, went on to be an important teacher in Cuba. His nephew, José Manuel Carreño, is one of the most elegant dancers on the stage today. I see how the American Ballet Theatre looks to him for solid technique and a sort of quiet artistry. He is a great partner and a wonderful example for young dancers.

Last year, I spent some time in Havana attending a gathering of regional ballet schools. For several days I got to see the same group of young men in class—they were twelve to fourteen years old. Their training was impressive to say the least, but this didn't surprise me. It really is true that Cubans today are producing the most interesting and best technically equipped male dancers—in my opinion, surpassing the French and Russians.

I think this is because Cuban dancers embody an interesting fusion of the Western and Russian schools. Alicia and Fernando Alonso both returned to Cuba from the U.S. early in their careers so there was a fresh American influence (remember Alicia was Balanchine's original *Theme and Variations* ballerina). But the company also benefited from the Russian training of dancers like Azari Plisetsky who, along with Fernando, shaped the early Cuban school. It's taken a few decades, but this different way of training has led to extraordinary results. It's impossible not to notice when a Cuban dancer walks into the studio.

What also makes the Cuban dancers stand out, I think, is their ethics. They have a respect for ballet from an early age. It's been said before that no one is born a dancer; you have to want it more than anything. These Cubans want it and feel privileged to be a part of it. They give themselves completely.

I know that Octavio Roca's love of Cuba is as profound as his knowledge of ballet, and I know this book is from his heart.

by Mikhail Baryshnikov

Loipa Araújo, Alicia Alonso, Mirta Plá, and Josefina Méndez in Alonso's
exquisite *Pas de Quatre*. Courtesy of Museo National de la Danza.

Acknowledgments

The gestation of this book has been long, and my debts are many. My heartfelt thanks go to Danny Bellas, a Cuban patriot living in Los Angeles, without whose love and enthusiasm for Cuban ballet and culture this book would never have happened.

For an insider's view I have been fortunate to count above all on Alicia Alonso, who first suggested I write this and gently has insisted so over the years; and also on her husband, the eminent Cuban philosopher and critic Pedro Simón, founder and director of the journal *Cuba en el ballet* and of the Museo Nacional de la Danza in Havana. The filmmakers Cynthia Newport and Andy García, in different ways, gave me living examples of translating love of Cuban culture into heartfelt artistic statements. Some artists and friends who are not part of this story must be thanked here for teaching me much about artistic integrity and resilience in the face of difficult odds; Renata Scotto, Julien Green, Roland Petit, and especially Mstislav Rostropovich. To have known these people as well as Alicia Alonso, to have seen them at work, and to have shared time with them is to me a privilege and a gift of the mysteries of art for which I am more grateful than I can express.

Thanks in part to Alicia Alonso's generous introductions, many of the key players in this story shared their experiences with me over the years, including Antony Tudor, Jerome Robbins, Igor Yousekevitch, Michael Maule, Lucia Chase, Sir Anton Dolin, Agnes de Mille, Antonio Gades, Brian Macdonald, Glen Tetley, Maurice Béjart, Galina Ulanova, Maya Plisetskaya, Azari Plisetsky, Vladimir Vasiliev and Ekaterina Maximova, Yuri Grigorovich; the Cuban choreographers Alberto

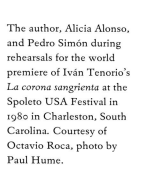

The author, Alicia Alonso, and Pedro Simón during rehearsals for the world premiere of Iván Tenorio's *La corona sangrienta* at the Spoleto USA Festival in 1980 in Charleston, South Carolina. Courtesy of Octavio Roca, photo by Paul Hume.

Méndez, Ivan Tenorio, and, working in Marseilles, the poet and choreographer Pedro Consuegra. Guillermo Cabrera Infante and Reinaldo Arenas each shared with me incisive observations of Alonso and her troupe. Among my fellow critics are two late friends I especially wish to remember. Walter Terry took me under his wing and frankly helped me negotiate the political and emotional thickets of my return to Cuba as an American critic for the first time; a mutual friend in Havana once joked at the height of the Cold War that he never could figure out whether Walter worked for the CIA or the KGB, but all I know is that his love of Cuban ballet was the real thing. Paul Hume generously allowed this cub critic a shared byline as we covered the Spoleto Festival together for *The Washington Post* when I was still in graduate school and, thanks to him, I published both my first ballet review and my first interview with Alicia Alonso in the *Post*. The first time I, as an adult, got to know Alicia Alonso was backstage at the first Kennedy Center Honors in 1978, and the John F. Kennedy Center for the Performing Arts was my hometown theatre for so long that to thank the officials and staff there is a bit like thanking my family. But I have to thank one friend from that family, Tiki Davies, with particular love and gratitude.

In Miami, the second largest Cuban city after Havana, Pedro Pablo Peña and Magaly Suárez have been both frank and sensitive about their difficult labors keeping Cuban culture alive in exile. In Cuba, both Fernando Alonso and Alberto Alonso were extremely generous in the early stages of my research, as were Laura Alonso, Lázaro Carreño, Orlando Salgado, Francisco Salgado, Loipa Araújo, Josefina Méndez and her son Victor Gilí, Angela Grau, Francisco Rey Alfonso, and most of all Miguel Cabrera, the Ballet Nacional de Cuba's official historian and one of the world's foremost authorities on dance in the Americas. I also owe

The author and Galina Ulanova at the Havana Libre, *neé* Hilton, Havana, 1980, before heading off to Varadero for the day. Courtesy of Octavio Roca, photo by Walter Terry.

thanks over the years to the American Ballet Theatre's Mikhail Baryshnikov and Kevin McKenzie, Boston Ballet's Mikko Nissinen, San Francisco Ballet's Helgi Tomasson, Ballet San Jose's Dennis Nahat, Houston Ballet's Ben Stevenson, Cincinnati Ballet's Victoria Morgan, the Royal Ballet's Antony Dowell, and the English National Ballet's Peter Schaufuss and Ivan Nagy.

My greatest debt of all is considerable, and my deepest love and thanks go to Luis Palomares, my partner for more than three decades, the friend with whom I rehearsed every line and every move of this book, and the lover without whom *Cuban Ballet* could not have been written. This book is for him.

Introduction

In dance, as in life, we fall in love all of a sudden and then, if we are fortunate, we can spend a lifetime working out the details. Ballet, much like deep enduring love, is nourished by memory at least as much as by its living, breathing everyday celebration. The first time we see *Giselle*, *Theme and Variations*, *Esplanade*, *Tarde en la siesta*, or *Le Parc*, we form timeless memories that inform the depth and meaning of subsequent experiences of these ballets. I mention this because this book is both a work of love and a work of memory—an exile's memory as much as that of a critic. My own personal memories are not part of this story, but they are part of the impulse behind the way I will tell it, and a few of them want disclosing if only by way of prelude.

I was born in Havana, where my mother María Luisa Rivero was a dancer with Ballet de Pro-Arte Musical, the precursor of today's Ballet Nacional de Cuba. *Giselle* with Alicia Alonso and Igor Yousekevitch was the first ballet I ever saw, and I was five years old.

Far from home and a bit of a lifetime later, I first interviewed Alicia Alonso for *The Washington Post* while I was still a doctoral candidate in philosophy at Georgetown University in 1980. I have followed the Cuban ballet adventure critically and passionately ever since.[1] I am fortunate that my dance memories are many. Two memories in particular, each of more recent vintage, in fact gave shape to this book. They were made by two beautiful sisters, both Cuban ballerinas to the core, dancing for two very different companies, the Ballet Nacional de Cuba and San Francisco Ballet.

I was lucky to witness the immensely moving triumph of Lorna Feijóo's 1999 American debut

Cuban Memories

as Giselle with the Ballet Nacional de Cuba, describing her in the *San Francisco Chronicle* as "an airy creature with monumental balances and a fluttery, breezy line, a terrifying vision of innocence in peril." Lorna Feijóo, who unbeknownst to me would soon herself defect and become an exile along with her brilliant husband Nelson Madrigal, embodied in Alonso's exquisite production everything a critic could hope for in bringing a great role to life, but also everything an exile could pray for in nourishing a cultural identity far from home.[2] Within months, by coincidence, I had the privilege of covering her sister Lorena Feijóo's first *Giselle* in Helgi Tomasson's new San Francisco Ballet production. Her performance, with memories of her sister's as well as of so many Cuban Giselles before her, was ineffably uplifting, personally life-affirming in ways I thought were as irretrievably lost to me as my homeland. The *San Francisco Chronicle* review of that performance read in part as follows:

> There are moments in the Theatre, and they are really very rare, that come as sudden and tender reminders of what art is all about: the best in all of us, the hopes and the dreams, the brutal limitations of time on human life and the majestic transcendence of the human spirit. Saturday afternoon brought such an unforgettable moment to the War Memorial Opera House. Lorena Feijóo danced her first Giselle, and it was clear that her whole life had been leading up to this role.
>
> Her line was exquisite, womanly in Act One and miraculously ethereal in Act Two. Like Alicia Alonso before her—and I do not make this comparison lightly—Feijóo understood the wildly different styles needed for the two acts, and she made sense of both in one heartbreaking, seamless characterization. Feijóo instinctively traced romantic outlines with her body, subtly presenting the torso slightly

OPPOSITE: Alicia Alonso in Act One of *Giselle*. Courtesy of the Ballet Nacional de Cuba.

ABOVE: Alicia Alonso in *La Fille mal gardée*. Courtesy of the Alicia Alonso Collection.

forward and conveying an impression of vulnerability . . . Her footwork was fluid, from her whispered batterie to her perfectly placed balances. Her upper body was eloquent and womanly, possessed of unassuming sensuality. Her acting was rhapsodic, inseparable from her dancing and drenched in detail.

The sweet way Feijóo played with her skirt in the allegros brought to mind Carla Fracci's legendary Giselle, except in the Italian ballerina's case the playfulness often disguised blurred articulation. The Cuban Feijóo has no such limitations. Technically, Feijóo was fearless.[3]

As I write this a few years later, Lorena Feijóo and Lorna Feijóo, ballerinas no longer with Ballet Nacional de Cuba but instead coast-to-coast in the United States, are epitomes of a curious, thrilling cultural spectacle. This much is undeniable: at its most sublime, dance can say things that cannot be said any other way, and ballet certainly is a universal language. It's just that lately that language has a strong Cuban accent.

The phenomenon embodied by the Feijóo sisters—from their respective home bases far from Havana in San Francisco and Boston as well as on their world tours alongside dancers from the Cuban diaspora—is changing the face of ballet in the twenty-first century. The sisters are a sign of the times. After nearly half a century of defections from Alicia Alonso's Ballet Nacional de Cuba, including that of twenty dancers in a new wave

LEFT: Lorna Feijóo and Nelson Madrigal dancing on the *azotea* of the García Lorca in Old Havana with the Cuban Capitol as background. Courtesy of David R. Garten.

OPPOSITE: Lorena and Lorna Feijóo with Grover, perhaps their hairiest partner, in an episode of *Sesame Street*. Courtesy of Sesame Street.

Havana's famed Malecón, with El Vedado and Miramar in the distance. Courtesy of Illume productions/Candela, photo by Christina Thompson.

in 2003 that represented a loss of nearly one-fifth of the full company, Cuban dancers and teachers are exerting a powerful influence on American and world dance that brings to mind the profound impact Russian dancers brought to the West as their defections mounted in the dusk of the Soviet empire. These dancers are creating for the world the beauty they too often cannot make in their homeland.

The spectacle has not gone unnoticed; the *San Francisco Chronicle* in 2002 took note of this "powerful new wave of dancers,"[4] while in 2004, *Dance Magazine* announced that "Latin is the new Russian."[5] In 2006, *Time* magazine summarized the development in an article focusing on the Feijóo phenomenon: "A generation ago, during the Soviet era, defectors like Baryshnikov, Rudolf Nureyev and Natalia Makarova were galvanizing the dance world. Russian dancers and this historic tradition they sprang from were the gold standard in international ballet. Today, however, the buzz is all about Latins . . . especially Cubans."[6] No less an authority than Mikhail Baryshnikov told *The New York Times* in 2006, "When you see a Cuban dancer, he moves like nobody else, but in such a simple, noble manner."[7]

The Feijóo sisters, an unprecedented team in the history of ballet, are just the tip of the iceberg. The growing diaspora of Cuban defectors everywhere is giving the tropical island a cultural importance that is miraculously disproportionate to its size. The entire Cuban population of eleven million could fit comfortably in greater Moscow, London, or New York. In addition to Lorena Feijóo and Lorna Feijóo, principal dancers from Cuba today star in the American Ballet Theatre, San Francisco Ballet, Boston Ballet, and Miami City Ballet as well as the Cuban Classical Ballet of Miami, Houston Ballet, London's Royal Ballet, Vienna State Opera Ballet, Buenos Aires' Ballet del Teatro Colón, and

Students practicing in the
García Lorca rehearsal
studios in Old Havana.
Courtesy of Illume produc-
tions/Candela, photo by
Deborah Harse.

INTRODUCTION

many other major troupes. Cuban ballet teachers, all formed in the rigorous pedagogical tradition of Alicia and Fernando Alonso, head faculties from the Royal Danish Ballet to La Scala, from Madrid to Mexico City, from Buenos Aires to Paris. The Paris Opera Ballet School, in 2003, sent a team of observers to Havana to study the teaching methods of Alicia Alonso's National School of Ballet.

There is of course not a little irony in that the Cuban School of Ballet, essentially invented and refined by one of Fidel Castro's strongest cultural supporters, is now being spread all over the world by Cuban artists who are fleeing Castro's regime. Alicia Alonso, while allowing that the recent defections "hurt us," is nevertheless adamant that her company and its one hundred and ten dancers will do just fine without them. "Besides," she told me in 2004, "this is what we have always wanted to do—to share our art, to share our Cuban ballet."[8] In truth, she has been doing just that since her own debut in 1931.

The influence is everywhere. Even as it seems that Cuba increasingly is unable to keep its own best dancers, and despite what seems to be a disproportionate dispersal of its artistic resources, each tour of Alicia Alonso's troupe guarantees a fresh platoon of defections and a stream of revelations of tomorrow's brightest dancing talents. The dancing of Lorena and Lorna Feijóo, each sister so different from the other and yet each so unmistakably Cuban, complements Alonso's living message and carries Cuban ballet to stages everywhere.

Many artists have been driven by cruel limitations, but Alicia Alonso's case is unique. In a field that depends so much on the mirror, on the body's self-image, and on visual presentation of the dancer's own body at the heart of artistic creation, here is a woman who was told at the outset of her career that she would soon be blind and she would not dance again. This was not late in life, either—Henri Matisse turned failing eyesight into a virtue in the glittering last phase of his career as

a visual artist; Beethoven lost his hearing by the time he composed his staggering thirty-second sonata; Nureyev lost control of his beautiful body near the end of his life on stage; Jean-Paul Sartre went blind and, though his self-image suffered tremendously, he nevertheless continued to write his sprawling masterpiece on Flaubert until his deathbed. But Alicia Alonso first suffered a detached retina in 1940, before her glorious prime. As she lay in bed blindfolded and with her head immobilized, recovering from the first of a lifelong series of eye surgeries, she ran through the role of Giselle in her imagination, moving her fingers in her lap to rehearse steps as well as feelings in the dark. She resolved to make real what her imagination dictated, to refuse to accept the material conditions of her existence. Sartre is right that freedom is what you do with what has been done to you, that consciousness and choice are one and the same thing.[9] Alicia Alonso was free, material conditions be damned, and blind or not she would become one of the greatest ballerinas in history.

Jorge Esquivel, Alicia Alonso's astounding partner in the Indian summer of her career—and now, in exile, principal character dancer of San Francisco Ballet and one of the company's most trusted coaches—touchingly confesses, "We will always be Cuban, and we will always miss our families, our country. But it is a new millennium," he continues, summing up the Cuban dancers' situation with hard-earned clarity. "We can no longer say that I am from this little piece of land and you are from the other one. Our real home is the world."[10]

Alicia Alonso's lessons do not stop with Alicia Alonso. Of course her example continues to represent a blueprint for Cuban greatness in dance—this is what a Cuban dancer looks like, this is what the New World can give back to the Old. But beyond Cuba, in fact especially in the Cuban diaspora, what these Cuban dancers have done and continue to do is one of the most entertaining

OPPOSITE: Alicia Alonso in Act Two of *Giselle* with her finest partner since Yousekevitch, Jorge Esquivel. Courtesy of the Ballet Nacional de Cuba, photo by Frank Alvarez.

and exhilarating spectacles of dance in our time. What has been done to them, to all of us exiles, is cruel. That exile is for so much of the world a natural condition is little consolation. But the consolation is there, in our imaginations. Reinaldo Arenas once told me, far from the tropics and sitting in his cramped Hells' Kitchen walk-up in New York, that they had taken away his beloved Caribbean sea but now he had the freedom to imagine it, to create it anew. He did just that, and his impossibly beautiful oeuvre stands as a monument of hope and possibility in Latin American arts.

That hope is alive in a generation of Cuban dancers in exile. There is, of course, a danger of perennial mourning for the path not taken—a danger to which both those who stayed and those who left may be vulnerable. What would have happened had these dancers not had to leave their country? What an even greater company the Ballet Nacional de Cuba might have been without Cuba's long nightmare. But with Jose Martí we say, *"No vamos a preguntar, sino a responder,"* "Let us not ask, but answer." What a gift to the world it has been that these dancers enrich and will continue to enrich one company after another around the world. That is our answer. There is vital momentum to their living history; there is hope. That, too, is our answer. They are exiles, artists who freely take up the sacred responsibility of an art that becomes universal precisely because it remains so defiantly Cuban. It is a responsibility taken up not so much by followers of the Cuban School of Ballet as by heroes and heroines in their own right, creating new worlds of dance even as they struggle to keep their own identities as Cuban artists. There is a sacrament of kindness bestowed in all its holiness each time they step on stage. They dance with a Cuban accent, and their dance is at home in the world.

Lorena Feijóo and Lorna Feijóo, Jorge Esquivel, Osmay Molina, Joan Boada, the ever-growing number of Carreños from Lázaro and Alvaro up to Alihaydée, José Manuel and Joel, Rolando Sarabia and Daniel Sarabia, Xiomara Reyes, Carlos Miguel Guerra, Miguelángel Blanco, Luis Serrano, Isanusi García Rodríguez, Carlos Quenedit, Hayna Gutiérrez, Adiarys Almeida, Gema Díaz, Cervilio Amador, Taras Domitro, and so many more dancing in Havana but soon to arrive on foreign shores as I write this, all of them are improbably at ease while splendidly, heroically creating a Cuban culture in the absence of the free Cuba they deserve. In the process, they are enriching the lands where at first they were strangers. American Ballet Theatre, Boston Ballet, San Francisco Ballet, Joffrey Ballet Chicago, Houston Ballet, Washington Ballet, Cincinnati Ballet, Miami City Ballet, Royal Ballet, Covent Garden and many more companies all are better for it, and different for it. There is beauty in the arduous, unwilling, often unacknowledged transformation of temporary exile into permanent immigration. There certainly is artistic fervor in these lives. This may offer little solace, an unsatisfactory substitute for the land we lost. But what a surprise it can be to find these labors are now part of the culture of new lands we might call our own. Again let us remember Jose Martí's dictum, that *"Hacer es la mejor manera de decir,"* "Doing is the best way of saying." Just as Alicia Alonso once refused to recognize her blindness as a brutal limitation for her art, dancers in the Cuban diaspora refuse to recognize the loss of their homeland. They are Cuban artists and they are free. What they do with what has been done to them is a touching, gripping tale. Theirs is a bittersweet victory, or perhaps just a sign of the inexorable momentum of history. Theirs is above all a true tale of the greatness of the human soul, of the indomitable spirit of dance. This is their story.

Lorena Feijóo in *Don Quixote*. Courtesy of R. J. Muna.

Alicia

We were all happy accidents.

—Fernando Alonso

$\mathcal{A}$ntonio Martínez de Arredondo realized as he prepared to leave the university that if he intended to make a living as a veterinarian he would have to acquire more patients than his shingle attracted in Havana in 1908. Cavalry horses were more common than house pets in those days, so he resolved to join the armed forces of the young republic. He was assigned to Campo Columbia, a military base where for six years he lived and carried out research on the care and breeding of horses.

Cuba had come late to independence, and her army was not thought to be very important. When the Spanish were defeated in 1898, the Cuban Army of Liberation was forbidden by the United States from entering Havana; and the members of the peace conference in Paris did not even have the good manners to invite a Cuban delegation. Cuba's future was discussed between Spain and the United States. When Cuban independence was eventually confirmed on May 20, 1902, the Platt Amendment insured that the United States had the constitutional right to intervene militarily in Cuba, as it had done twice in 1899, whenever it deemed it to be necessary. After two such invasions in 1906, President Tomás de Estradapalma was forced to step down from office under pressure from the American government and see

OPPOSITE: Alicia Martínez at age eleven—Nicolai Yavorsky's pupil. Courtesy of the Ballet Nacional de Cuba.

The architectural *vaivén* of Old Havana—as Spanish Baroque meets the tropics—from the film *Dance Cuba*. Courtesy of Illume productions/Candela, photos by Christina Thompson.

his country run without the benefit of elections by the American Governor Charles F. Magoon, the infamous former governor of the Panama Canal Zone. Most disturbances among the Cuban population were handled swiftly by the United States Army, and the Cuban forces often had little to do but to take care of their horses. By the time of the enlistment of Antonio Martínez de Arredondo in 1908, the foreign armies had just left Havana, and Cuba, in truth, would fare much better than many of her neighbors. The price of sugar rose dramatically, and Cuba remained peaceful and prosperous while the United States invaded Nicaragua in 1912, Mexico in 1914, Haiti in 1915, and Santo Domingo in 1916. The only exception was in 1917, when the crucial sugar crops in Santiago de Cuba were endangered by a peasant rebellion that President Mario G. Menocal was unable to suppress. The United States Army stepped in to take care of the problem, but at least both countries felt compelled to give a reason for the invasion; the Cuban peasants were said to be German

sympathizers, even if most of them had not heard of Germany.

Young Antonio was glad that the Cuban Army was not yet trusted with such internal problems. He was a veterinarian miscast as a soldier; he loved horses and he held a good job while holding the happy belief that he might never be required to do what soldiers are supposed to do. In the spring of 1910, he met Ernestina del Hoyo y Lugo and immediately fell in love. Aggressive and unassuming, not poor, but not much better, Ernestina was a well-educated seamstress with ambition. She radiated an aura of elegance which was afforded by her profession and enhanced by her low, smoky voice. She was a bit stocky but nicely proportioned, with porcelain skin and large dark eyes. She enjoyed reading Dickens and Pérez Galdós, those phenomenal twin lovers of urban humanity; and she loved the city of Havana. The shy young soldier's family had been among the conquerors of the New World, founders of the city of St. Augustine in Florida. Most of those ancestors moved to Cuba in

Alicia's mother, Ernestina del Hoyo y Lugo. Courtesy of the Alicia Alonso Collection.

grows wild in Cuban fields. It was Ernestina's favorite flower and Antonio would bring her mariposas each Saturday when he came from Campo Columbia for his chaperoned visits with the del Hoyo family. Some evenings he would bring them to her room, where they shared long talks through the elaborate iron filigree of her window, he standing on the cobblestones and she pretending to sew. Silent movies and loud musical plays were very popular, and the couple often would stroll under the elms of the Paseo del Prado before letting Ernestina's sister Alicia, who always accompanied them, choose a theatre for the afternoon. Later they would drift through the columns and arcades of Old Havana, down El Prado past San Lázaro towards the ruined city walls and what was even then known as the Parque de los Enamorados, a colonial lovers' lane where the metropolis flirted with the seashore; then to the Malecón where the tropical moonlight always clings to the ocean. They would listen for the cannon, which boomed from the other side of Havana Bay at nine o'clock, as it does to this day, and Antonio would set his pocket watch, which was always a bit slow. The couple shared the sweetness of discovering an old city in a new country, as well as a romantic longing for the finer things of which they only dreamed. The courtship of the seamstress and the soldier was as long as custom dictated but no more, and they were married on January 14, 1914, at the Church of the Holy Angel. Antonio's work required that they live near Campo Columbia. Ernestina would not hear of living on the military base where their housing would have been free, so the couple settled in Reparto Redención, a suburb in Marianao only a few miles from Havana, in a small wooden house on the narrow corner of Pasage Central and 3rd Street. The house still stands today with its neighborhood engulfed by metropolitan Havana and its two million citizens, its address now a more complicated No. 3703, 90th Street, on the corner of 37th in Marianao.

the 1720s, escaping the British and beginning the long ascent to the middle class in a new country. Ernestina's own family were Spanish citizens who had migrated to Cuba from Asturias only one generation before; and they settled in a small house in Old Havana, on a narrow hilly street in view of the flying buttresses of the Church of the Holy Angel.

The national flower had just been chosen: the mariposa, a dainty cousin of the orchid that

It would take the couple ten years to afford a finer home, and Ernestina did the best she could until her return to her beloved Havana. She and Antonio had a carefree and loving marriage. It was cozy in their home, with lace antimacassars over every chair and table and images of saints blessing almost every wall. The gregarious Ernestina hosted *tertulias* several times a week, where friends would gather in a noisy salon of homegrown music, creaking rocking chairs, and flapping silk fans. Her sister Alicia would sing imitations of whatever diva she had seen in the Teatro Payret or the Tacón. Ernestina herself would recite poetry, often her own; and all would talk, eat, and smile into the night. During the day she did her sewing in virtual darkness, since she treasured the Spanish habit of closing the shutters in order to keep out the heat, and it was always hot. Antonio could come home early for lunch and dinner, his work went well, and they were very happy.

Their first child soon arrived, a boy named Antonio. Blanca came two years later, nicknamed Cuca, and quickly became her father's favorite. The boy Elizardo followed. Then their fourth child, a girl, was born on December 21, 1920. She was named Alicia, for her aunt, and Ernestina for her mother. With her baptism, she received additional references to Our Lady of the Caridad del Cobre, Patroness of Cuba, although these names did not appear on the birth certificate registered by Antonio in the city of Marianao the following week.[1] Her godparents were her aunt Alicia and her cousin, the young lawyer Manolo Alonso. This seven-pound little girl with a tuss of black hair, Alicia Ernestina de la Caridad del Cobre Martínez del Hoyo, would become one of the greatest ballerinas of all time.

No sooner had she learned to walk than she danced. Her earliest memories would be of movement and of music, recalling that she "danced before knowing what dancing was." Alicia quickly grew into the most restless of four very active

Alicia's father, Antonio Martínez de Arredondo. Courtesy of the Alicia Alonso Collection.

children, and Ernestina discovered that the way to keep her little girl quiet was to play music, any music, and leave her alone. The trova had invaded Havana from the Cuban countryside, and it was now that Cuban music acquired the rhythm and flavor in which the world has delighted since. The radio had begun in Cuba in 1920, and by 1933 there were thirty-four stations in Havana.[2] Music was everywhere and Alicia loved it. Listening to the strains of the latest danzón by Barbarito Diez, or mouthing a song by Esther Borja or Rita Montaner on the radio, Alicia would sway and swoon around the house, tying loose strands of Ernestina's silks and velvets around her bobbed hair, imagining stories told in motion, and pretending to have long flowing tresses that followed her every step. "*Es una húngara*, a gypsy," Cuca said one evening, as much for her sister's constant dancing as for her deep dark eyes. "Unga," then, would remain her particular nickname for Alicia throughout their lives. There was a definite attraction in the household toward the arts, if not especially toward dance, and the children joined in the nocturnal gatherings, staying up until all hours in fine Cuban fashion, reciting or singing or dancing through exotic fantasy worlds for their friends in Marianao. They also loved the movies, with Alicia and Cuca fascinated first by the piano in the silent films, and later by Hollywood dance extravaganzas or the later tango pictures from Argentina. Music always made them smile.

Antonio rose to the rank of captain, and Ernestina could afford to take in less sewing and take more time to make dresses for her little girls. They nurtured in their home the aspirant's fervor towards the values of higher class, and the children were required to dress for dinner as well as for all family gatherings: Elizardo and Toñiquito had their blue suits for winter and white for summer, all part of their uniform dress for Sunday mass at the Colegio De La Salle; and the girls would change out of the brown plaid jumper dresses of the Escuela de las Hermanas Teresianas and step into Ernestina's frilly creations. Both La Salle and the Teresianas were among the best and most exclusive preparatory schools in Havana, and the financial sacrifice was great by the time

the third and fourth child entered school—again it seemed as if Ernestina would sew all day and all night in order to meet the tuition payments. That Ernestina would one day make the first tutus for her daughter's company and later become one of Cuba's leading ballet costume designers was not even suspected then.

What was suspected was that Alicia was rather unusual. With the help of Ernestina's tutoring she could read at the age of four, and her memory for long poems was thought of as remarkable. She was a funny child, joking in her precociously deep and raspy voice, making fun of her own thin arms and her long legs, which always made her seem taller than she really was. As for her schoolwork, only ballet class would eventually satisfy her, and for now, she was not doing as well at the Teresianas as her sister Cuca was. Alicia would never feel at home in this world of tiny pine desks with crucifixes in every classroom, old maps and older images filling the walls, brown and white dresses, and habits. Although the initials J.M.J. were scrawled dutifully on the margin of every sheet the little girls wrote, Alicia's mind seemed to the nuns to be not at all close to Jesus, Mary, and Joseph but elsewhere and far away. Her irreverence landed her in trouble more than once with the good Teresian sisters, but Alicia would find a way to make them laugh each time. While Cuca was and always would remain a devout Catholic who once wanted to be a nun, Alicia was not religious even if she did eventually take to the images and private rituals that are as cultural as they are spiritual in Latin countries. Many years later, the critic Anne Barzel would recall with affectionate amusement how all the little saints that were staples of the great Cuban ballerina's dressing room somehow vanished after the revolution. But that's getting ahead of the story. When it came to religion, the young Alicia disliked being on her knees, and she resented it very much when the nuns asked her to tell her parents to come to church more often. Antonio was a Freemason, and

With the help of Ernestina's tutoring, Alicia could read at the age of four.

Ernestina simply preferred to let her children go to the school chapel with their mates on Sundays, without the parents.

When it came time for Alicia's first communion in the winter of 1927, she found it so difficult to master the fine art of swallowing the sacramental host without chewing it, that she decided it was better not to take communion again. Anything she could not do correctly, she would not do at all, but she hated to cheat. If she learned anything from the Teresian order, it was an obsession for self-discipline.

It was in the first grade at the Teresianas that Alicia first stepped on the stage. She was only supposed to remain in the background and look nice in some sort of school pageant, but she improvised instead, reciting and singing the way she had learned at home, moving to whatever lines came to her mind. Her voice made everyone laugh, which surprised the little girl who had not yet learned that she was hopelessly tone-deaf. But although the bemused nuns chastised the first grader, her daring drew applause—and little Unga liked that very much. Cuban ballet curtain calls, which could themselves grow into extravagant spectacles that the great Anton Dolin jokingly referred to as *Giselle, Act Three*, may have had their roots on that little Havana private school stage.

Her sister suffered from the vapors. When she fainted once in school that same year, a nasty older girl told Alicia that Cuca died. Alicia cried and wailed and would not be subdued until she too was sent home to see that Cuca was fine. "Let's not go back, not ever," she made Cuca promise. As it turned out, they did not go back in the fall.

Captain Martínez de Arredondo twice took part in a military exchange program, traveling to the United States to further his specialization in horse breeding for the Cuban army. A long six or seven months in 1926 at Walter Reed Army Hospital in Washington, D.C. were followed by summer visits to Carlyle, Pennsylvania, and St. Louis, Missouri. Alicia's memories of these trips would be important

if not vivid: Antonio would not let the children speak English at home—a mixed blessing for her in later life—and he would be fond of reminding them of the splendor of the Cuban beaches and the warm Havana woods as they strolled through Washington's leafy 16th Street near the hospital. "He taught me how to feel Cuban, and he taught me how to grow," Alicia would remember more than seventy years later. She, Cuca, and the boys managed to tie their knees and learn the Charleston from neighbors before returning to Cuba. And when they did return, it was not to the dreaded Marianao, but to El Vedado, one of Havana's most beautiful and prosperous parts. If the Spanish, who built old Havana, preferred elms and mahoganies and oaks in formal lines, in El Vedado the tropical flora was invited to adorn the elegant nineteenth century houses and later the classic revivals and modern buildings that came with prosperity of each dramatic increase in sugar prices after the first World War. Art Deco found a home among the royal palms, coconut trees, and elephantine rhododendrons that always mocked any architect's attempt at severity. Technology from the United States was as much the rule as culture from Europe. The Nobel Laureate Vicente Blasco Ibáñez was struck by the uniqueness of El Vedado and remarked,

> . . . in these new neighborhoods small private palaces are ever more numerous. The old Spanish architecture, with the added comforts of North American living, is usually the rule of these buildings, and the tropical shrubbery sounds a note of originality in the construction, which recalls at once the courtyards of Seville and the wooden palaces of Long Island.[3]

Around the new mansions arose a fringe of apartment buildings, the first in the city, accommodating the rising middle class. The Martínez de Arredondo y del Hoyo family moved to a modest apartment on the edge of Vedado, on 6th Street

Alicia's teacher Mari gave her a pair of castanets, hoping to keep her hands still.

between 21st and 23rd, not far from what is today the headquarters of the Instituto Cubano de Artes e Industrias Cinematograficas (ICAIC), Cuba's film institute. This was only a temporary home, since at Ernestina's insistence they soon were established in the gracious shade of 14th Street between 19th and 21st, in a large third floor apartment in a grey Bauhaus box of a building where the family would remain for almost twenty years. The boys could walk uphill to the Colegio De La Salle and the girls to Teresianas, accompanied by a maid named María. They were now very near the recently built Teatro Auditórium, the same theatre which later would be named Amadeo Roldán and become the home of Alicia Alonso's ballet company, and which later still, in 1975, would be destroyed by counterrevolutionary arson. In the late 1920s, the enterprising Sociedad Pro-Arte Musical filled the theatre nightly with resident or visiting entertainment, and Ernestina was overjoyed that her children could see these things more easily now. They had arrived.

In 1929 Antonio Martínez de Arredondo was given the rather pleasant assignment of spending a year in Spain with his family, choosing horses for the Cuban army and participating in experimental research on the improvement of various Arab breeds in Jerez de la Frontera.

Alicia's maternal grandfather missed and often spoke of all things Spanish, but his health kept him from going on this trip. It was Ernestina's idea to surprise the old man with dances from his memories, and she decided that Cuca and Alicia would take dance lessons in Spain. The girls surely would enjoy them, as they had enjoyed seeing the dance troupe of Ana María y sus Bailes Españoles in Havana that same year. And it would be a beautiful present for their grandfather.

After a week with distant cousins in the rocky Cantabrian beaches of Santander, and another week further south in Madrid, they settled in Jerez de la Frontera, an austere and beautiful town near

Cádiz. They lived in the outskirts of town, south of the bull ring and just off the road to Ronda. Their walks to Antonio's stables would take them past the vines of the old Alcázar and the enormous bodegas of sherry—Jerez being the city that first gave the world that drink three centuries ago. The girls were handed over not only to a school run by the ubiquitous Teresians, but also to a Spanish dance teacher. The boys were matriculated in a Jesuit school for the year, liking it so much that Toñiquito convinced his parents to let him withdraw from the Colegio De La Salle upon returning to Cuba to finish high school at the Jesuit Colegio de Belén—the same school that years later educated the young Fidel and Raúl Castro. For Cuca and Alicia, it was the dance lessons that would fill their memories of the trip.

The girls first met what they remember as a tubby Andalusian lady whose pregnancy caused her in two or three weeks to be replaced by a young flamenco dancer named Mari Emilia. The older Cuca was first given more complicated steps to learn, while Alicia followed the teacher in simpler motions. But in a few afternoons Alicia had learned all the other dances by watching them, performing them to her teacher's surprise. From then on the slim nine-year-old grew more graceful with each new challenging step, learning to improvise within each rhythm formation and mastering much of the jota, the malagueña, and the sevillana. Her teacher gave her a pair of castanets, partly to teach the little Cuban to keep her hands still. The girl wrapped this wooden treasure between thumb and forefinger and almost never took it off, taking the castanets to bed with her, learning to play them in any position, and with each tilt of the wrist.

"These were the first dance lessons I ever had in my life," Alicia would recall, "and I was smitten—I didn't let the castanets out of my hands for days, and my progress was so fast that the teachers started giving me steps that they had thought were much too complicated for an eight or nine-year-old." Alicia loved Spain: the open skies as blue as those of the tropics, the proud serenity of the dancers' line, the frothy ruffles of their dresses, majestic peinetas in their hair; that marriage of Europe and the Middle East that is known as Spanish music, its constant heart always beating to the pulse of dance itself. The stomping and fast footwork of the sevillana came easily to Alicia; drawing lines with her hands and whispering phrases with her feet were tasks she treasured, and she dreaded that her dancing lessons would stop when they returned to Cuba. The year was 1930.

There was a sense of security and intimate warmth as the Martínez family moved from place to place during Antonio's three years of travel. The serenity, along with that of many other Cuban families, soon would be shattered in Cuba. In his first administration, President Gerardo Machado y Morales had taken steps towards conscientious urban planning, employing the unemployed by building the Capitol, the present campus of the University of Havana, and many of Havana's monuments. Cuba's debts to foreign banks, especially to Chase National Bank of New York, grew enormously with the approaching world economic depression; sugar prices fell from an already low three cents a pound to less than three-quarters of one cent per pound.[4] A devastating hurricane destroyed all of the crops in 1926, and later conscious efforts to increase sugar prices by limiting production were voided by increased sugar production elsewhere. Virtually all Cuban and Spanish banks on the island were bankrupt by 1929, with the only solvent banks being from the United States. Yet, when it was suggested to the President that there should be a moratorium on payment of foreign debts, Machado's fear of the Platt Amendment and its threat of American invasion in defense of American interests, led him to raise taxes and oppose labor reforms that he himself had encouraged at the time of his election in 1925.[5] The result

was discontent among the workers and the students; and their discontent was met with frequent massacres by Machado's police. Once the youngest general in Cuba's War of Independence from Spain, Machado became a dictator, to be surpassed in sheer brutality and oppressiveness years later only by Fidel Castro and his younger brother Raúl.

In 1930, the year Antonio and his family returned to Cuba, a general strike paralyzed Havana; the universities were closed. Finally on August 12, 1933, a coalition of workers, students, and military officers forced Machado out of the country in what proved to be only the beginning of the bloody revolution of 1933. At this time Ramón Grau San Martín came to the aid of the country, not for the last time, becoming president and naming the socialist leader Antonio Guiteras to his cabinet. Grau's was the first Cuban presidential administration established without the approval of the United States government. Progressive laws, most of which would remain in effect after the 1959 revolution, were enacted: the autonomy of unions was guaranteed along with high standards for working conditions[6]; maternity laws were enacted, guaranteeing women's rights to child care and maternity leave; and free public education was established from elementary through university. It is worth noting that all this progress in Cuba happened in 1933, not 1959. Machado's own proclamation to the presidency for a second term without elections was repudiated, and, significantly, the Platt Amendment was eventually repealed. Most Latin American countries recognized Cuba's new government, but the United States did not.

President Franklin Delano Roosevelt did not invade, as previous American presidents most assuredly would have. But he surrounded the island with a blockade of warships. Roosevelt's ambassador, Benjamin Sumner Welles, personally chose a sergeant whose previous experience included mostly typing and other smaller tasks in Campo Columbia, and he helped him in organizing a coup d'état. The sergeant's name was Fulgencio Batista y Zaldívar. He proclaimed himself head of the armed forces on September 4, 1933. There followed an uneasy coexistence of Grau, Guiteras, and Batista, when it was not clear where the power would rest. In fact, a string of weak administrations would follow Grau, with presidents Carlos Hevia y de los Reyes Gavilán, whose name is almost as long as his twenty-four hour presidency; Manuel Márquez Sterling, Carlos Mendieta, José Agripino Barnet, Miguel Mariano Gómez Arias, and Federico Laredo Bru, all before the constitutional reforms of 1940, and Batista's own accession to the presidency that same year, with the United States approval.

Meanwhile a group of discontented army officers, including Alicia's father, gathered at the Hotel Nacional in Havana to plot against Batista's takeover of the army. On October 2, 1933, Batista's forces attacked the hotel, using full artillery from land as well as constant bombardment from the warship *Patria* anchored in Havana Bay. The Hotel Nacional stands on a high promontory overlooking La Rampa and Old Havana to the east, El Vedado to the west, and the ocean to the north. Its beautiful walls still bear the scars of that battle, as does the country.

Antonio Martínez de Arredondo was not on the winning side of that fight. Although his role was not important enough to warrant more drastic punishment, he was imprisoned briefly in the old Spanish fortress of La Cabaña; his health suffered, and his spirit was broken. Young Cuca would be sent to visit her father at La Cabaña, carrying tins of rice pudding to jail, bringing news and family stories, involving herself irretrievably in her family's problems, and her country's politics.

Alicia was sheltered from these problems. She never went to La Cabaña in those five months of her father's imprisonment; her mother thought it a blessing that Alicia was busy with ballet by now, taking classes at Pro-Arte and far away from the gloom of the family home. And not for the last time, Alicia would lack the time to be preoccupied with politics; her concerns would be only with dance. "I don't know why they bother asking her about Cuban politics when she comes here," Antony Tudor told me once about the press coverage of one of Alicia's few appearances in New York after the Cuban revolution. "All she knows about is ballet."

Antonio's military career was finished. Not without bitterness, his daughter Alicia would say much later that "he was too honest ever to be anything more than a captain; he was too good." He lost none of his gentleness with his family, even when growing quieter and sterner, and he took up such then unheard of causes as the conservation of Cuba's multicolored beaches and the replanting of trees in the Bosque de La Habana. Many years later, when Alicia Alonso filmed her production of *Swan Lake* in these lovely woods, the background of much of the film consisted of trees her father planted.

Her father's quiet perseverance taught Alicia much. Yet it was at this time that Ernestina del Hoyo's strength blossomed and she became the most powerful influence in the formation of Alicia's character. When Antonio was in prison, Ernestina refused to move in with her parents and worked without respite to keep her apartment in El Vedado. She saw to it that the lives of her children were not disturbed unnecessarily and she remained combative and even joyful, her tenacity contained only by economics. This vibrancy with a touch of madness was learned by her youngest daughter, who herself would face several trials in her day. Ernestina supported Antonio when he stubbornly ignored the advice of friends who suggested their moving to Spain or the United States, where he was not without connections. "We belong here," Antonio would say to them. "All the bad will pass, and we will be fine in our own country." Life did go on as uneventfully as possible for them. There were distractions and books and the radio, and there were motion pictures when they could afford to go. Ernestina did not discuss politics at home. "It was easier to do that then, of course," Cuca would remember in exile half a century later. "That everyone would become so obsessed with politics is something that happened only after 1959. It wasn't like that before in Cuba; things happened, but people just lived or at least tried to live normal lives." And it is true that the 1959 revolution would be the first to leave no Cuban family untouched, one way or another, by loss. For now the Martínez del Hoyo family would do its best to keep itself alive, together, and happy. And earlier, as their trip came to an end in 1930, the main thing on Ernestina del Hoyo's mind was joining the exclusive Sociedad Pro-Arte Musical so that her daughters might go on dancing.

Also headed for Cuba in 1930 was Nikolai Yavorsky, a Russian émigré and former Cossack who would become Alicia's first ballet teacher. Yavorsky was born to the aristocracy of St. Petersburg in 1891. Still in his teens, he escaped the Russian Revolution and shed his czarist uniform in favor of theatrical costumes in the West. As a dancer, he was an amateur with memory and good taste. His striking figure and Russian name carried him far at first. He gave lessons in ballroom dances in Yugoslavia, and in the early 1920s he briefly became a soloist with the Ida Rubinstein Company, which took him to Paris and to lessons with Olga Preobazhenskaya. Here he met and

mingled with many of the artists he had admired in Russia, and he witnessed another revolution—a revolution in the art of dance. He would also recall with fondness meeting a youngster named Igor Yousekevitch at this time.

In Paris he met Georges Milénoff, a young Bulgarian pupil of Nicolas Legat with whom he established what in the cant of the day was called a "romantic friendship." The two young lovers saw an excellent opportunity for their talent in a new opera company called Opéra Privé de Paris, which was to perform the Russian repertory on tour in America with a mostly émigré cast of singers and dancers. Milénoff became the premiere danseur and Yavorsky the dance master of the ensemble.

In Cuba at this time, the arts in general and the Sociedad Pro-Arte Musical in particular were caught in an economic dilemma. Pro-Arte needed money, and it needed to expand its artistic scope in order to obtain it. The previous seasons had been increasingly successful since Pro-Arte's founding in 1915 by María Teresa García Montes de Giberga, an event which coincided with the first Cuban season of Anna Pavlova and Alexander Volinine at the Teatro Payret. Things were going so well, in fact, that the plans were executed for the building of the Teatro Auditórium in the Vedado, on the Paseo de Calzada and D Street at the top of Parque Villalón. There Pro-Arte could continue to present opera, ballet, and concerts to the Havana public as well as to provide a gathering place for its aristocratic membership. After a brief set of preview performances, the Auditórium opened with a gala concert on December 2, 1928. The evening included the premiere of a commissioned tone poem, *Anacaona* by Eduardo Sánchez de Fuentes, showcasing the Pro-Arte Musical Chorus and the Havana Symphony Orchestra directed by Gonzalo Roig, whose own 1932 operetta *Cecilia Valdés* would change the course of the Cuban lyric theatre. The hall became the home of the orchestra, which rented it from Pro-Arte, as well as of the Society for Popular Concerts and all of Pro-Arte's presentations.

These included Yavorsky's Opéra Privé de Paris. The company began its tour in January of 1930 with two weeks in Havana, during which the Russians gave the Cuban premieres of *Prince Igor* by Borodin; *The Fair at Sorochinsk* by Moussorgsky; *The Tale of Tsar Saltan, The Snow Maiden (Snegouroshka)*, and *The Invisible City of Kitezh* by Rimsky-Korsakov. The operas were well received, but this would be the last foreign company that the Pro-Arte could afford to engage for some time. There were brief visits by Anna Duncan, Irma Duncan, and Ruth Page, and there was a successful presentation of a local flamenco troupe, but it was not a very full season. In February, all economic aid from the Commission of Tourism was withdrawn, as the global economic crisis reached Cuban shores.

The depression also affected the Opéra Privé, which disbanded soon after its Cuban tour and after a week in Mexico City. None of the artists was paid. Milénoff had met a gentleman in Mexico who lured him to St. Louis, Missouri, to help start a conservatory of music, which he did. Yavorsky was left alone and with little money; he had liked his brief stay in Havana and told a friend later that he would "rather starve there than in Mexico," so he used what savings he had to return to Cuba in March of 1930.

At first it was difficult for the Russian to meet the acquaintances he had made while performing at the Auditórium. The theatre was dark for most of April that year, and the wealthy officers of Pro-Arte along with many Pro-Arte patrons he knew happened to be vacation. He did not know of Pro-Arte's financial worries, nor that these worries might give him a new career.

Plans were being made by Pro-Arte's president, Oria Varela de Albarrán, and by the board of directors, which was headed by Natalia Aróstegui de Suárez and Laura Rayneri de Alonso, to attract new members to the society. They decided the way to attract them was not by presenting more performances, since there was little money circulating at the time and since the political tenor of Machado's Cuba was scaring away foreign impresarios, but rather the ladies decided it would be appropriate to offer dance, drama, and music lessons for a modest fee to members. They could keep the initiation cost at its present high rate, but the lessons themselves would be inexpensive. Thus they hoped to solve a cash flow problem. And thus, they would found the first successful ballet academy in Cuba, the Escuela de Ballet de Pro-Arte.

In 1918, the dancer Ina Claire had come with Anna Pavlova to the Teatro Nacional and remained behind with an Italian impresario name Braccale who used the named Fernán Flor to open the Academia de Ballet Fernán Flor; it was not successful. Throughout the 1920s, Anna Mariani of the Cecchetti School tried to persuade the Municipal Academy of Music in Havana to incorporate dance in its curriculum; but she would prevail only after Pro-Arte's success. And the socialite and Cuban dance pioneer Margot Párraga also had plans for a ballet school, which would be realized only in the mid 1930s. Pro-Arte's school would be the first and the best.

Nikolai Yavorsky met Sras. Aróstegui and Rayneri in his first visit, and he called on them several times when he returned to Havana, persisting when he was told that they were on vacation abroad. He worked briefly at the food concession of the Teatro Payret, which the economic depression had turned into a movie palace. He joined the Circo Pubillones as an acrobat, and for three weeks, the lonely Russian traveled with this modest circus tent to Matanzas and Las Villas. As summer approached, he returned to Havana. He was without a job and was forced to sleep in the park when his money ran out, appropriately preferring Parque Villalón in El Vedado, across from the Auditórium. He finally met again with Laura Rayneri de Alonso.

It did not take much to convince her to hire Yavorsky. While it never entered the minds of anyone concerned that the idea for a school would lead to any sort of professional training for dance or music, it was a wonderful way to further the cultural education of many young people while at the same time providing Pro-Arte with much needed money. The membership would surely increase. "That Russian may solve our problems," Laura told Natalia, recruiting her old friend to convince the rest of the board of directors—a bit of family history that Laura's granddaughter, Laura Alonso, would enjoy retelling years later. The two women helped Yavorsky with their own money until matters could be settled; they sought three other teachers for piano, guitar, and drama; they hired the pianist Luis Borbolla to accompany Yavorsky's classes; and they began a membership drive announcing that lessons would be available in the summer of 1931. What had been occasional flirtations would soon become the Cuban public's lasting passion for ballet.

Ernestina had joined Pro-Arte as soon as the family returned from Spain. The news of the drama and dance classes for her girls was an answer to her prayers, since both Cuca and Alicia had bemoaned the end of their Spanish dance lessons and already missed them. They would like the ballet school, and they surely would meet many socially respectable people while growing up gracefully. The extra six pesos a year for each girl was not very much at all, especially when it was payable so easily as fifty cents a week and the splurge of the initiation fee was already accomplished.

On June 30, 1931, Ernestina took Alicia by the hand and they went down the street to the Teatro Auditórium. They walked up the marble steps crowded with dozens of little girls and their mothers, and once inside the atrium Alicia had a surprise. This was to be the day of matriculation,

and classes of drama and music were to begin later that week. But Nikolai Yavorsky introduced himself and gathered all his new students for a class picture, then declared that they might as well start right then. "*¿Te atreves, Unga?*," Ernestina asked Alicia, "Do you dare?" And the girl answered by running to the stage where a barre had been set up at the center and on each side. Ernestina was ushered to the auditorium with the other mothers where they would watch each dance class. On stage, Alicia stood at the end, the smallest girl with the largest bow in her hair. Through a thick accent of Russian-flavored Spanish she heard, "No talking, no talking at all. Stand up very straight, watch your backs. Watch what I do. We call this first position." The Escuela de Ballet de Pro-Arte Musical had begun.

Alicia was the smallest but surely the happiest girl in that class. She was thrilled from the first step and ballet was all she could talk about, all she could do. She felt at home on the large stage of the Teatro Auditórium, where she would dance so often through much of her life.

Cuca joined her sister within the week. Ernestina also enrolled the girls in drama and music lessons, and once each week for the next year, Alicia walked upstairs to the tiny recital hall that hosted the Escuela de Declamacíon de Pro-Arte. There classes were taught by the Spanish actor Jesús Tordesillas. On another afternoon, she attended the class of Clara Romero de Nicolá in the same hall, where Alicia was given a choice of piano or guitar lessons. She chose piano, but finger exercises proved vastly dull for her compared with the endless joys of demi-plié in five positions; and by the end of November she dropped out of her music class in order to take more dance.

Alicia Martínez, kneeling, fourth from the left, on the opening day of the new Escuela de Ballet
Pro-Arte Musical under Nicolai Yavorsky (center). Courtesy of the Alicia Alonso Collection.

More dance, in fact, was all she wanted. Although Alicia was almost always late for class—a habit she would cultivate as an adult—she was eager and worked well, and the watchful Yavorsky soon took her aside for extra tasks. These were not always successful. The Russian would prepare little dance stories for small ensembles of his girls, ways to keep them entertained and interested while giving them glimpses of what the arduous class routine could become some day. He set one of these to Strauss' *The Blue Danube*, in which he had two ladies and a child throwing a balloon to the waltzing beat of Borbolla's piano and Yavorsky's wooden stick. The two ladies were Cuca and Delfina Pérez-Gurri, the latter a gifted girl who would join the Ballets Russes de Monte Carlo in five years. The child was played by Alicia. The little girl was supposed to catch the balloon as it was passed from one lady to another, and then throw it back in time to the music. Alicia missed, but when she finally caught it, she could not throw it back in time. Yavorsky shouted at her from his customary chair at the center of the stage, and then he ran upstage where Alicia stood embarrassed. "I said catch it and throw it this way," he said, slamming the balloon down on the pins of her white cotton bow. The explosion stunned her. And Cuca, seeing her little sister near tears, said, "Come on, Unga, we're leaving."

When Yavorsky went backstage to persuade the girls to return, Cuca said that they would not unless he apologized to Alicia in front of the whole class. He did. He rather liked the two Martínez girls.

He liked all of his students, really, and he found that he was happy teaching and that his pupils enjoyed his class. Many of them would stay late and he would spin tales of St. Petersburg and Paris; of Tamara Karsavina; of the great Anna Pavlova, who died on January 23 of that same year; of how much harder a teacher Preobazhenskaya was than he. He also told stories of how Vaslav Nijinsky seemed to fly.

Ernestina liked him too, and so did Antonio when they met at dinner in the Martínez home. The army captain did not know anything about ballet but was pleased to find that the old Cossack loved horses. When he discovered that Yavorsky had not ridden since leaving Europe, Antonio set out to remedy the situation immediately. Yavorsky was grateful for that as well as for finding good friends in his new country. Noting Ernestina's talent, he suggested that she might design the costumes for a production he hoped to stage with the Pro-Arte students near Christmastime. Ernestina agreed.

As classes progressed, Alicia's natural gifts became apparent. The arch of her foot, though usually hidden by the white tennis shoes in which she danced at first, was perfect. Her turn out was wide, logical, and easy. And her legs followed from that line with lean strength. Her extension too was natural, and incredibly high—and this in the days before the pedagogic insistence on the prowess of extension by such masters as George Balanchine and Fernando Alonso. Her arms and head soon drew images in motion with unaffected simplicity and grace. Many of these virtues came without the help of Yavorsky, whose technical vocabulary was not rich. Certainly the good outweighed the bad, and Yavorsky nurtured Alicia's love of ballet and guided her first steps. "I think he was a dancer of great facility and inventiveness," Alicia would recall. "He was a great rider and he had a beautiful body. And he had a fabulous ear for music." It is this last quality which most influenced the young dancer. Yavorsky drummed and drummed the beat insistently until it could be taken for granted, then he tried to teach his students to add layers of melody to their movements. It was a useful lesson for Alicia, one which would be evident, as she later would describe, in "the way I dance today, the way I try to assume the rhythm and keep the timing but don't really dance to their rules. What I most use is the phrasing, living the melody in my body, letting it be felt in my movement."

When the Escuela de Ballet de Pro-Arte opened its doors in Havana ballet supply shops had not yet opened theirs. There were no slippers and the girls danced in tennis shoes. Yavorsky advised Pro-Arte that this was unacceptable, and the ladies of the board promised to correct the situation soon. In the meantime, one of them returned from an Italian vacation with a pair of shoes for Yavorsky's inspection. "These are fine," he said. "Let's order more and let's give these to one of the girls now." Pandemonium happened on the dance floor as the budding ballerinas tried on the shoes. Alicia, arriving late, was greeted by her friend Leonor Albarrán, "Hurry up, Unga, run. There's a pair of ballet shoes, see if they fit you." Now, there was no reason for the shoes to fit Alicia if they did not fit the rest, since several of the girls must have been more or less the same size. But only Alicia noticed as she grabbed the pink satin treasure that cotton balls were stuffed down where the toes were supposed to go. She removed the cotton, slipped on the slippers, and stood up smiling. "*Mira, mira,* I'm on my toes." She was the first girl in her class to wear such things. That night she took the slippers to bed with her, and that night, Alicia Martínez promised herself that she would be a ballerina. "I took them to bed with me; I put them under my pillow," she would recall. "I searched for them half asleep to make sure they were really there with me."

Dancing around the apartment was nothing new, but now there were fancy ribbons on her feet. Alicia seemed never to take off her new shoes. "Ernestina," Antonio shouted one day, "I don't think this girl will ever walk like a normal person." But Unga was so excited and happy that even he could not tell her to stop. Her mother mended the satin shoes and mended them again, until Alicia wore them to shreds. Then she went back to tennis shoes.

Many years later Alicia Alonso would remember that great ballet shoe shortage of 1931 and, not entirely in jest, she would trace the provenance of her famous slow turns and endless balance to her tennis shoes because they made her feet feel as if they had been glued to the floor and she was forced to hold her balance in order to complete a turn in Yavorsky's class. "And we were without shoes for a very long time." Much would be made about Alicia, tennis shoes, and other signs of humble origins, but truthfully this is one memory of underdevelopment that time has clouded somewhat. By December of 1931, Pro-Arte had imported shoes for the whole class, in time for Yavorsky's holiday production.

Yavorsky chose to stage scenes from *The Sleeping Beauty,* a ballet that had not been seen in Cuba since Pavlova and Alexander Volinine had danced it in 1918. As rehearsals began, Ernestina was busy designing and cutting patterns for the costumes and sewing for her girls, so she did not watch class as often as she used to. Cuca and Alicia were old enough to take care of themselves, and María could always go and bring back Alicia when she stayed late after class. Early in December Alicia had a problem. Yavorsky had edited the Tchaikovsky score into a version of Act Three, known as "Aurora's Wedding," with additional music from the opening of Act One. For one of the numbers he picked the best girls in the class, including Dinorah Agudín, Leonor Albarrán, Delfina Pérez-Gurri, and the sisters Cuca and Alicia Martínez. They executed a string of arabesques to frame the opening and closing tableaux, and in rehearsal Alicia's leg went up much higher than those of the other girls. Too high, thought some of the jealous mothers watching as the class applauded this little girl. After class, some of these ladies took Alicia aside and explained to her that it was very vulgar to raise her leg so high, that it was "*muy chusma, una ordinariez,*" that it was unladylike and she should not do it again. Alicia was crushed and did not even tell Cuca until they were home. By then someone had called Ernestina with the story that Alicia had behaved in a very vulgar fashion in class. But Ernestina knew her daughter and could not believe this. She and Alicia walked back to the Teatro Auditórium to see Yavorsky.

"Is it vulgar to dance like this? Go ahead, Unga, show us." And Alicia produced her extension as before.

"No, not at all," replied Yavorsky.

"And how high should a dancer raise her leg like that?"

"Frankly, Sra. del Hoyo, every dancer I have ever known raises it as high as she can."

"Thank you, that's all we wanted to know."

Yavorsky had not even heard of little Alicia's bout with her censors. Ernestina hugged her daughter and told her, "You go ahead and learn the dance and do it the way they told you. But at the performance, *ponte la pierna en la oreja o enfréntate conmigo*—raise your leg to your ear or else you'll have to answer to me."

The holiday season was hectic and full of expectations that year. On December 21, the family celebrated the double birthday of Alicia and her older brother with Ernestina's customary two cakes: strawberry for Unga and chocolate for Toñiquito. Christmas came and Alicia's favorite present was the costume that Ernestina made for her debut. Soon the night arrived, December 29, 1931. Orchestral music of Liszt and Mendelssohn filled the first part of the evening. Then came *The Sleeping Beauty*, choreographed by Yavorsky after Marius Petipa, presented by the Escuela de Ballet de Pro-Arte Musical. Gonzalo Roig conducted the Havana Symphony Orchestra and the Teatro Auditórium was sold out of its three thousand seats. The occasion was at once elegant and truly popular, with balcony seats costing as little as fifty cents; and as much of the excitement came from what this might mean for ballet in Cuba as from what the evening itself might bring.

Alicia felt too good to be nervous. She would never be nervous on stage. She stood in the wings with her sister by her side, looking splendid as a Lady of the Court in the blue and white satin costume sewn by her mother. After the overture came the sweet Act One allegro known as the Garland Dance, and with this waltz the eleven-year-old Alicia stepped into her first ballet.

The year 1932 was filled with dance and little else for Alicia. Her schoolwork did not suffer, but neither did it shine. Her playmates were all from the Pro-Arte school, except for her neighbor and best friend Manón Toñarely, who herself would soon be taking class at the Margot Párraga Academy. Alicia's life revolved around Yavorsky's classes and she spent all of her free time at the Auditórium. In the second year, classes moved from the stage to a fourth-floor studio overlooking Parque Villalón. Luis Borbolla's piano accompaniments were themselves amusing musical lessons, ranging from classical music to $3/4$ and $4/4$ adaptations of popular melodies of the day. So to Chopin, Gershwin, or Lecuona, Alicia prepared her five positions at the barre, intuitively easing from fifth to fourth with a smile. Always keeping her figure straight, she would move from battement tendu in demi-plié to the same flutter in fifth position under Yavorsky's watchful eye. She learned early on to feel the center of her body's weight as it shifted from torso to leg, and back to the body, while traveling from first to second positions as well as in all the other exercises. She was taught to use the barre as an aid in centering her body, and her knowledge of her own space seemed as preconscious as her body was flexible and limber. In the center of the room, Yavorsky's exercises lacked the rigor that Alicia would demand later from her other teachers, but he did stress the strict rules governing the different poses in classical ballet and the concept of épaulement and port de bras. These two details in particular, notoriously not cultivated by American neoclassicism in the School of American Ballet in New York, would become benchmarks of the Cuban School of Ballet. Young Alicia learned to use the mirror to shade the lines that she could create by turning her body in a croisé then, for example, uncrossing the lines in the mirror in an effacé. The arms, head, and face were as important as the legs in Yavorsky's intentions, and Alicia from the outset was taught to offer the serene appearance of grace even while executing the most strenuous routines. By the end of the first year she was allowed some pointe work, and it never entered her mind to do anything but dance.

Fifty years later, in revolutionary Cuba, it would be claimed that although Alicia was able to take classes at Pro-Arte, "her road was not an easy one. . . . In the bosom of that institution she would know the discrimination that allowed giving principal roles to pupils of superior economic means without taking into account the value of true talent."[7] In truth, Alicia was lovingly groomed by her teacher, as were Cuca and the other talented girls and boys in Yavorsky's classes. By the time of the school's second staged presentation, on November 26, 1932, little Unga was given the important role of the Bluebird and was taught a version of that difficult Petipa variation by Yavorsky for his staging of the complete *Sleeping Beauty*. In a feature interview in that morning's daily *El Mundo*, Yavorsky praised in particular "one of my students who has done the work of three years in one. The development and artistic enthusiasm of young Alicia Martínez are a living example of the purest in classical dance."[8] And all this before the girl's twelfth birthday.

After the 1932 Bluebird, Alicia began looking pale and weak, and doctors suspected tuberculosis; she was told that her ballet lessons must stop. Yavorsky's concern quite matched that of the Martínez family, and he followed them from doctor to doctor until they found out that indeed it was nothing more serious than exhaustion. It would not be the last time that Alicia would be told by doctors that she could not dance again, and the support of her mother and teacher made a deep impression. She promised to turn over a new leaf, to do better in school, to rest and gain weight. She promised anything as long as she could continue her beloved classes. And continue she did.

For the three world premieres of Yavorsky's own ballets that followed in the next years, Alicia was given a principal role in each. In *The Circus*, she struck a humorous series of attitudes and arabesques as The Girl on the Tightrope. On the same evening of November 4, 1933, Alicia and Cuca had parallel adagio variations in a classroom piano ballet called *Ejercicios*. The following year *Polka Coquette*, set to a score by Joseph Joachim Raff, gave Alicia another solo; and Yavorsky's *Tartaritos*, his staging of Fokine's "Polovetsian Dances" from *Prince Igor*, first showed off her high jump on the stage of the Teatro Auditórium on June 1, 1934.

That summer, Pro-Arte received a visit from Antonia Mercé y Luque, "La Argentina," one of the great dancers of her generation and the one most responsible for the revival of Spanish dance in our time. Yavorsky asked Alicia to perform for the veteran dancer her variation from the *Polka Coquette*. Her shoelace was loose that morning, a rare thing for Alicia, and it became untied during a turn. Undaunted, in character and without missing a beat, Alicia improvised and managed to tuck the offending lace, rejoin the music, and finish Yavorsky's choreography as if nothing unusual had happened. Antonia Mercé was charmed. She told the old cossack that the girl's physical attributes and technique were impressive enough, but that such *gracia* and spontaneity were truly gifts to treasure. She asked Alicia whether she knew any other piece and was delighted when the little Cuban

Alicia Martínez in her first solo role, the Bluebird in Yavorsky's *The Sleeping Beauty*, Ballet Pro-Arte, 1932. Alicia's costume was created by her mother, Ernestina. Courtesy of the Alicia Alonso Collection.

plunged into a sevillana that she had learned in Jerez de la Frontera but that Yavorsky had never seen. When the dancing was finished, La Argentina turned to Alicia and said, "Little girl, I believe you are a genius. Let me know if ever I can help you, and please let me know when you dance your first ballerina role. I promise that if I can I will come to see you."

In less than one year, Alicia was given such a role, although by now La Argentina had fallen gravely ill and would remain at home in Bayonne, France, until her death in 1936 at the age of forty-eight. She would have been pleased with Alicia dancing her first Swanilda in a new staging by Yavorsky of the romantic comedy ballet *Coppélia*. Partnering her for the first time that night of March 20, 1935, was a boy named Alberto Alonso, and in the audience was his older brother Fernando. From that night on, the name Alonso and the fate of those two boys would become inseparable from that of Alicia Martínez del Hoyo.

Fernando Alonso was born to Matías Alonso and Laura Rayneri de Alonso on December 17, 1914. Three years later, on May 22, 1917, his brother Alberto was born. Blessed with independent means that had not yet begun to dwindle, Matías and Laura led a charmed and charming life. When the Sociedad Pro-Arte Musical was founded in Havana in 1918, Laura Rayneri was one of its strongest financial supporters, and it was she who, together with Natalia Aróstegui de Suárez and Oria Varela de Albarrán, conceived the Pro-Arte schools of ballet, drama, and music. They lived on the Paseo de Calzada only steps away from the Auditórium, and the rosters of their evenings at home were at least as prestigious as those of the theatre itself. Names like Gigli, Bjoerling, Scotti, Rachmaninoff, Horowitz, and Schnabel could be found in the guest book. The composers Joaquín Nin, Gonzalo Roig, and Amadeo Roldán were family friends. And Anna Pavlova, once Laura's houseguest in 1918, rocked the toddler Fernando

in her arms. Laura herself was a gifted pianist, although after her marriage she confined her concerts to playing for her sons before bedtime.

The Havana society of the 1920s encompassed a world of horse races, regattas, and fast motor cars; of fancy dress balls and street carnivals; of money made from sugar or selling real estate to North American interests, which then made more money from sugar. The Alonso family was not quite so rich as some of the older families, but there was no such thing as very old money in a new republic, and life could, as Cuca Martínez said, be quite unaffected by politics. This was also a time of cultural growth in Cuba. The presence of Cuba's northern neighbor in the country meant that hostility towards Spain was quickly erased and the *Madre Patria* would remain with France, the cultural guiding light. A new romanticism was revived with all its nostalgia for European values, and a cosmopolitan atmosphere persisted in its effervescence despite the infusion of technology and values from the United States. The separation of the popular and the serious arts took longer than in many countries, with the Spanish *zarzuela* permanently bridging the gap between opera and vaudeville. A publishing boom occurred that would last until the strikes of 1930; university reforms began and there seemed to be a spontaneous intellectual revolution. The poet Rubén Martínez Villena publicly declared that intellectuals had a patriotic duty to criticize society, and literary *peñas* filled the outdoor cafés of Old Havana and El Vedado, setting the tone for the urban intellectual life. Verlaine and Mallarmé were translated, and Unamuno was worshipped. The public response to the arts was genuine and broad, uniting politics and culture in very practical ways. The Sociedad Pro-Arte Musical was

Anna Pavlova once rocked the toddler Fernando Alonso in her arms during a visit.

the least overtly political of Havana's organizations, being mostly in the business of bringing foreign artists to Cuba. Yet when it needed money, the standard warning against raising ticket prices too much was "Remember Caruso!" It seems that in 1920 Enrico Caruso received the highest fee of his career for singing Radames in Verdí's *Aida* in the Teatro Nacional's opera season; stall seat prices were raised to an unprecedented thirty-five pesos. The audience response included a very loud bomb that exploded during the Triumphal Scene in Act Two, apparently hurting no one but sending the tenor in costume running out of the theatre, across El Prado and swiftly back to the Hotel Inglaterra, from whence he did not emerge except to be taken to the ship and out of Cuba forever. No, Pro-Arte was not going to make that mistake.

Before the success of the Pro-Arte schools in 1931, Laura Rayneri de Alonso had sunk so much of her capital in the organization's artistic enterprises that she often found herself too short on cash even to pay for the children's tuition at the Colegio De La Salle. In one of several amusing letters from the dean, she was politely told, "Dear Sra. Rayneri, as we have waited already for last semester's matriculation payment for your son Fernando, we find it very difficult to comply with your request for a deferment of this payment again for the present school year."[9] She quite literally had put everything into Pro-Arte and fought vigorously for its success. In three years she would become its president, guiding Pro-Arte through fifteen golden years and later being awarded the prestigious Order of Carlos Manuel de Céspedes, Cuba's highest civilian honor, for her pioneering work in the cause of culture in Cuba.

In 1932, the fourteen-year-old Alberto joined Yavorsky's class and immediately showed promise. Fernando at first could not understand why his brother would want to leave gymnastics, swimming, and basketball, their favorite sports, for ballet. But he adored his little brother and would

pick him up after class as the flamboyant Alberto would jetté across the streetcar tracks of Calzada and double turn into El Carmelo's terrace café for lunch. Alberto was exceptionally handsome, with large brown eyes and swarthy Latin complexion. He was hairy to the point of being almost furry, and he would soon shave his body hair for ballet class. My own mother, María Luisa Rivero, who was Alberto's frequent partner later in the Ballet de Pro-Arte, would recall how much the young man's prickly torso made her itch during lifts. The green-eyed Fernando was fair, and his smooth and leaner body was toned almost to perfection by years of gymnastics and swimming. Alberto chatted constantly and was already quite popular with his class, while his older brother was serious and more than a bit shy at first. "It's funny, Fernando really was the shy type, even as a teacher," Lorena Feijóo, one of his last and brightest pupils, would recall in exile in 2009. "One just wanted to take him home," Lorena laughed, realizing that this is exactly what another young pupil did in 1976, causing the breakup of what was by then one of ballet's legendary marriages.

Fernando did not make many friends of his own and he shared Alberto's happily, so when his kid brother's life became centered on ballet, the dance crowd became his own. Some of these friends included Delfina Pérez-Gurri, Leonor Albarrán, Dinorah Agudín, Manón Toñarely, and Alicia and Cuca Martínez. The inseparable Alicia and Manón were young mascots to these teenagers, and Fernando would not pay much attention to Alicia yet, although he would recall of those days how very funny that little girl was with the large white bow in her hair.

Fernando was sent to preparatory school in Asheville, North Carolina, while Alberto prevailed on this mother to let him remain in Havana so that he might continue his ballet class. In the United States, Fernando's perfect English, green eyes, and sandy hair made many of his classmates

think that he was an American, sometimes sharing with him ethnic jokes about his fellow Latin American students. In later years, Fernando Alonso would trace the beginning of his political education to the first time he heard the word "spic," there in his North Carolina prep school. An excellent athlete, he organized an extracurricular Latin basketball team, and was nicknamed "Cuba." (This would be Alberto's nickname in the Ballets Russes years later as well.) He remained in North Carolina and put aside an early interest in literature, earning a degree in business and becoming a certified public accountant. He began to collect books on art and music, which he would send to the home of his parents for safekeeping. And he joined the Communist Party in 1935, something he felt his parents did not need

to learn. That same spring of 1935, Fernando suffered an attack of acute appendicitis and returned to Cuba after his operation to recuperate.

In Havana, his father arranged for a job with the Ministry of State, a nicely salaried clerical position in the department of international relations, which Fernando would keep for two years. On the week of his arrival, on March 20, 1935, he went with his parents to see his brother Alberto dance the role of Franz in *Coppélia*, with young Alicia Martínez as Swanilda. It was a night that would change his life.

The ballet was Yavorsky's biggest success at Pro-Arte. His staging was based on memories of Petipa's arrangements of the original 1860 choreography by Arthur Saint-Léon, shortening the final divertissements and somewhat simplifying

the work of the corps. The E.T.A. Hoffman tale was rescued from Teutonic darkness by Delibes' ebullient score, and the Havana Symphony under Amadeo Roldán received high praise on this occasion. The lavish costumes were designed by Ernestina del Hoyo and executed by the haute couturiers of Havana's exclusive fashion house Fin de Siglo. Yavorsky drilled his young cast well for the night, from the opening mazurka through the final apotheosis. Alberto's energy and his jumps were outstanding. Alicia's quick beats and precision, her lightness, her naughty innocence as the mechanical doll, and her sweet passion as a maiden in love made her Havana's sensation at the age of fourteen.

Years later, as the chief author of her own myth, Alicia Alonso would downplay her comic gifts in favor of her undeniably powerful breadth as a romantic tragedienne. Yet those who witnessed her *Coppélia* over the years—from the very young Mikhail Baryshnikov through Igor Yousekevitch, Walter Terry, Anne Barzel, Alberto Alonso, and Pedro Simón—agree that her outrageously funny, *viva* Swanilda was as brilliant in its way as her Giselle.

That night in 1935, Fernando Alonso could hardly believe that the ballerina holding his brother's hand at the curtain call was little Unga from the neighborhood. He was not prepared for such beauty. Almost half a century later he would remember in vivid tones that "there was in her a quality totally out of the earthly, something not present in any of the other girls. Her technique was there very early, you know; she had a beautiful, natural jump. And her body, even that night . . . that girl had a tremendous force but not necessarily from muscles developed too soon, no. Even then she had long, well formed limbs. And above all I remember her great gift for communication. I felt as if she were talking to me alone as she danced."

That night Fernando decided to dedicate himself to dancing. He had become quite thin during his illness and convinced himself that ballet was just the thing to return his physique and vigor. He began classes with Yavorsky at the same time he began his job with the Ministry of State, and soon he found toiling at the barre superior to typing at the office. In little over a year, on June 22, 1936, he made his stage debut, partnering with Alicia Martínez in a new pas de deux by Yavorsky set to Beethoven's *Clair de Lune*. Afterwards, he began courting the fifteen-year-old ballerina. He was completely in love.

In 1936 the Ballets Russes de Monte Carlo was brought to Havana by Pro-Arte, largely through the office of Laura Rayneri. The ensemble had been reorganized only five years earlier by the Colonel Vassily de Basil following Serge Diaghilev's death in 1929. It was the first major ballet company to appear in the city since Pavlova's three seasons of two decades before. It was a thrill for Yavorsky's young dancers to see the great Alexandra Danilova and Leonid Massine as well as the famed baby ballerinas Irina Baronova, Tatiana Riabouchinska, and Tamara Toumanova. There was Massine himself in his *Three-Cornered Hat*. Baronova interpolated her famous fouettés in "Aurora's Wedding" from *Sleeping Beauty* and each unsupported turn dazzled Alicia and Fernando. There were *The Blue Danube*, *Petrouchka*, *Les Présages*; Massine as the Poet in *Les Sylphides* and Toumanova in *Prince Igor*. Alicia, Alberto, and Fernando watched each performance as well as each company rehearsal, and the feeling invaded them that all they were doing at Pro-Arte perhaps was not enough. The thought of dancing professionally had not occurred to them; it was not something that the Sociedad de Pro-Arte Musical encouraged. But the possibility of dancing better did.

Cuca was still a devout Catholic, while Alicia had abandoned all religious trappings.

During the Ballets Russes' visit, Yavorsky obtained an audition for Alberto Alonso and Delfina Pérez-Gurri with Colonel de Basil. They were immediately accepted into the company. Delfina's family prevailed against her leaving home, but within three weeks the jubilant eighteen-year-old Alberto left for Paris with the blessings of Laura and Matías to join the Ballets Russes in its European tour.

Without his brother, Fernando grew even closer to Alicia. And for her part this marked the beginning of a lifelong habit of analyzing her dancing with Fernando; they would talk endlessly. She needed his friendship very much as well. At fifteen, as Alicia later remembered, she was

> going through a difficult period in my development as a dancer. I had been concerned with technique so much and now I wondered if I was really dancing at all. As a little girl everything felt good and was easy, and then as class became more and more demanding I had to concentrate on separate details, the body position, the head, the port de bras, the correct fifth, the right jump. It took me some time to realize that to conquer technique *is* to dance, and that I would be conquering it not once and for always but each day again and again, and that in that way I would truly begin to dance.

Until Fernando, it was also a lonely time for Alicia, and not only because of her need to talk about ballet. Cuca had finished high school by 1933; but for Alicia the political turmoil of those years and her father's fall from grace meant having to withdraw from the Colegio de las Teresianas during what should have been the eighth grade. Her school work had been poor, and the nuns were not inclined to give her a scholarship. What she could not give up was dancing, and that scholarship was easily arranged at Pro-Arte. In fact, Alicia took advantage of her glowing press notices and obtained a job teaching a ballet class of rich girls, earning thirteen pesos a month at the Margot Párraga School of Ballet on 4th Street not far from home. Antonio Martínez de Arredondo did not like to have his teenage daughter working at all— he thought it was disgraceful. But he had been jailed and was out of work; and his daughter was determined and his wife seemed to agree with her. So the old soldier said little. Alicia would never again have any other work but dance.

She also would never ask her family for money. Her independence at this time surprised her and it was not entirely welcome. Of this year she would remember, "Cuca was always my father's favorite, Toñiquito was the darling of my grandparents on my father's side, and Elizardito was my mother's. I don't think I was anybody's favorite then." She even felt distant from Cuca for the first time, since her sister was growing up faster than Alicia. Cuca had several interests outside the dance, so she stopped going to class. Alicia could talk of nothing else but dance. Cuca was still a devout Catholic, while Alicia had abandoned the religious trappings of her Teresian education even before dropping out of school. Cuca was politically engaged and once acted as an underground courier during the Hotel Nacional siege. Alicia was apolitical and never even read a newspaper except for the music and dance reviews. Cuca had met a boy, a bright student activist from the University of Havana called Raúl Chibás. She fell in love with him, and when his family thought it prudent that he leave Cuba in 1936 after the general strike against Colonel Fulgencio Batista failed, Cuca followed him to Columbia University in New York as his wife.

Alicia was left alone, her only confidant being this older boy who was already in love with her. He disliked the name Unga and soon called her "my Alicita." They talked incessantly. What with dancing and working, and the turbulence of the times, Alicia was given more freedom than girls her age usually had in those days; she spent her

freedom with Fernando. The romance grew naturally, logically. Fernando convinced her that they needed new opportunities that they could not enjoy in Cuba at the time. She had never dreamed of anything except dancing, but it was in conversation with Fernando that the strategy of pursuing a career was crystallized. Particularly with the example of Alberto still quite recent, it became obvious that they should leave Cuba. "After all, Pro-Arte did not want a professional company; it founded a ballet academy in a moment of vision and for economic reasons: it needed new members. It allowed the petite bourgeoisie to participate in the arts," a revolutionary Fernando would recall years later in his own well-bred bourgeois voice, "and it brought the best of world culture to Havana. But it never meant to train professional dancers. We were all happy accidents."

On May 10, 1937, Nikolai Yavorsky staged a version of *Swan Lake* in three acts, with Alicia as Odile-Odette and the Ballets Russes' Emile Laurens (using the name Robert Belsky for contractual reasons) as Siegfried. Fin de Siglo again constructed the costumes after Ernestina's designs, and Amadeo Roldán conducted the Havana Philharmonic for this gala occasion. Alicia's ethereal White Swan Queen was a sensation, as were the thirty-two piqués that crowned her Black Swan variations. She was, at sixteen, Cuba's top ballerina. This incidentally was the first full-length *Swan Lake* in the New World.

That summer Fernando convinced his family that he needed to return to the United States to refresh his English and to establish some business connections. He left for New York in September and found an apartment on West 174th Street one block off Broadway. He found a job as an accountant and typist for a firm that manufactured X-ray film and other medical supplies in the Bronx. Finally, in his second week in New York City, he was given an audition and then a job with the Mordkin Ballet.

He announced to his family and Alicia to hers, that they wished to marry and that Alicia should join him in New York. The news was "a disaster," as Cuca would recall. Alicia was still a child; she had barely discovered boys. She still had dolls, "she even still wet her bed"—a problem that would persist for years. Her father Antonio was devastated and it took all of Ernestina's tact and persuasion to make peace between father and daughter. On Alicia's part, there was no turmoil. There was remarkably little need of confrontation. She was not asking for advice or permission. She was not a teenager running away with her boyfriend but a woman who had made an important choice, a unified choice of Fernando and of ballet. She did not endeavor herself to think of guilt or of consequences, she did not mean to oppose her father and she would consent to any explanation which made him the least unhappy. She also did not intend discussing the matter.

Ernestina decided that it would be better not to mention the dancing at all. Her daughter was, after all, marrying a responsible young man from a very good family and who had a position in New York. Her father, though unhappy to see Alicia go, could accept her following a husband more readily than her following a career in dance. Conveniently, Laura Rayneri pointed out that the husband of Natalia Aróstegui de Suárez had been named Cuban Consul to the New York delegation, and Natalia was now preparing to leave for New York as well. And of course, Cuca and her husband were in New York, he at Columbia University Law School and she studying modern dance with Martha Graham.

On September 28, 1937, Alicia and Fernando were married by proxy in Havana, with Matías Alonso standing for his absent son. In early October, Alicia, chaperoned by Natalia, sailed from Havana Bay to meet her husband in New York. She had not told Ernestina and Antonio that she was pregnant with Fernando's child.

Interlude

Before the Alonsos

I was just a child then, and God's irony in
creating the universe was unknown to me.

—Heinrich Heine

The premiere of Nikolai Yavorsky's production of *The Sleeping Beauty* at the Teatro Auditórium del Vedado on December 29, 1931, with the young Alicia Martinez beaming as a Lady of the Court, is doubtless a landmark in Cuban dance history. Although the importance of this occasion cannot be overestimated, it was not by any means "the first performance of classical ballet by Cuban dancers in the history of the country," as Beatrice Siegel states in her book about Alicia Alonso.[1] Cuba's first ballet season occurred long before, in 1803, when the choreographer Jean-Baptiste Francisqui organized a small company for the Teatro Coliseo de La Habana, which had been built in 1776, and was renovated and renamed as the Teatro Principal de La Habana in 1804. Although Francisqui came from a French theatrical family and was himself probably from New Orleans, his company featured as principal dancers the Cubans Francisco Henríquez and Luisita Borrosí, who studied in Havana with the Catalan teacher Joan Guillet. Guillet himself had staged pantomime ballets in 1800 at the Teatro del Circo

(later called Teatro Villanueva) and was partly responsible for a flurry of opera and ballet visits between Havana and New Orleans in the early part of the nineteenth century.

By 1811, there was a resident Cuban ballet company directed by Joaquín González. This company gave the Cuban premiere of *La Fille mal gardée* at the Teatro del Circo on February 14, 1816. The New York premiere of this ballet, it is worth noting, would not be until the Mordkin Ballet's production in 1937, with Fernando Alonso in the corps de ballet while his young wife Alicia was at home with their baby Laura. Fanny Elssler came to Cuba in 1841 with her own company, but by 1843 she was employing Cuban dancers in the corps for her productions of *La Sylphide*, and *Natalia* or *The Swiss Milkmaid* at the Teatro Tacón.[2] Elssler's *Jaleo de Jerez* that first season proved popular enough to merit restaging in several provincial Cuban cities for many years to come.

Augusta Maywood brought her version of *Giselle* to Cuba in 1849, also performed at the Tacón, only eight years after the world premiere in Paris. She used a Cuban company and thus insured the popularity of that theatre, which is known today as the Gran Teatro García Lorca and is the home of the Ballet Nacional de Cuba. The rising popularity in Cuba as well as in Spain of zarzuelas, that uniquely satisfying Spanish hybrid of musical theater, high and low, led from the 1850s on to a decline in the hegemony of classical ballet and opera. Opera tastes could still be satisfied by French and Italian visiting performers, but the number of ballet performances dwindled. A brief resurgence occurred in 1904, with Aldo Boreilly's company of forty Cuban dancers, reportedly popular because of its beautiful women; and again with the seasons of Anna Pavlova and Alexander Volinine, beginning on March 13, 1915, and returning in 1917, 1918, 1919, all at the Teatro Payret.[3]

Pavlova, who bounced the toddler Fernando Alonso on her knees at his mother's house, would

Alicia in her stage debut as A Lady of the Court in Yavorsky's *The Sleeping Beauty,* at Ballet Pro-Arte, 1931. Courtesy of the Alicia Alonso Collection.

exert a strong influence on Cuban dance tastes among the intelligentsia before the founding of Pro-Arte Musical in El Vedado. Incidentally, Yavorsky's *Sleeping Beauty* with his Pro-Arte pupils was performed at the Teatro Auditórium and not at the García Lorca, as is reported incorrectly in Walter Terry's otherwise impeccable *Alicia and her Ballet Nacional de Cuba.*[4] Pro-Arte never used the competing García Lorca, which was known as the Nacional in those days, preferring to use the Teatro Payret until 1928 and using its own Teatro Auditórium exclusively until 1959. Only the paucity of ballet and opera caused by the political atmosphere of Machado's regime can explain the public and critical adoration that Havana showered on Pro-Arte's lovely ballet school presentation and debut of Alicia Alonso, which ten years earlier might have had difficulty being noticed.

Ballet Nacional de Cuba: A New Company for a New World

> My sister Alicia always wanted one thing, from the beginning,
> for as long as I can remember. It was her ideal, her dream
> above everything else, to have a company in Cuba. Few
> people are so lucky, to reach their ideal so well.
>
> —Cuca Martínez

Alicia and Fernando's whirlwind adventures in New York, like those of Alberto with the Ballets Russes, strictly speaking are not part of the tale of Cuban ballet. Still, the young couple's life would never be the same once they hit the Big Apple. The sixteen-year-old mother would stay away from ballet only until her daughter's second month, she and Fernando both would find themselves at the birth of American classical ballet, and their experiences would help shape Alicia's dream of a ballet company in her own country. Alicia Alonso, as she was billed in her debut in the United States at Jones Beach, Long Island, would, alongside her husband Fernando Alonso, dance in the historic beginnings of Lincoln Kirstein's American Ballet Caravan—a forerunner of today's New York City Ballet—as well as of Richard Pleasant and Lucia Chase's Ballet Theatre, the magical seed that would grow into today's American Ballet Theatre. It was in New York that the Alonsos took lessons from Enrico Zanfretta, Michel Fokine, Léon Fokine, and Alexandra Fedorova, from Léonide Massine, from Antony Tudor, and from George Balanchine. They created dances for Balanchine and Tudor, and also for Agnes de Mille, William Dollar, Eugene Loring, and Jerome Robbins as well as for themselves. In other words, these two Cubans were integral to the story of American ballet in much the same way that

OPPOSITE: Surely one of the twentieth century's most beloved dance partnerships—Alicia Alonso and Igor Yousekevitch. Courtesy of the Alicia Alonso Collection.

59

ABOVE LEFT: Alicia Alonso performing in *La Fille mal gardée* in Havana. Courtesy of the Alicia Alonso Collection.

ABOVE RIGHT: Alicia Alonso and John Kriza in *La Fille mal gardée*. Johnny, Alicia's favorite partner for comedy in the 1940s and '50s, was in both Ballet Theater and the new Ballet Alicia Alonso. In 1948, Kriza also played the Young Pastor opposite Alonso's murderous Lizzie Borden in the world premiere of *Fall River Legend*. Courtesy of the Alicia Alonso Collection.

OPPOSITE: Alicia and Fernando practicing in their first New York apartment. Courtesy of the Alicia Alonso Collection.

their American colleagues would become integral to the story of Cuban ballet, of Alicia's dream of a new company for the New World. It is a tale worth telling by way of groundwork for the foundations of the Cuban School of Ballet. It is also worth putting in context: the details of Alicia and Fernando's life in New York and Havana before the 1959 revolution in Cuba, and the life of their Ballet Nacional de Cuba after 1959, half a century later form part of a complex universe of art and politics, of bliss and violence, of the serenity of ballet and the turmoil of revolution. Alicia Alonso herself is a living study of ambiguity and extremes—an embodiment of the predicament of the arts in a world where clean hands may be a luxury and where hope nevertheless must be kept alive.

Before turning to 1938, it is worth noting that virtually every form of art in Cuba today is an art in exile—except dance. It is also worth noting that at a time when misguided Cuban Communist Party loyalties insistently make a cultural virtue out of vulgarity that the Ballet Nacional de Cuba remains a refuge for taste. A decade into the twenty-first century, the Cuban troupe's productions of *Swan Lake, The Sleeping Beauty, Coppélia, La Fille mal gardée, The Nutcracker, Shakespeare y sus máscaras*, and above all *Giselle* continue to flower at home and abroad. The success of Alicia Alonso

and her Ballet Nacional de Cuba has grown continuously in artistic and political significance since Fidel Castro's coup d'état in 1959. In the last forty years, the Cubans have gathered critical praise and sold-out crowds in New York, London, Paris, Venice, Moscow, Barcelona, Madrid, Athens, Mexico City, and of course Havana. The International Ballet Festivals in the Cuban capital have, since 1960, shown visitors that art doesn't always seem to imitate miserable life in Cuba and that the Ballet Nacional works when nothing else does in Cuba. In particular, the 1990 International Ballet Festival, held at a time when most of the communist world was well on the way to crumbling, sounded a spectacularly defiant note by attracting international stars of every political persuasion to a celebration of dance. Since the demise of Soviet communism, Alonso's festivals in Havana have continued, with an occasional, daring influx of a Cuban-American exile artistic presence that must count as an extremely rare instance of glasnost in what remains a stubbornly Stalinist state. This much is undeniable: No event in recent history has been as controversial or influential in the Americas as the Cuban revolution. One extraordinary woman has been and continues to be at the center of that revolution, and the effects of her influence on world dance and culture will linger

On Broadway in *Great Lady,* 1938. From left to right is an impressive chorus line of Nora Kaye, Jerome Robbins, Fernando Alonso, and Alicia Alonso. Courtesy of the Alicia Alonso Collection.

long after the revolution itself has been consigned to the dustbin of history.

That is what the future held for the sixteen-year-old Alicia Alonso as she sailed for New York in 1937, pregnant with Fernando's child.

Fernando got an office job, but soon he also joined the Mordkin Ballet, a small but by all accounts good troupe led by Mikhail Mordkin, Anna Pavlova's partner in her New York and Havana seasons in 1910. Alicia and Fernando's daughter Laura—named after Fernando's mother—was born in the spring and soon became a fixture in the rehearsal studio. The young mother first just watched, then, barely a month and a half after Laurita's birth, Alicia joined the company. After a less than glamorous professional American debut with the Mordkin Ballet in Jones Beach, Alicia and Fernando appeared in two Broadway shows. The first of them, *Great Lady*, was choreographed by the recent Russian exile George Balanchine.

Balanchine was by this time no stranger to the musical, having choreographed Josephine Baker's star turn in the Ziegfeld Follies of 1936 and, in the same year, the landmark Richard Rodgers-Lorenz Hart production *On Your Toes*. *Great Lady*, despite Frederick Loewe's lovely score, was not a hit in 1938. But it nevertheless boasted spectacular solos by André Eglevsky, Leda Anchutina and Annabelle Lyon, as well as the Broadway debuts of Alicia Alonso, Fernando Alonso, and Jerome Robbins—in retrospect not at all a bad bunch of Broadway gypsies.

The Alonsos' next Broadway job, *Stars in Her Eyes*, in 1939, was an Arthur Schwartz-Dorothy Fields backstage musical directed by Joshua Logan, starring Ethel Merman, Mildred Natwick, and Jimmy Durante. This one was rich. Tamara Toumanova, whose dancing was choreographed by Carl Randall, played a ballerina named Tata. Alicia and Fernando were featured and got first billing after the stars, as principal Lady of the Ballet and principal Gentleman of the Ballet. Alicia recalled

how Randall would laugh whenever she and Maria Karnilova would try the time-step. Apparently they were awful, but unintentionally very funny, and the choreographer left their bit in the show. Marusia, Alicia's neighbor and lifelong friend, was at the time in the corps de ballet of the Metropolitan Opera and was still being billed as Maria Karniloff. Two other Upper West Side neighbors of the Alonsos were in the chorus, Jerome Robbins and Nora Kaye. It was around this time that Fernando befriended a wealthy ballerina named Lucia Chase, then a fellow dancer with the Mordkin Ballet.

When not rehearsing or auditioning for shows, the Alonsos would take lessons for fifty cents a

Alicia Alonso with the Ballet Caravan in Lew Christensen's *The Debutante*. Courtesy of the Alicia Alonso Collection.

ABOVE: A portrait of Alicia Alonso in *Billy the Kid,* taken in Havana. Courtesy of the Ballet Nacional de Cuba, photo by Eugene Loring.

RIGHT AND OPPOSITE: Alicia Alonso as Juliet in Alberto Alonso's third version of *Romeo and Juliet,* 1970. Courtesy of the Ballet Nacional de Cuba.

day from Enrico Zanfretta at the Works Projects Administration. The Italian Zanfretta, trained in the Cecchetti method, would prove the first of a triumvirate on influences on what would become the seed of the Cuban style. The Fokine training was next, as both Alicia and Fernando took classes from not only Michel Fokine but also from Michel's brother Alexander, his wife Alexandra Fedorova, and their son Léon Fokine. That powerhouse group with all their Maryinsky and Diaghilev cultural baggage would soon be followed in Alicia and Fernando's life by the towering influence of Antony Tudor.

While taking a class with Fedorova, the new School of American Ballet noticed Alicia's talent and offered her and Fernando full scholarships. Through Robbins, Alicia met Lincoln Kirstein, who invited her and Fernando to join the American Ballet Caravan in 1939. Her first principal role there was that of the Mother and the Mexican Sweetheart in Eugene Loring and Aaron Copland's *Billy the Kid,* which would become an American ballet classic. When the Caravan's season ended in 1940, Alicia joined in the founding season of Ballet Theatre, receiving rave notices for the pas de trois from *Swan Lake,* danced with

Alicia Alonso in *Dioné*
at Ballet Pro-Arte, 1940.
Courtesy of the Ballet
Nacional de Cuba.

Leon Danielian and Nora Kaye. It was after that performance she first experienced double vision and had several minor accidents offstage.

It was Lucia Chase and Antony Tudor who asked the Cuban couple to join Ballet Theatre. Tudor, originally from England, would become perhaps the strongest artistic influence on Alicia Alonso's style, although this aspect of her art has been overlooked as the Tudor ballets have fallen out of the repertory on both sides of the Atlantic. Alicia took the leading role in Tudor's *Romeo and Juliet*, created *Shadow of the Wind* for him, and brought a new dimension to the despicably sexy adolescent Ate in *Undertow*. "It was a whole new world with Alicia," Tudor told me. She and Nora Kaye even made Tudor crack up laughing in his *Gala Performance*, "until some reviewer told them they were funny," said Tudor. "Then they stopped being funny." That Alicia would be singled out

from Ballet Theatre's rich ensemble seemed inevitable to Fernando. "Her physical proportions, her muscle tone, and her capacity to recover from any injury all astounded people as much as her extension and speed," recalled Fernando a lifetime later when looking back at their youth. "So did her character and her discipline. She was a gifted athlete. She was a complete artist."

"She was very funny," remembered Robbins, "with that accent. She was always very open about what she did and didn't know—and she didn't know English. She called me Yawi." She also cooked for him, since he was helpless in the kitchen on tour. Robbins grew close to the Alonsos when the three took on a brief season with the Chicago Lyric Opera right after *Stars in Her Eyes* closed. The three budding Ballet Theatre members landed principal roles with the opera ballet and danced in Verdi's *Aida*, *Il Trovatore*, and *La Traviata*. All three would remember this as a very happy gig. Robbins told me how the chorus was miffed by the ovations the dancers were getting, and one night they started closing in on Alicia mid-fouetté in the Spanish dance of Act Three of *La Traviata*. He and Fernando held back the singers with their banderillas and lances. They were asked not to take a curtain call that night.

Alicia's eye troubles began early, and surgery after surgery followed. The Japanese attack on Pearl Harbor found Alicia blindfolded and convalescing in New York's Presbyterian Hospital. Her return to the studio, however, was swift. In 1943, a few months after another eye operation in Havana, Cuca would remember, "Dr. Alamilla had tears in his eyes when he told my sister she would never dance again." Nonsense, thought Alicia. She went against her doctor's advice and wired Lucia Chase that she was ready to return to Ballet Theatre. Léonide Massine took turns with Jerome Robbins partnering Alicia in Massine's own classic *Capriccio Espagnol*. On November 2, 1943, after the reigning classical ballerina of

the day, Alicia Markova, became indisposed, the fiery Alicia Alonso learned the role of Giselle with only three days' notice, danced the opening, and became an overnight sensation in the ballet she would own from that day on. The tale at this point becomes in fact at least two: one of Alicia Alonso the American ballet star, and another of Alicia Alonso the pioneering founder of Cuban ballet.

Dividing her time between Havana and New York, Alicia Alonso, the American ballerina, went on to create not only standard versions of the classics of the repertory, but also the world premieres of such modern masterpieces as Agnes de Mille's *Fall River Legend*, Antony Tudor's *Undertow* and *Shadow of the Wind*, Bronislava Nijinska's *Schumann Concerto*, Alberto Alonso's *Romeo and Juliet* and *Concerto*, and George Balanchine's legendary *Theme and Variations*.

But Alicia, the Cuban ballerina, had not stopped dancing in Cuba, even during her first season with Ballet Theatre. Hers was, from the start, a Cuban world. In 1940, Alicia and Fernando Alonso created *Dioné* in Havana, the first ballet choreographed to an original score by a Cuban composer, Eduardo Sánchez de Fuentes. That same year, while convalescing from her third eye operation, she and her husband helped to

organize the Agrupación Teatral La Silva, together with several Spanish communist exile actors and dancers. With this troupe she staged her own first choreographic efforts, *La Condesita* and *La Tinaja*, both ballets with Cuban themes. These ballets mark the beginnings of a lifelong project to find Cuban expression for classical European dance forms, something Alberto Alonso later raised to new heights in the 1950s and 1960s, followed by Alberto Méndez in the 1970s and 1980s. It is a project that today the Cuban *danseur noble*, Carlos Acosta, is attempting, with deep affection for his roots, in London and around the world.

By 1946, Alicia Alonso was prima ballerina of the American Ballet Theatre, and the company gave her top billing in its first European tour to London, Paris, and Vienna. Ruthlessly, Alicia connived to have her rival Rosella Hightower leave the company; Alicia Markova and Anton Dolin also left. Igor Yousekevitch joined the company in 1946, becoming Alicia's principal partner, and her lover, for the next fifteen years. Dance meant everything. In 1947, when Alicia's father died, she danced that very night.

When Alicia and Igor danced the 1947 world premiere of George Balanchine's *Theme and Variations*, the ballerina began defining her artistic

Alicia Alonso and Igor Yousekevitch in Balanchine's original *Theme and Variations*. The ballet has never left the repertory of the American Ballet Theatre and the Ballet Nacional de Cuba since its creation in 1947. Courtesy of the Ballet Nacional de Cuba.

OPPOSITE: Dama de la República Alicia Alonso after receiving the medal of the Order of Carlos Manuel de Céspedes, then the highest civilian honor of the Republic of Cuba, 1947. Courtesy of the Ballet Nacional de Cuba.

ideals: She was convinced that ballet is theatre and that it is always humane, that it cannot be the abstract art form envisioned by Balanchine. While she had taken well to Tudor's rhythmically free approach to choreography, Balanchine's strictly ordered musicality was at first difficult for Alicia. "I always had a feeling of being just behind the music when I worked with Balanchine," she told me, "of the music escaping me." She would conquer that particular hurdle. There were bitter clashes during rehearsals, followed by triumphant notices on opening night. "Mr. Balanchine kept giving me and Igor more and more complex steps to do, hoping our personalities wouldn't show through," Alicia recalled. "But we couldn't help it. Maybe that is the reason *Theme and Variations* is Balanchine's most sensual ballet. That is just the way we danced."

When ABT's leading dramatic ballerina, Nora Kaye, fell ill, Alicia took over the role of Lizzie Borden in the world premiere of Agnes de Mille's *Fall River Legend*. With the best reviews in the romantic, classical, and modern repertories, an assertive Alicia Alonso now owned every major role in the company. Encouraged by her acclaim internationally and back home by receiving Cuba's

highest civilian honor, the Order Nacional de Carlos Manuel de Céspedes, Alicia founded her own ballet company with Fernando Alonso as director, Alberto Alonso as resident choreographer, and herself as prima ballerina.

On October 28, 1948, the Alonsos' beloved Auditoríum del Vedado was the scene of a debut that few then could imagine would lead to so much. It was the first performance by the Ballet Alicia Alonso. Its composition was cosmopolitan, its reach urbane, and its pedagogical impulse real and humane, as it is to this day. The school was hand in hand with the company from the start, and Fernando, having absorbed lessons from Fokine, Tudor, and Balanchine, would himself become a ballet master and model for generations of dancers to come. Alberto, the most widely traveled and in many ways the most Cuban of the three, aimed to bring a Cuban accent to the substance of the classics, the distinctive fusion of Spanish and African strengths at the heart of Cuban movement. He began teaching at his mother's Pro-Arte in 1940, in between Ballets Russes dates, and choreographed for Ballet Pro-Arte, *Preludes* (1942), *Concerto*, Jose Lezama Lima's *Forma*, *The General's Daughter*, *Skyscraper*, and *Sinfonia* (all in 1943), *El mensaje*

BALLET NACIONAL DE CUBA

Alicia Alonso in Alberto
Alonso's *La Valse*. Courtesy
of the Ballet Nacional de
Cuba.

(1944), *Sombras* (1946), *Antes del alba* (1947), and *La Valse* in 1948—all as prelude to his career with the company he founded with his brother and his sister-in-law. It was Alberto Alonso who began a nationalist movement in choreography that continues to influence all of Latin American dance. Cuba had something unique. When Alicia, Alberto, and Fernando opened the doors to the Academia de Ballet Alicia Alonso, the path was set for what Arnold Haskell and others would pronounce the youngest school in the history of this venerable art, the Cuban School of Ballet.

President Carlos Prío Socarrás' administration granted the company a small state subsidy, and there was a conscious outreach across class boundaries in performances, from glittering galas to free dance recitals at the University of Havana. The Ballet Alicia Alonso enjoyed strong labor and student support, particularly from the FEU (Federación Estudiantil Universitaria), Cuba's politically powerful student union. In 1954 the company staged the first complete *Swan Lake* in the Western Hemisphere, starring Alicia Alonso and Royes Fernández, a gifted protégé of Anton Dolin. Alberto Alonso, partly out of concern over the neglect of Cuban folk dance within the company, formed his own Ballet Nacional for two seasons and prophetically complemented the repertory of what was then still called Ballet Alicia Alonso.

Stylistic homogeneity would come later, but the Ballet Alicia Alonso—later called Ballet de Cuba, and now known as the Ballet Nacional de Cuba—was a new force in the Americas. Its aim was high. The company toured at home and abroad with great success until Fulgencio Batista's brutal regime withdrew all financial support from the company and forced Alicia into exile in 1956.

OPPOSITE: Alicia Alonso
as Odile from *Swan Lake*.
Courtesy of the Ballet
Nacional de Cuba.

Alicia Alonso as the Snow
Queen with Igor Yousekev-
itch in the 1959 Ballets
Russes de Monte Carlo's
version of the *Nutcracker*.
Courtesy of the Ballet
Nacional de Cuba.

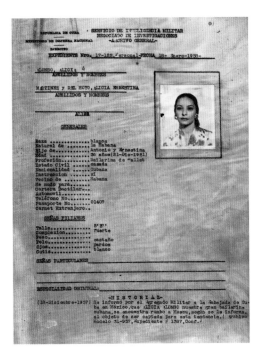

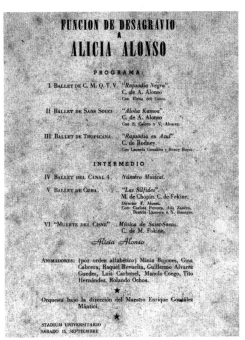

LEFT: This is the first page of the extensive SIM (Servicio de Inteligencia Militar) secret file on Alicia Alonso, ordered by the Batista government after her invitation to become the first Western dancer to appear with the Bolshoi Ballet. The epithet "our great Cuban ballerina" is used repeatedly in the report, and Alicia calls it one of her favorite reviews. Courtesy of the Ballet Nacional de Cuba.

RIGHT: The program from the historic Función de Desagravio held on September 15, 1956 at the University of Havana. Alicia Alonso danced Fokine's *The Dying Swan* and vowed never to dance in Cuba again as long as Batista remained in power. Courtesy of the Ballet Nacional de Cuba.

While Alicia danced abroad with her partner and lover, Igor Yousekevitch, first with ABT and then with the Ballets Russes de Monte Carlo, Fernando remained in Cuba with his mistress, the dancer Leonela González. Sixteen of the original dancers of the Ballet Alicia Alonso were Cubans, but twenty-four were taken from the roster of Alicia's friends from American Ballet Theatre and Ballet Caravan. Among these was the nineteen-year-old Michael Maule, who became Alicia's lover as well as her partner when Yousekevitch was not around. Fernando had been consistently unfaithful, but this was Alicia's first affair that Fernando saw as a threat. It was meant to be just that; "I did it to punish Fernando, that's all," Alicia told her friend Angela Grau. For Alicia, the choice soon became one not only between husband and lover but also perhaps one of keeping her ballet company alive or not. After a series of unpleasant scenes involving Alicia's mother, daughter, husband, and lover, Michael Maule was sent packing to New York, where he joined New York City Ballet. Leonela González also was fired, though

not before Alicia's mother, Ernestina, attacked her backstage with a pair of scissors. Alicia resigned herself to an unhappy marriage that years later would end up in divorce. But after that episode, she would never be so indiscreet or vulnerable again. Leonela was replaced by Menia Martínez, the next woman in what Fernando and Alicia's daughter, Laura, would remember as a series of "cruel little revenges" for Alicia's increasing fame.

While their marriage was saved for the time being, the ballet company faced ruin for different reasons. From 1953 to 1959, Fernando Alonso used the ballet school and the company's travels abroad as covers for clandestine activities against the Batista regime. By 1956, the Cuban secret police as well as Fulgencio Batista's own Bureau for the Repression of Communist Activities, supported by the American CIA, had compiled extensive intelligence files on the dancers.

The Cuban government tried to pressure Alicia Alonso to travel as part of a propaganda campaign to aid the troubled Batista regime. After she refused, the company lost all its financial support

Alicia Alonso performing in the Ballet Nacional de Cuba's *Swan Lake* with the Kirov's Sviatoslav Kuznetsov. Courtesy of the Ballet Nacional de Cuba.

from the Cuban government. The influential magazine *Bohemia* courageously stood against Batista's governmental decision and, in an editorial, called the withdrawal of funds from the Ballet de Cuba, as the Ballet Alicia Alonso was called by now, "an attack on our national culture."[1]

An outraged artistic community joined the FEU in organizing an *Acto de desagravio*, a mass rally and benefit concert, September 15, 1956, in Havana's Stadium Universitario to protest the treatment of the arts in general and of Alicia Alonso in particular. An audience of more than 25,000 braved the police lines and other intimidation to attend the unique spectacle, which proved to be a turning point in the fight against Batista as well as a remarkable chapter in the story of Cuban ballet.

The program opened with Fokine's *Les Sylphides*, with Carlota Pereira, Ada Zanetti, and Beatriz Lismore. Fernando Alonso danced the role of the Poet—even though by this time he had effectively retired from dancing and had devoted himself to teaching ballet. Alicia danced *The Dying Swan*, which Fokine himself had taught her, for the last time in her career. The student leader Fructuoso Rodríguez, who acted as master of ceremonies in the *Acto de desagravio* was assassinated within days by Batista's police. The Ballet Alicia Alonso left for the Western province of Pinar del Río the day after the event, on a previously planned tour of the entire length of the island. Alicia Alonso returned to Havana in October, as a guest on the popular CMQ network television show *Casino de la Alegría*, where she surprised the television audience as well as her family with these words:

> I am sure that ballet will not perish because I am leaving it in hands that will defend it with all they have, in the hands of the Cuban people, the same people who work in the land and work in the arts. I want you all to know that I will be there at your side, whenever I am able to, that I will return to Cuba, that I will continue fighting for the Ballet de Cuba, for the arts in Cuba, and for these dancers who danced today. *Hasta pronto.*[2]

With those unexpected words of farewell on television, Alicia was forced into exile along with many of her dancers. Fernando remained in Havana to run the ballet school, courageously continuing his political activities. The Academia de Ballet Alicia Alonso continued its classes and would do so until it became the National School of Ballet after 1959. The ballet company did not perform again in Cuba until 1959.

An ironic, sad footnote may be added here; fifty years after the historic *Acto de desagravio*, as the culmination of a series of events the FEU organized to commemorate that page in Cuban ballet history, there was a special performance of the Ballet Nacional de Cuba in the very same Stadium Universitario. The program included not only *Les Sylphides*, by now a signature piece for the company, but also Brian Macdonald's new *Prologue to a Tragedy*, and Alicia Alonso's own *Gottschalk Symphony*. Among the principal dancers that night were the young stars of Cuban ballet Carlos Quenedit, Yolanda Correa, Joel Carreño, and Taras Domitro, the youngest and perhaps most brilliant of them. Domitro had the honor of acting

as Alicia's cavalier, presenting her a memorial plaque from the FEU at the evening's end. That was on December 18, 2006. Three years later, Domitro, Quenedit, Correa, and Carreño would all be Cuban exiles in the United States.

Back to 1956, and now on to a bit of comedy. Alonso's Cuban dancers landed in the Greek Theatre in Los Angeles for Alicia Alonso's *Coppélia*, a historic staging that would set the model for future productions of the ballet both at the Ballet Nacional de Cuba and—not credited—in Enrique Martínez's version at the American Ballet Theatre. The ballet would emerge, like *Giselle*, as another of history's sweetest surprises; a French stage masterpiece based on a German story, once best known through Russian interpretations, that came

Alicia Alonso and Rodolfo Rodríguez in Act Two of *Swan Lake*. **Courtesy of the Ballet Nacional de Cuba.**

down to us in ideal form as spectacularly recreated by a Cuban ballerina. Alonso did this with the heartbreaking *Giselle*, and she did it again with the rambunctious *Coppélia*. Here was real comedy, with some of the most wickedly funny pantomime in all ballet. Here, in her version, also was high-voltage virtuosity, heart-stopping bravura of the sort that makes one believe that dance has no limits. The staging, remarkably consistent for half a century, remains as vital a part of the Cuban repertory to this day as Alonso's *Giselle*, *Swan Lake*, and *The Sleeping Beauty*. George Balanchine once declared *Giselle* to be ballet's great tragedy and *Coppélia* its great comedy. It is no accident that both became signature pieces for Alonso and her dancers. The Cuban people's love of these two works runs deep, and Alonso has spent a lifetime refining each to perfection.

Alonso's involvement with *Giselle* is legend, but she in fact danced Swanilda in *Coppélia* first, in Nikolai Yavorsky's shortened 1935 Pro-Arte Musical production in Havana when she was only fifteen. She later collaborated with Leon Fokine, at the time a teacher at the Academia Alicia Alonso in Havana, on her first *Coppélia* staging, in 1948, with the inimitable Igor Yousekevitch as her loving Franz. In 1957, with André Eglevsky as her Franz, came the historic *Coppélia* mounted at the Greek Theatre in Los Angeles. Alicia once confessed to me that Eglevsky was if anything even more exciting than Yousekevitch. Then the 1968 Alonso *Coppélia* for her Ballet Nacional de Cuba became, like her definitive 1972 *Giselle*, for both the Paris Opera Ballet and the Ballet Nacional de Cuba, the standard by which other choreographic versions must be judged.

Why is this so? The reasons are as varied as they are joyful. It is no coincidence that Alonso worked with Michel Fokine, with Leon Fokine, and with Alexandra Fedorova. The Fokine influence on Cuban ballet is at least as strong as that of Antony Tudor or of any later Russian artistic

Alicia Alonso and Royes Fernández in *Coppélia*. Courtesy of the Ballet Nacional de Cuba.

forces. The sensual and exquisite boundaries of the Cuban style are defined by Alonso's *Coppélia* as much as by her *Giselle*.

Alonso's historically informed reconstruction of the original 1870 Arthur Saint-Léon, and later Marius Petipa, versions of *Coppélia* carries the unmistakable post-Romantic line and flavor that marked the Fokine revolution in the early twentieth century. The superhuman demands on virtuosity are there, more than in any other *Coppélia* production from New York to London to Saint Petersburg. Swanilda's Act Three solo alone demands the technical fireworks of a couple of Rose Adagios with Giselle's Act One extended pointe solo added for good measure. But more than all the classical complexity—and Alonso's Cubans routinely toss off impossible steps with aplomb—there is real humanity in the reconstruction. Like the Alonso *Giselle*, her *Coppélia*

OPPOSITE: Alicia Alonso and Royes Fernández dancing *Coppélia* on tour. Courtesy of the Ballet Nacional de Cuba.

ABOVE: Alicia Alonso and
Azari Plisetsky in Alberto
Alonso's *Carmen.* "Azari
became one of us, a real
Cuban dancer," Alicia
would recall. Courtesy
of the Ballet Nacional de
Cuba.

OPPOSITE: Alicia Alonso
and Igor Yousekevitch in
Alicia's version of the *Don
Quixote* pas de deux. Courtesy of the Ballet Nacional
de Cuba.

has been a training ground in humanity for some
of the most humane of Cuban dancers, long after
Alonso and Yousekevitch's own Swanilda and
Franz, the roles have been filled by every available Carreño, Sarabia, and Feijóo; by Carlos
Acosta, by Osmay Molina; by Joan Boada, who
became the youngest Franz in the Ballet Nacional de Cuba's history before leaving home; by
the even younger Taras Domitro, and by Hayna
Gutiérrez. That all of them now take this gift to
the world's stages far from Havana only speaks of
the reach of their dancing with a Cuban accent.
Alonso's *Coppélia* matters because it makes one
believe in the power of dance to reaffirm the best
in all of us.

After the success of *Coppélia* in Los Angeles
in 1956, Alicia abandoned the American Ballet
Theatre when faced with an offer from the Ballets
Russes de Monte Carlo, which not only let her join
Yousekevitch again—a crucial incentive—but also
made her the highest paid dancer in the world.

In 1957, in the midst of the Cold War, Alicia
Alonso became the first dancer from the Americas
to appear with the Bolshoi Ballet. This signaled
a historical series of performances in Moscow,
Riga, and Leningrad that not only broke the ice
artistically with the Iron Curtain but also insured
her place as the world's *prima ballerina assoluta.*
The anti-communist Igor Yousekevitch was also
invited, but he turned down the offer. Politics were
not terribly important to Alicia Alonso at first. "In
fact, Alicia was never very intelligent when it came
to politics," Fernando Alonso told me in Havana
after their divorce. "You have to remember that
she barely has an eighth-grade education. She is
not a sophisticated political thinker." Even to this
day, Fernando remains one of his ex-wife's severest
critics inside of Cuba, publicly worrying about the
loss of Cuba's greatest dancers to exile and, in an
especially cruel gibe, about "Alicia not seeing what
is going on."[3] Sophisticated or not, however, Alicia
has cultivated shrewd co-production partnerships
with European theatres such as Venice's La Fenice
and Bologna's Teatro Communale that have given
the Cuban ballet access to economic resources
otherwise non-existent in Cuba since the end of
Soviet economic support. In 2005, Alonso's Cuban
production of *Don Quixote* became the cultural
centerpiece of Spain's celebrations of the four
hundredth anniversary of Cervantes' masterpiece.

After Fidel Castro's coup d'état, January 1,
1959, Alicia returned to Cuba. Her grandson, Iván
Monreal, was born to Laura and her then husband
Lorenzo Monreal that February. The Ballet Nacional de Cuba was reorganized with a strong political identification, eventually touring the world as
cultural ambassadors of the revolution. Alicia's

BALLET NACIONAL DE CUBA

BALLET NACIONAL DE CUBA

mother died that summer, on the opening night of the first International Ballet Festival in Havana. It was that night Alicia was to dance Fokine's *The Dying Swan* wearing the costume her mother had so carefully made for her. *The Dying Swan* had a particular place in Alicia Alonso's repertory and is drenched in significance for her company's ballerinas. Alicia learned it from Fokine, and she nurtured the four-minute jewel with real affection. Her arabesques began higher than most; her *pas de bourrés* were almost imperceptible, floating with serene anguish. Silence usually followed the close, a gasp then leading to applause that usually lasted longer than the piece. Like Pavlova before her, Alicia took these curtain calls in character. She never encored it. After Alicia danced *The Dying Swan* in 1956 in Havana, she did not repeat the role as long as she could not dance it in her native country. She began rehearsing it for the 1959 International Ballet Festival in Havana after the revolution, and her mother made her costume as she had made every one of her costumes since her debut. When her mother died of cancer before the festival opening, Alicia cancelled the performance, effectively giving up the role after the death of Ernestina del Hoyo. Pavlova kept her swan costume near her and called for it before her death in 1923. When Alicia returned to ballet in 1974 following her last eye operation, she confided to her friend Angela Grau that she would dance *The Dying Swan* one more time, as her farewell to ballet. In Havana a few years later, as she showed me many of her souvenirs and treasures, mementos of a long and beautiful life in dance, I saw that there was only one costume in Alicia's home and that costume is the delicate swan tutu made by her mother on her deathbed. It is lovely, fresh and pressed, and never used.

Shortly after the festival, all the doors to the West were suddenly closed as the United States began its economic blockade of Cuba. In 1958, *Dancemagazine* gave Alicia Alonso its coveted annual award; one year later there was a ban on that publication and others of the mere mention of her name in print. Press releases from the Ballet Nacional de Cuba mailed to the United States were returned, sealed, with the pages torn to pieces, according to Angela Grau. A 1960 Anniversary Gala for the American Ballet Theatre was the last time she would dance with Yousekevitch for twenty years. Even her close friends, Anton Dolin, director of the London Festival Ballet, and Erik Bruhn, director of the Royal Danish Ballet, turned their backs and failed to extend invitations to Alicia to dance with their companies. "Nobody, nobody would ask me," Alicia told me. ABT's Lucia Chase did not forget Alicia, but her efforts to obtain a visa for her friend to dance in New York were blocked by the U. S. State Department. Alicia Alonso was not allowed to return to her New York public until 1975.

Ballet was not a high priority in the early days of the revolution, and Alicia languished in her prime without a stage. Soon, however, the political value of such a dancer became obvious. Fernando Alonso was photographed in his militia uniform giving ballet class with a gun at his side; Alicia and her dancers were shown in newsreels cutting sugar cane. They would not, it must be said, be forced to do that for long. Fidel Castro himself became a familiar backstage figure as performances were organized again in Havana. Alicia accompanied Fidel on fishing trips and rumors flew about a love affair between the ballerina and the bearded leader. In 1960, Alicia traveled to Nice as Fidel Castro's personal envoy to an homage to Pablo Picasso.

Also in 1960, the company staged its first political ballet, *Despertar* (*The Awakening*) in Havana, a dance agitprop portraying the revolutionary struggle of the Cuban people. The artistically mediocre piece would not remain in the repertory, but its premiere achieved its purpose of securing generous government funds for new productions.

OPPOSITE: Alicia Alonso in a studio portrait of Michel Fokine's *The Dying Swan*, wearing the costume designed by her mother. Courtesy of the Ballet Nacional de Cuba.

These included a restoration of all the *divertissements* from *Coppélia*, making it the first complete production of that nineteenth-century comic masterpiece in the twentieth century.

The year 1966 was another turning point in the career of Alicia Alonso and the history of Cuban ballet; Alonso received the Grand Prix de la Ville and the Prix Anna Pavlova for her *Giselle* choreography and performance during the Ballet Nacional de Cuba's Paris debut. The historic visit

was not all the Cuban government hoped for, however, and it marked the beginning of harsher security measures within the company. The Paris 1966 engagement would be remembered as the first and most public defection from the company, as ten leading male dancers of the BNC sought political asylum on the day of the *Giselle* gala before the president of France. It took a while for the political import of the Paris incident to be felt, and there was time for levity in France There was a happy incident with Maria Callas in Paris, or rather an episode involving a fan who was convinced Alonso was Callas and asked for her autograph—both women favored turbans and

huge dark glasses at this time. This later inspired Alicia to portray the Greek-American diva in the Alberto Méndez ballet, *Maria Callas: In Memoriam*. Somewhere in Paris there is an opera fan with a Callas autograph signed by Alonso. Back in Havana, the ICAIC (Cuban Film Institute) produced a film of Alicia's *Giselle*, and the ballerina ignored the Cold War on all sides by managing to donate a print of the film to the New York Public Library's Dance Collection in 1963—so that "my public will not forget me." It became the most often requested film in the Lincoln Center collection. Dance and film in Cuba grew with the filming of *Génesis*, which was a collaboration between Alicia Alonso and the Italian avant-garde composer Luigi Nono, and with theatrical

films of *Swan Lake*, *Grand Pas de Quatre*, and *Don Quixote*.

Good news came from the Soviet Union the following year. Alberto Alonso choreographed *Carmen* for Maya Plisetskaya and the Bolshoi Ballet, a commission that was at the time a unique honor for a non-Russian. On August 4, 1967, the ballet was adapted for Alicia with the blessings of her Soviet colleague. *Carmen* became one of the staples of her repertory, her most sensual and Latin role.

Also in 1967, Alicia danced Giselle with the Grands Ballets Canadiens staged by Sir Anton Dolin during Expo '67. It was an emotional event, with many of her friends from the United States seeing her for the first time in many years. Few in the audience knew or noticed that Alicia danced the entire performance with a hairline fracture in her right foot, an injury suffered in the dress rehearsal. Influential critics including Anne Barzel, Clive Barnes, and Walter Terry began a campaign in the American press to allow Alicia Alonso to return to dance in the United States. During her Canadian visit, friends noticed that Alicia had given up signing autographs, embarrassed by her awkward blind scrawl. Already at home, shortly before the tour, a cruel incident with a fan shocked Alicia into facing her blindness and almost accepting the inevitable: a little girl at the stage door shouted to her mother, "*Mami, es una ciega*—the lady's blind!" That night in the small Cuban city of Sancti Spiritus, Alicia began seeing herself as her public might see her, resolving not to make any allowances to acknowledging her own blindness. News of that blindness as well as of her incredibly youthful dancing reached the American public.

Her tale of a blind monarch, *Oedipus Rex*, was a major success in 1970, in Havana and in Paris, though her many changes to the role of Jocasta led the choreographer Jorge Lefebvre to take his name off the ballet. The title role was made for Jorge

BALLET NACIONAL DE CUBA

OPPOSITE: Alicia Alonso as Jocasta, seduces Jorge Esquivel's Oedipus in this scene. Courtesy of the Ballet Nacional de Cuba.

Jocasta has just learned that Oedipus is her son. Courtesy of the Ballet Nacional de Cuba.

Esquivel, securing his place as Cuba's leading male dancer. In 1972, Alicia was accorded the commission of choreographing *Giselle* for its original home, the Paris Opéra Ballet. She staged the ballet for the Parisians and danced the title role in the premiere opposite the impulsive Albrecht of Cyril Atanassof, to great critical and popular acclaim. By now all she was able to see were a single red light placed downstage center and two blue lights on the sides. The audience was unaware of the ballerina's blindness. Her husband, Fernando, convinced her that another operation would mean the end of her career, so she continued to dance in total darkness. She agreed to undergo surgery for the fourth time to restore her vision when she had completed the 1972 season. Close friends from all over the world were told in confidence of what would be Alicia's last performance, and many flocked that September to the Herkel Theatre in Budapest for the most daring and passionate *Carmen* of her career. By now she was totally blind. After the performance she flew to Barcelona for surgery, believing that her life as a dancer was over.

At first she kept up her spirits. Jerome Robbins, who had not seen Alicia since before the revolution, had a tearful reunion with her during the Moscow Ballet Competition in 1973, when Alicia was still getting used to having some of her sight back after surgery. He went into the elevator of his Moscow hotel and out of nowhere, he "heard this voice, with a heavy Cuban accent I recognized instantly, saying 'Mr. Robbins, I presume'." They hugged, cried, and caught up. They did not discuss politics "because we never had," Robbins told me. "She was never political when I knew her, not at all."

Robbins was touched by Alicia's initial astonishment mixed with fear upon being able to see again, even a little. "She told me the only thing that didn't scare her were the trees, that everything else was so different and unexpected. The faces and the colors were not what she remembered."

Alicia Alonso and Azari Plisetsky filming the *Don Quixote* pas de deux at the Plaza de la Catedral in Old Havana. Courtesy of the Ballet Nacional de Cuba.

Alicia Alonso, dazzling in a new Oscar de la Renta costume, in Jerome Robbins' lovely *In the Night*. Courtesy of the Alicia Alonso Collection.

Ever on the lookout for her company, Alicia, as she chatted with her old friend in Moscow, secured a gift of his sublime *In the Night*, which eventually would be staged by Sarah Leland in Havana for the Sixth International Ballet Festival in a new production with costumes by the Dominican designer Oscar de la Renta.

Between 1972 and 1974, Alicia regained partial sight in both eyes, a form of tunnel vision that allowed her to focus on her immediate surroundings; she was told by doctors that any sudden movement of the head would cause her weakened retinas to become detached again, this time irreparably. She was fifty-four years old and her muscles quickly lost their athletic tone; dancing, was of course, out of the question. Her artistic inactivity forced her to see Fernando's infidelities in a cruel new light and her marriage became very uncomfortable. She

befriended Pedro Simón, a handsome ballet critic twenty years her junior, in whom she confided her hopes of returning to the stage.

It was while she was for all purposes retired from the stage that it seemed as if other promising ballerinas would have a few more opportunities in the company. It was in 1973 that Alberto Méndez created his *Tarde en la siesta*, the same season that Azari Plisetsky made *Canto vital*. When Alicia Alonso was commissioned by the Paris Opéra Ballet to reconstruct the Grand *Pas de Quatre*, it was Josefina Méndez who danced the role of Mme. Taglioni, as a guest star with the French company. La Méndez also starred as Giselle in Paris, and returned home to Havana in triumph for *Tarde en la siesta*. The same year, Amparo Brito won the gold medal at the Moscow International Ballet Competition, the first of many international honors

that would be showered on Esquivel's young bride. Marta García was made a principal. It was a singular honor for Cuba as well as for the company that Alicia Alonso was commissioned *The Sleeping Beauty* by the Paris Opéra Ballet, and both Paris and Havana premiered her version in 1974.

Although she could not dance, emotional and physical discomfort convinced Alicia that she must return to the studio, even if only for mild exercise. She suffered from symptoms of ulcers, she was moody, she quarreled with her staff, and she lost her managing director, her old friend Angela Grau, who went on to become director of Cuba's National Theatre. "I loved her too much to stay and fight with her like that," Grau told me in Havana in 1980. Cautiously at first, Alicia Alonso returned to ballet class; she spent hours at the barre without moving her head, simply executing *pliés*

and *relevés*, returning to the slow arabesques and balances of her days in class with Antony Tudor. When Laura Alonso was forced by diabetes to abandon a promising ballet career of her own, Alicia offered herself to her daughter as a pupil for Laura's birthday. Laura's farewell performance had been a moving occasion: Just before Alicia's operation Laura danced the role of Giselle's mother, with her own mother, Alicia, playing Giselle. Soon Laura Alonso became one of the most noted ballet pedagogues in the world, responsible for pioneering work in the field of dance therapy. It was in 1974, as Alicia choreographed *The Sleeping Beauty* in Paris, that something changed. Encouraged by all the excitement of so much success, she met secretly with Laura and the choreographer Alberto Méndez, and from Paris to Havana the word was out that Alicia was planning something new.

Alicia Alonso and Andre Eglevsky in the Bluebird variation from *The Sleeping Beauty.* Courtesy of the Ballet Nacional de Cuba.

Rumors spread of a possible comeback, and during a November 24, 1974, salute to the women's movement at the IV International Ballet Festival, Alicia made an unannounced solo appearance in the new ballet, *Mujer*, by Alberto Méndez. Her doctors had not been wrong about the dangers of dancing, and the ballet in fact caused her to lose sight in her right eye forever. In every performance for years to come, she would dance at the risk of losing what little remained of her sight. But that night in 1974, Alicia Alonso returned.

The brilliant Méndez, whose debut in *Plásmasis* in 1970 already had signaled the arrival of a major choreographic talent, became chief choreographer in residence of the Ballet Nacional de Cuba. His style, though the young man had seen little ballet outside Cuba and the Soviet Union, would recall that of Antony Tudor over the subsequent years. "The human being is the essential presence in all my ballets," Méndez told me, echoing Alicia's own aesthetic. "The style depends on function, on who is doing the searching. I think all human roads are the best road." It was Mendez's *In the Middle of the Sunset* that would bring to a close Alicia Alonso's dancing career with a spectacularly nostalgic flourish.

While Alicia was in Paris with *The Sleeping Beauty*, Fernando was with the Ballet Nacional de Cuba on a tour of Eastern Europe. From Warsaw, Alicia anonymously received some unpleasant photos of her husband with Aida Villoch, a fifteen-year-old dancer from the corps de ballet. By the time she returned to Havana, Alicia learned that Aidita was pregnant with Fernando's child. In a rage, Alicia ran to the Minister of Culture, the youthful revolutionary veteran Armando Hart Dávalos, and delivered the ultimatum: "Fernando goes, or I go. Choose!" Alicia's divorce preceded Fernando's literal banishment from the company he founded and from Havana, along with his new wife. Aidita became prima ballerina of the Ballet de Camagüey, where Fernando hoped to mold her

Fernando Alonso and his second wife Aida Villoch, prima ballerina of the Ballet de Camagüey, Havana, 1980. Photo by Octavio Roca.

into a new Alicia. Her *La Fille mal gardée* would be legend. But it is no accident that, fine as the Ballet de Camagüey is, neither Villoch nor the company are known abroad. "I don't have a company in Havana, you see," a bitter Fernando Alonso told me in 1980. "I don't even have a house in Havana anymore. I stay with my father-in-law when I'm here."

Pedro Simón's rise in the Cuban intelligentsia followed, as did his romance with Alicia Alonso. Simón began publication of the magazine *Cuba en el ballet* and helped to organize the Center for the Documentation and Study of the History of Dance, later also founding the Museo Nacional de la Danza in Havana. A voracious scholar of interdisciplinary reach, Simón also has done extensive work on behalf of Cuban poets and in 1993 published a critical edition of the neglected feminist genius Dulce María Loinaz.[4]

OPPOSITE: Alicia Alonso backstage at the Spoleto USA Festival with her husband Pedro Simón and daughter Laura Alonso in the background. Photo by Octavio Roca.

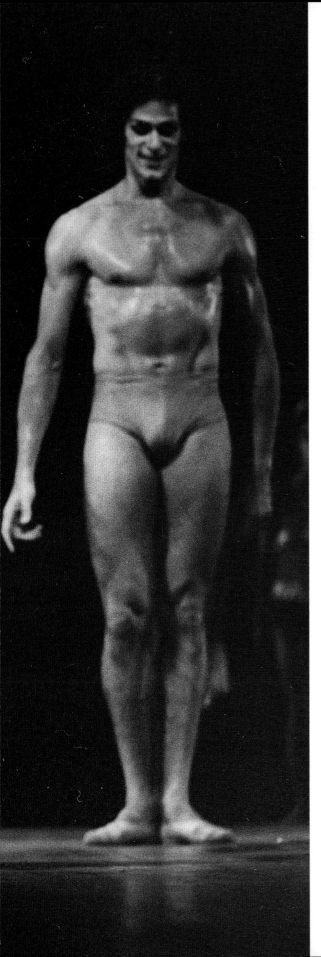

Only Alicia's grandson Iván Monreal knew of his grandmother's plans before she eloped with Pedro Simón. Years later in New York, Igor Yousekevitch would remain convinced that Pedro Simón was little more than a guard dog of the Cuban secret police or the KGB, with the intimate assignment of reporting on his wife. "I'm sure he works for state security," Yousekevitch told me, "and I think it is such a pity that I could never again just sit with Alicia alone and just talk, by ourselves, like old friends." I understand why one might think that, and I also understand the crucial role Simón has played in helping Alicia and her company walk on the eggshells of Cuba's volatile political scene. Especially after 1989 and the fall of the Soviet Empire, the Cuban Left was in a state of dismemberment and the political intelligentsia was always hard to predict. Trained in philosophy, Simón would be an asset. "Pedro is the real director of that company," Lorena Feijóo has said, echoing the opinion of many current and former members of the Ballet Nacional de Cuba. But I also have observed Alicia and Pedro together over the years, and I think Yousekevitch was wrong. This is a loving marriage, and Pedro's devotion to his *monstre sacré* of a wife is itself a life-affirming spectacle.

With Fernando remarried, with Alicia remarried and back on stage, the Alonsos, it seemed, were nevertheless growing old. Alberto, always the most underrated, and politically the most vulnerable of the three, at this time was the happiest. He was married to his muse, the inimitable dancer Sonia Calero, and he was left alone. Calero, who coached Lorena Feijóo for her 2009 performance of *Carmen* in Miami, told the young ballerina how every morning she would get up before her

95

husband, get all *emperifollada*, then jump back in bed perfumed and in full makeup so her husband would find her *bonita*. "Alberto told me he loved me every day and every night until the day he died," Calero told Feijóo.

Following the defection of Alicia's partner, Miguel Campanería, a young orphan named Jorge Esquivel became the first dancer since the days of Igor Yousekevitch to match Alicia Alonso's own stage magic. History smiled at them at this point. The U.S. State Department gave Alicia and Jorge a visa at last, and they danced in the thirty-fifth Anniversary Gala of the American Ballet Theatre in New York on July 28, 1975. She had just returned to dancing after her operation, and the only ballets in her active repertory at this time were the *adagio pas de deux* from Act Two of *Swan Lake* (which until now had never been danced out of context), *Mujer*, and *Oedipus Rex*. She chose the *Swan Lake* piece for all her appearances outside Cuba in 1975, while rebuilding her repertory and preparing her return to *Giselle*. I remember that night in New York, the strangely serene aplomb of that adagio, the way time stood still even as the impossibly difficult double ronds de jambes seemed simply to happen, effortlessly, as Alonso became simply Odile, an enchanted swan free even in the hunter's grip. In truth, Alicia would become more assured as both her limited eyesight and seemingly limitless technique returned, though a new suggestion of caution was apparent and was perhaps in part responsible for the very slow tempos. The gala was especially rich for ABT, including not only Alicia's return to New York but also the company's showcasing a Cuban exile who had studied in Havana alongside Jorge Esquivel: Fernando Bujones.

By this time Bujones, perennially boyish and precociously sensitive to any partner's needs, was on his way to becoming one of the finest dancers of his generation. Rudolf Nureyev, in his prime, was also at the gala. I remember realizing in retrospect that the seeds of Jorge Esquivel's defection were planted that night, not because of any eye-opening to the possibilities abroad, but rather because of the way Cuban state security treated Alicia's young partner. He wanted to have his picture taken with Nureyev and Bujones, and he was told in no uncertain terms that he could not. "They treat me like a kid," Jorge told me backstage after the incident. "They always do that." That gala also was a revelation of another sort: Gelsey Kirkland and Mikhail Baryshnikov had joined the company, and another era had begun. Suffice it to note here that Baryshnikov, in Leonid Jacobson's 1969 solo, *Vestris*, gave notice that a new sort of complete artistry and a revolutionary new chapter in male dancing had begun for American ballet in 1975. It is also worth noting, if only to smile at the passage of time and the sweetness of living history, that the only other dancer to dance *Vestris* besides Baryshnikov would be the Cuban exile Joan Boada, coached by Jacobson's widow in San Francisco a lifetime later. The 1975 ABT gala at the Metropolitan—and its preview gala at the Kennedy Center—was historic by any standard; Alonso and Esquivel, Nureyev and Kirkland, Baryshnikov and Noella Pontois, Bujones, Cynthia Gregory, Marine Van Hamel, Ivan Nagy, and Ted Kivitt were all there. This was the ABT of the glory days that Alicia remembered, and she was ineffably happy to be part of it once again. If *Mujer* in Havana was her official return to dance after her surgery and divorce, the ABT gala was her real homecoming.

"I had recovered everything by that night," Alicia told me. "It was beautiful." True, as she confided to Jerome Robbins, the technical challenges were as surprising as they were vast; she could see her partners now, but she had had to find a new center when she was blind and now she had to learn all over to find a center and redefine her balance while seeing. Sometimes she still would close her eyes in the middle of a turn. "It was like having written my memoirs," she told me, "and then suddenly reading them."

The Ballet Nacional de Cuba studios in Havana's El Vedado. Courtesy of the Ballet Nacional de Cuba.

Lucia Chase gave a party in her apartment after the 1975 ABT gala, an amazing gathering of living chapters of American ballet history. "The butler was not on duty, so we all had to go to the kitchen and make our own drinks," Antony Tudor reminded me. "There I was when I felt these fingers slowly moving upwards from my shoulders then scratching the back of my neck." He recognized his old friend before he turned around to see her. "She has the most miraculous touch," Tudor told me. They had never really enjoyed each other's conversation outside the studio and they did not socialize the way Robbins and the Alonsos had in the old days, but the dance memories were powerful, and suddenly they returned. "There is pure sensuality in her hands, in her whole body." Tudor said. They would see each other again, after another ABT gala, at the Met in 1980, when Alicia stopped the show with her fluttery *entrechats* in a scene from Act Two of *Giselle*. "Alicia has total sensuousness in her muscles," Tudor told me a few days later. "That is why they were so perfect, so miraculous."

Her sensuality was of course integral to the Cuban School of Ballet. "The Cuban style comes from deep within the Cuban spirit," Alicia Alonso told me for a 2003 interview in *The Miami Herald*,

"from our joys and from our sadness. Some people are always turned inward. The Cubans are always out, sensual. The Cuban ballet style comes from me, from my way of projecting my whole being."[5] That political control was and is tight remains besides the point for the artistic integrity of the Ballet Nacional de Cuba. The Cuban School of Ballet was there before Castro and will surely survive his passing. And, there always was method in the madness of Alicia Alonso's project. Of her refusal to accept a well-known Soviet dancer in favor of the young and yet unformed Azari Plisetsky as a partner in 1960 when no Western dancer would join her, she noted incisively that "what would look natural on the Soviets would have looked mimetic, like a mannerism on us. We had a hard time explaining that to our Soviet friends." Alicia's careful attention to stylistic purity and to the development of a distinctive consistency in her Cuban dancers would tell over the years. So would her consciousness of being a Hispanic artist, and of fighting ethnic prejudice as well as friendly foreign influences. The Hispanic race, a vast culture that runs from the Pyrenees to the Tierra del Fuego, finds its emblematic dancers and its style in The Cuban School of Ballet. It is the first Hispanic school of ballet and its place in history is

Alicia Alonso and Jorge Esquivel in the world premiere of Iván Tenorio's intense *La corona sangrienta* at the Gaillard Auditorium in Charleston, S.C., 1980. The electronic score was composed by Georges Barboteu. Photos by Octavio Roca.

established alongside the Russian, Soviet, Danish, and English schools.

Even as Cuban ballet enjoyed triumphs abroad and artistic growth at home, however, political realities marked it. The Teatro Amadeo Roldán, formerly Pro-Arte's Teatro Auditorium del Vedado and the home of the Ballet Nacional de Cuba, was burned to the ground by counterrevolutionary arsonists. The company, after that loss, moved to its present home, the Gran Teatro García Lorca in Old Havana. The Ballet Nacional de Cuba made its United States debut in 1978. The reception at the Kennedy Center in Washington and the Metropolitan Opera House in New York was ecstatic. Other appearances in the United States followed, through the election of Ronald Reagan and the deterioration once again of Cuban-American relations. The 1980 Mariel Exodus, when more than 125,000 Cubans left the island by boat for Florida, again tested the company, as it tested both the Cuban and the American people. Miami became the second largest Cuban city in 1980. It was at this time that, among others, the young dancer Pedro Pablo Peña got on a boat to Miami and began his journey toward keeping Cuban ballet alive in exile through what would eventually become the Cuban Classical Ballet of Miami.

After the Spoleto USA Festival in 1982, when she danced the world premiere of Iván Tenorio's *La corona sangrienta*, Alicia confessed secret despair at knowing that she might never again dance with the American Ballet Theatre as long as its director was Mikhail Baryshnikov, a Soviet defector to whom, ironically, she had awarded the first prize in the first Moscow Ballet Competition years earlier. In truth, Baryshnikov would have been the last person to keep her away; but it was the Castro government's own sporadic and unpredictable security tsunamis that she and the rest of the company feared with good reason.

In the United States, Alicia's political views were muted, or perhaps merely frank, and she told me for a 1982 profile in *The Washington Post*, "Politicians can travel and they are never asked about ballet. Why should I be asked to speak about politics? I just want to dance."[6]

Alicia Alonso became the first dancer to receive the UNESCO Award for service to humanity. Maurice Béjart was among the speakers at the ceremony in Paris, and he recounted how many times the end of Alicia's career has been foretold and how each time "she rises like a Phoenix in all her glory." On a tour of Nicaragua in 1980, she performed the political ballet *Avanzada* under the Sandinista flag. From 1984 to 2009, the International Ballet Festivals produced new ballets amid tense and uncertain political developments. I remember being told by local balletomanes how subdued the responses were at the 1980 festival, given how many ballet fans had been put on a boat in the Mariel harbor. There was a riot before the appearance of Julio Bocca's popular Ballet Argentino in Havana at the 1990 festival. The threat of decreed vulgarity in a revolutionary environment became as strong as the threat of political terror. Alicia Alonso staged *The Sleeping Beauty* for Milan's La Scala, a reprise of her Paris and Havana stagings, and the Cuban influence on international theatres only grew. Cuban choreographers, albeit briefly, showed immense promise: Alberto Méndez, and of course Alberto Alonso, but also Iván Tenorio and Jorge Lefebvre. Alicia Alonso herself grew as choreographer, in original works from *El Pillete* through *Génesis*, *Shakespeare y sus máscaras*, and in reconstructions such as not only *Giselle*, *Swan Lake*, *The Sleeping Beauty*, and *Coppélia* but also the *Grand Pas de Quatre*, *Flames of Paris*, and others.

The 1995 world premiere in San Francisco of *In the Middle of the Sunset* at once celebrated and made history, offering up the then seventy-six-year-old Alicia Alonso dancing alongside ballerinas as young as sixteen in a heartbreaking confessional ballet. The setting of the ballet is telling: it is the

OPPOSITE: Alicia Alonso and Igor Yousekevitch in Act Three of *Swan Lake*. Courtesy of the Ballet Nacional de Cuba.

Alicia Alonso's *Shakespeare y sus máscaras,* among her loveliest and most successful late choreographies. RIGHT: Víctor Gilí as the Seller of Masks. BELOW RIGHT: Javier Torres and Bárbara García as Romeo and Juliet. OPPOSITE: The Ballet Nacional de Cuba celebrating the genius of Shakespeare and the glory of dance. Courtesy of Museo National de la Danza.

The company today—the Ballet Nacional de Cuba's corps in Alicia Alonso's version of *Swan Lake*, Sala García Lorca del Gran Teatro de La Habana. Courtesy David R. Garten.

end of the day and dancers of all generations making up the Ballet Nacional de Cuba shared their lives and memories with the founder of their company. The cast was a golden book of Cuban ballet—Alicia Alonso, Loipa Araújo, Marta García, Maria Elena Llorente, Aydmara Cabrera, Alihaydée Carreño, Lienz Chang, Jorge Vega, Orlando Salgado, Vladimir Alvarez, and William Castro. A romp in a Cuban garden bathed in the light of dusk portrayed a freedom that was as distant a memory as Alonso's youth. Choreographed by Alberto Méndez with nostalgia for his own youthful *Tarde en la siesta*, it was set to the music of Ernesto Lecuona and made the most of the rubato that is the birthright of Cuban dance. The heartbreaking new ballet revealed layers of feeling—the references to an era's end and the urbane nostalgia of Lecuona's gentle piano—that were utterly Proustian. With this ballet, a final gift to his muse Alicia Alonso, Alberto Méndez fused memory and imagination, step by step, sigh by languid sigh. His sense of place, his love for Cuba, is alive in this ballet, which would have made both Alberto Alonso and Antony Tudor exult with recognition. Like the closing pages of *Time Regained*, this valedictory Alonso world premiere performance accepted the inevitable with a melancholy smile. The sadness was brief, the pleasure immense. It remains for me one of the most moving, devastatingly beautiful theatrical experiences of my life. Shortly after *In the Middle of the Sunset*, Alicia Alonso stopped dancing.

"The hardest thing for a dancer to learn is the ability to look at herself in the mirror and see the truth,'" Alicia Alonso told me. "But it is that truth that keeps a career going. My own habit of self-criticism, my own discipline, comes from having been alone so often. I had to learn a lot about myself, as a dancer and as a woman," Alonso says. "And I had to learn it early. I think dancers today tend to take support for granted, so they rely less on themselves. I try to teach my dancers self-reliance. That is part of their discipline, the part that builds character. Yet, you see, our style is sensual."[7]

Her performances and her teachings, her style and her choreography, her technique and refinement have revitalized and recreated tradition and made revolutionary changes concrete. The historical recreation of a major ballet into a wildly popular spectacle that also happens to be authentic requires more than scholarship and imagination: It requires the intuition of genius. Fascinating questions arise from Alicia Alonso's staging of *Swan Lake*, *The Sleeping Beauty*, and especially *Giselle*, where the influence of her performance practices and choreography cannot be underestimated. The vital historical question is one of choreographic meaning of the danced text, and of Alicia Alonso's artistic aims. That is to say, does *Giselle* seen through a Marxist lens, with class-conscious peasants and oppressive aristocrats, carry that political meaning to audiences in Paris or New York? Or does the balletic text regardless of the context remain faithful to its tradition and history? In either case, Alicia Alonso's fastidious construction and deconstruction of the minutest detail in these narrative ballets continues to fascinate and captivate, as well as to inform the very soul of the Cuban School of Ballet. The possibility of different readings by different audiences has increased alongside her influence in the international ballet scene. Following a Ballet Nacional de Cuba run of *Giselle* in Granada in 2009, Pedro Simón told a Spanish newspaper how Alicia "always has a surprise in store," even in *Giselle*, "because she is constantly distilling, purifying her concept. She constantly works on the classics but she is never quite finished, rather she renews them and tries to clarify the work as she accentuates our style."[8]

More than anyone else in the second half of the twentieth century, Alicia Alonso managed to be at once relevant and faithful to the traditions of ballet. Her unique attributes have made her both the most traditionally brilliant ballerina of our time and perhaps the most profoundly revolutionary dancer. In 1981, Alicia Alonso celebrated the fiftieth anniversary of her stage debut by dancing; in 1983 she celebrated the fortieth anniversary of her first *Giselle* by dancing her favorite role yet again, an unprecedented feat of longevity in dance history. With tears in her eyes, Galina Ulanova told me as we stood to cheer Alicia's *Giselle* in Havana, that her performance was "a miracle, truly a miracle."[9]

Alicia Alonso's place in history is secure, but the world cannot have her forever. There was never talk of retirement, but the inevitable happened, and it was not her blind eyes but her deteriorating hips that brought down the force of time on her career. Her doctors recommend a hip replacement operation, but the reality is that surgery in her eighties would have put her out of commission for some time, and that her company might not survive the political and economic climate without her. In 2010, she is running her company from her wheelchair. Unlike Fidel Castro, who anointed his little brother Raúl as his heir when time slowed him down at last, Alicia Alonso has no obvious successor in Cuba.

"I helped my country take the first strong, certain steps towards a future of dance," Alonso told me the first time I interviewed her for the *Washington Post* in 1980. "I am very proud of our company. Most of all I believe in the human being, and I believe that art makes us human. I have learned to trust that, over so, so many years."[10]

Today, Alicia Alonso and Pedro Simón live in Madrid most of the year, far from Havana and in tacit anticipation of the inevitable changes to come. Dissatisfaction and unrest in the ranks of the intelligentsia in Havana since the dawn of the twenty-first century have reached a degree of openness that is quite rare in the annals of the revolution.[11] The Bolshoi Ballet and the Kirov Ballet have survived the fall of the Soviet Empire, and there is every reason to expect that the Ballet Nacional de Cuba will survive the fall of Fidel and Raúl Castro. The Cuban diaspora, too, has a life of its own: in the American Ballet Theatre, San Francisco Ballet, Houston Ballet, Miami City Ballet, Cincinnati Ballet, Joffrey Ballet Chicago, the Royal Ballet, Covent Garden, and the Cuban Classical Ballet of Miami. The Cuban School of Ballet is already an inextricable strand in the fabric of dance history. Cubans will go on dancing, and the world will go on loving Cuban dance. But what will Cuba do with Alicia Alonso? How will history regard her legacy?

Alicia Alonso, like every other Cuban, must face the delicate question of how Cuba will change. Will it be a peaceful process from communism to democracy? Will it emulate Czechoslovakia or Yugoslavia? Will Cuba's culture suffer the post-communist hangover that even today maligns the arts in Russia? How will Cuba's richest cultural legacy to the world, its Ballet Nacional de Cuba, endure? Alicia Alonso's tenacity and charisma, and the loyalty of Cuba's dancers—whether living in Cuba or in exile—suggest that Cuban ballet will survive. It may well be in exile, but it will survive.

The Ballet Nacional de
Cuba in all its glory at
the season opening *défilé*
at the VII International
Ballet Festival, Gran
Teatro García Lorca. Alicia
Alonso, artistic director and
prima ballerina is in the
front row; Aurora Bosch,
Josefina Méndez, Mirta
Plá, Loipa Araújo, and
María Elena Llorente are in
the second row; José Zamo-
rano, Lázaro Carreño, Jorge
Esquivel, and Orlando Sal-
gado are in the third row;
and the entire company and
school are behind them.
Courtesy of the Ballet
Nacional de Cuba.

Theme and Variations

In art, there are no rules,
there are only examples.

—Julien Gracq, *Lettrines*

A breathtakingly beautiful dance, straightforward yet always surprising, exuberant, and unmistakably American, *Theme and Variations* is a jewel in the crown of at least three very different companies, two in New York and one in Havana: The American Ballet Theatre for whom it was made; New York City Ballet, where its creator made his home; and the Ballet Nacional de Cuba, which adopted it as its own within months of the world premiere. It was also, from the start, both a symbol and living proof of the close cultural ties ballet helped nurture between the neighboring countries. More than half a century after its creation, it remains a blueprint of limitless possibilities.

George Balanchine choreographed it to the final movement of Tchaikovsky's *Suite No. 3 for Orchestra in G major*. It was a commission from Ballet Theatre and a vehicle for Alicia Alonso and Igor Yousekevitch. The world premiere at City Center on November 26, 1947, was followed within months by the Cuban premiere with virtually the same cast—not only Alonso and Yousekevitch, but also Melissa Hayden and Fernando Alonso, all four company members of both Ballet Theatre and the newly formed Ballet Alicia Alonso, the predecessor of today's Ballet Nacional de Cuba. It has remained in the repertory of those two companies ever since, and it entered New York City Ballet's at City Center in 1960, this time with Violette Verdy and Edward Villella. It was transformed in 1970 and integrated by Balanchine into his *Tchaikovsky Suite No. 3*, with Villella and Gelsey Kirkland. When the great Kirkland defected to ABT, her partner there was Mikhail Baryshnikov, and they danced the piece together for the first time at the Kennedy Center in 1974. The *Theme and Variations* tradition was revitalized once more at the American Ballet Theatre. By the time Alicia Alonso and her trusted ballet mistress Josefina Méndez coached ABT's Angel Corella and Paloma Herrera for the George Balanchine Foundation in 1999,[1] Alonso could say with confidence that *Theme and Variations* is "a masterpiece . . . one to which the audiences of the future have every right."

It was originally hailed as a triumph for Balanchine, "The aristocrat of contemporary ballet," as Walter Terry endearingly dubbed the choreographer after the premiere.[2] But in fact, it took a bit of time to understand the magnitude of this dance and what it meant for its dancers. Terry himself grew even more enthusiastic within a few years, and his 1952 analysis of Alonso's interpretation in particular proved visionary of what would become the Cuban School of Ballet. "In George Balanchine's *Theme and Variations*," wrote the young critic,

> Miss Alonso moves softly through adagio passages and sharply through allegro sequences and in both one is aware of the sensuousness of movement. A leg, for example, may float easily upward but the exhilaration of stretching is also present in its execution just as the daintiest of steps speak of the pleasure of contact as well as of lightness.

Alicia Alonso and Igor Yousekevitch in Balanchine's *Theme and Variations*. Courtesy of the Ballet Nacional de Cuba.

Miss Alonso is not always ethereal and her poetry is usually passionate rather than romantic, for she is the kind of ballerina for whom the art of balletic display was invented, a feminine virtuoso, an actress, a vivid personality. If it were a different day and age, fans would probably unhitch the horses and pull Miss Alonso in noisy triumph through the streets . . . .[3]

Terry's perceptive review was onto something. Alonso, particularly before she grew into the role of Giselle after 1948, was at first a classical perfectionist who willed herself into becoming a romantic ballerina (Lorena Feijóo years later would be very much in this Alonso mold—Lorna Feijóo, like Gelsey Kirkland before her, is a born romantic ballerina). Balanchine, who could size up a great dancer's possibilities at a glance, I suspect saw

Theme and Variations

this in Alonso. What Balanchine understood was Alonso's fiendish virtuosity in allegro dancing, and by exploiting it, improbably created an illusion of adagio serenity within all the frenzy of movement. The results may have surprised everyone involved. There is a sensual quality to *Theme and Variations* that is often absent from many subsequent plotless Balanchine works. That Balanchine meant it to be an abstract ballet was made clear by him to his two leading dancers. Alicia remembered:

> We couldn't help ourselves, no matter how many more difficult combinations Balanchine gave us, Igor and I could not eliminate our personalities. Balanchine would take a rhythm and play with it—if it was ⁴/₄ he would add another step, then another, in such a way that he would steal time from the next measure and then from the next. That's murder for a dancer—*para el que baila, es pedirle la muerte*. And all Balanchine ballets are like that, a game between technique and music.

> Igor and I tried to interpret within the technical demands, giving a sense of carrying the theme in the melody, of humanizing the dance. Balanchine did not criticize this at rehearsals, but he also did not approve. He would just look at us and say nothing.

And yet, Alonso recalls how *Theme and Variations* helped her bring together the various strands of her training up to that point. As she saw it in retrospect, the Zanfretta Italian precision and speed from the waist down, the Fedorova and Fokine aura of delicacy from the waist up, and the overall humanity of her approach to dance from Antony Tudor all came together as she rehearsed this ballet. That a dancer would bring lessons learned from Tudor to a Balanchine ballet would not have pleased either choreographer. But dancing Balanchine with a Cuban accent began with *Theme and Variations*.

As Alicia later commented, "I actually learned a lot from that ballet, from Balanchine. From him I learned to listen to each instrument individually even as I heard the whole orchestra. I learned to follow the sound that meant the most to my phrasing—and later when my eye problems got worse, listening this way became more and more important. I got that from Balanchine. But I know we made him a little mad with *Theme and Variations.*"

Yousekevitch, whose interpretation of this ballet remains legendary, was secure enough to remain playful with both Alonso and Balanchine. He would push Alicia gently off balance whenever he felt her "feminine instincts" took her a tad too far into over interpretation, for example, momentarily infuriating her but in fact bringing out her fiery best. There were sexual sparks in their dancing together, even in this unlikely evocation of Petipa's glory. Yousekevitch's partnership with Alonso was solid, and their conversational approach to *Theme and Variations* would remain the model at ABT as well as in Cuba. Older fans who remember Yousekevitch in the piece have remarked how much José Manuel Carreño, at both the American Ballet Theatre and the Ballet Nacional de Cuba, resembles him. "I believe that our romanticized interpretation did not quite please Mr. Balanchine," recalled Yousekevitch, "but fortunately or unfortunately (depending on the point of view), we could not divest ourselves of our overwhelming instincts to express rather than just execute."[4]

Yousekevitch and Alonso had a point. The impulse to abstraction often simply materializes artistic creation, that is, keeps it earthbound. In restricting the syntax, human connections can fail or disappear. The strain works on the memory as well, and images of technique unaided by human emotion tend to fade soon after the curtain falls. When memory persists, it is usually thanks to the failure of abstract dance ever to be abstract in the first place. The performing arts come alive through association in performance, and these associations

OPPOSITE: Alicia Alonso speaking at the sixtieth-anniversary celebration of the American Ballet Theatre in 2000. "We were so full of illusions," said Alonso. "We had the beginnings of everything." Courtesy of David R. Garten.

are always unpredictable, always human. It is not the technical details—brilliant though they doubtless were—that one remembers of a great *Theme and Variations* performance, from Alonso and Yousekevitch right through Kirkland and Baryshnikov or Corella and Herrera. It looks different in Havana than it does in New York or Paris and of course it looks different everywhere these days than it did in 1947. Audiences, too, are different. Even if this or any other ballet could stay frozen in time, our perception would be drastically changed by our knowledge of what came later, just as we could never hear Bach the same way after Beethoven, never see Goya the same way after Picasso.

Theme and Variations is quite possibly the most stirring dance Balanchine created. The piece certainly has remained close to everyone's hearts, and the associations it carries for its first ballerina and her companies are rich. For the sixtieth anniversary celebration of the American Ballet Theatre in 2000, *Theme and Variations* was of course the centerpiece of the starry spring gala at the Metropolitan Opera in New York. At the point in the program when everyone expected the ballet to be next, there was instead a surprise—the Met's golden curtain parted to reveal the beautiful eighty-year-old Alicia Alonso alone on stage, and the cheers were deafening. It fell to the Cuban ballerina to recall the optimism, the sense of adventure, and the eternal youth that ballet in the New World embodies, and to recall the days when this ballet was created. "We were so full of illusions," she said. "We had the beginnings of everything."[5]

Then, as the tears and cheers abated at the end of Alicia's speech, the familiar strains of Tchaikovsky resounded from the pit and the company appeared in the last movement of *Theme and Variations*. It was, and always is, a glorious new beginning.

"Ballet is like a rose," Balanchine once said. "It is beautiful and you admire it, but you don't ask what it means." In the colorful garden of twentieth century ballet, Balanchine cultivated the

American rose; exuberant, optimistic, and triumphant. The worldly confidence of Balanchine's choreography can withstand, and in fact, will continue to grow with such national and international cultivation.[6] His *Theme and Variations* is a living masterpiece and that is as it should be. Yet this is one Balanchine ballet that will always have a touch of Cuban *sabor*.

Cuca's Story
and the
Paris Incident

They asked that man for his time
So he could join it to History's own.
They asked for his hands,
Because nothing beats a pair of hands
in difficult times . . .
They asked for his legs . . .
They asked for his chest, his heart, his shoulders . . .
They asked for his tongue . . .
And finally they asked him, please, just to keep going,
For in difficult times
That, without doubt, is the decisive test.

—Heberto Padilla, *En tiempos difíciles*

Our story so far might give the impression that the Cuban ballet was a world apart from the realities of post-1959 Cuba, and in some ways this was true. Certainly the Ballet Nacional de Cuba was, and remains, among the few things in Cuba that work well and seems not to have been influenced by the Soviets. In crucial ways, however, dancers and their families suffered and still suffer the uncertainties and terror inherent in a Stalinist regime. Many of them, like three million other Cubans, would leave their beloved country.

The Havana where the beautiful dancer Lupe Calzadilla married José Lorenzo Feijóo Menéndez and raised two dancing daughters was very different from the city where Ernestina del Hoyo and Antonio Martínez first took their daughters, Alicia and Cuca, to ballet class. This is not the place for a political history of those years, but a tale or two from the early days of the revolution should suffice to suggest the constant base line of fear that has underscored the gorgeous melodies of the dance scene in Cuba.

Not all of Alicia's family was united in supporting the revolution, although I hasten to add that Cuca Martínez and Alicia Alonso did not make a habit of discussing politics, and in fact did not ever discuss each other's politics on the record. They loved each other deeply, across a political divide, like many Cuban families. I promised Cuca I would not repeat what follows until she was gone. She is, sadly, and

her story is worth telling. Cuca was always much more politically active than her sister, since the days when she would take meals and letters to her father in the political prison of La Cabaña while the younger Alicia was kept innocent of these dark days and busied herself with ballet.

After the January 1, 1959 coup d'état, Cuca taught modern dance at the University of Havana—she had been, after all, a pupil of Martha Graham in New York—but also became active in the FEU (Federación Estudiantil Universitaria), quickly becoming disenchanted with the revolution as early as the end of 1959. She slowly began contributing to the resistance in small ways at first, mimeographing pamphlets, organizing meetings, and helping form the underground Movimiento Ideológico Cubano in 1960. She never could forgive Fidel Castro "the cowardice of shooting Manolo Castro," her friend, in the back of the head, point blank, at the Cinecito in Havana. Rafael Díaz Hanscom, known affectionately as Ricky, Laura Alonso's first husband and Cuca's nephew-in-law and friend, worked alongside her in the resistance. On April 17, 1961, the failed Bay of Pigs invasion not only dashed the hopes of many in Cuba who had expected anything besides a regime more brutal than Fulgencio Batista's, but it also gave license to the revolutionary government to round up dissidents. Only months earlier, in Jean-Paul Sartre and Simone de Beauvoir's historic 1960 visit to Cuba, the French Nobel Prize winner had warned the writer José Lezama Lima that "your time of terror is still to come." It came very soon, and it was presaged clearly in Castro's now infamous "Words to the Intellectuals" speech.[1]

Ricky divorced Laura Alonso in 1961, in order not to compromise Alicia Alonso's daughter. Days after the Bay of Pigs invasion, he was arrested, speedily tried overnight, and shot by firing squad the next day. Alicia Alonso was dancing in Hungary at the time and could do nothing,

call no one, use no influence. By the time she heard of Ricky's murder, Cuca already had been the one to claim the body for the family at La Cabaña prison.

Cuca herself grew more daring and more active in the counterrevolution, perhaps unwisely given that the entire Alonso family was being closely watched. She talked a tad too openly against the government, although she also made sure not to tell Alicia anything of her activities. For years later, Alicia remained convinced that Cuca in fact never took part in any counterrevolutionary activities. In 1962, at a time when Cuca happened to be hiding two resistance fighters in her apartment, the police knocked on the door one night. What followed was swift—the two young men jumped out the window, one of them broke his leg, but both managed to escape. Cuca was arrested and put in the back of a police cab where she succeeded in swallowing her address book. "I was so afraid of what would happen to everyone I had in that book," she told me.

Alicia was convinced of Cuca's innocence and at first was not worried—there were worse things than being arrested. Alicia Alonso herself was above suspicion. Cuca was freed that time, but she was kept under surveillance. The case against her was not difficult to make, and soon enough it was made again. Alicia got word that her sister would be arrested a second time and called Cuca to let her know she "had to leave immediately." In those days, as often since, it only took a suggestion that someone worked for the CIA to ensure a swift death sentence. Cuca had nowhere to go. She tried two European embassies and was turned away, and then the Mexican ambassador himself took her to his home to avoid her imminent arrest. A tormented Cuca, knowing that her sister's house was being watched, left Alicia waiting and only called her after she was inside Mexican territory. The stand-off was not easy; Cuca was safe, but she was not guaranteed safe passage out of Cuba.

OPPOSITE: Alicia Alonso as La Niña de Guatemala (from José Martí's poem) in *Versos y Bailes,* choreographed by Cuca Martínez. Courtesy of the Ballet Nacional de Cuba.

Many Cubans would languish for years in friendly embassies in Havana in such situations. The prospect of the scandal of Alicia Alonso's sister being exiled, particularly after her son-in-law had been executed, did not make matters smooth. There were television cameras already poised at the airport in Mexico City waiting Cuca's arrival, whenever that might be.

That is when Alicia Alonso spoke to Fidel Castro and struck a deal to keep her family safe. Cuca would be allowed to leave as long as she swore never to discuss the matter in particular or Cuban politics in general on the record for anyone in the press. Alicia would remain in Cuba as usual and would also let the matter drop. Only Alicia could act as intermediary, given that no one in the regime would trust a known counterrevolutionary and that Cuca "couldn't believe Fidel, couldn't trust Fidel or any promise he might make." Alicia told her sister, "That's what Fidel says about you, but you both have to trust me."

Cuca voluntarily left the Mexican Embassy and remained under house arrest and under guard in her apartment in El Vedado. Alicia wanted Cuca to stay in Cuba and tried to smooth things out politically, but to no avail. One morning in 1964, with no explanation, she came to Cuca's in tears and told her, "Now you should leave." Alicia was about to leave on a tour of China and Korea, and she had reason to believe her sister might suffer Ricky's fate while she was gone. That September, Cuca left like so many other Cubans including my own family, with her dog and little else. She stayed in Mexico for two months and then made her way to the United States in December in time for the religious Cuca to celebrate Christmas in Miami. That holiday was by then outlawed in Cuba and would not be celebrated legally again until decades later, after Pope John Paul II's historic 1998 visit to the island. Cuca kept her word and never discussed Alicia's deal with Fidel or Alicia's politics in public as long as she lived. Alicia also has kept her word.

She never left Cuba, and she never distanced herself from the revolution.

"My sister was always very naïve about politics," Cuca told me over coffee at her house in Miami. "Not Fernando, he knows exactly what he is doing and he always has. But Alicia . . . it is surreal—I think she lives in a romantic fantasy world, she lives in a world of illusion. She has to, to be able to create what she creates. Look how she calls her backyard hens *mis nubes blancas*, my little white clouds. She can't see. She won't see. But I love her so much."

Alicia, for a long time, could not get used to not being able to simply drop by and talk to her beloved sister. Eventually, phone calls became possible. Time passed, the ballet company grew, and Alicia kept busy. The 1965-1966 season of the Ballet Nacional de Cuba was a whirlwind of venues for the increasingly acclaimed troupe. They went to Moscow and Leningrad, Volgograd, Kiev, and Tbilisi, then on to Beijing, Tsunan, Shanghai, Hanshow, Canton, and Wujan. They also went to war-torn Hanoi and to Ulan Bator. Then the company traveled to East Berlin, Erfurt, Hallet, Bitterfeld, Greifswald, Stralsund, and Rostock. Fall began with engagements in Bucharest, Cluj, Giurgiu, Loesti, Budapest, Mishkold, and Warsaw. Then came Paris.

The Festival International de la Danse in October of 1966 was a proud and beautiful moment in Alicia Alonso's career and a landmark in the history of Cuban ballet. The Cuban company of seventy-five dancers performed *Giselle* in the birthplace of that most exquisite of ballets. Dancers from the New World came bearing gifts to the Old World, bringing the most musically complete staging of *Giselle* since its world premiere.

Alonso was awarded the Grand Prix de la Ville from the hands of Serge Lifar, and she was honored as well with the Prix Anna Pavlova for her choreography and performance of *Giselle* during the Ballet Nacional de Cuba's Paris debut. The

OPPOSITE: Alicia Alonso as the Swan Queen. Courtesy of the Alicia Alonso Collection.

Alicia Alonso and Royes Fernández with Mary Skeaping backstage in Havana. Skeaping, who was on the Ballet Nacional faculty, was responsible for Alonso adding the long-lost fugue to Act Two of her *Giselle* in the 1960s. Courtesy of the Ballet Nacional de Cuba.

last thing on her mind was security. To her chagrin, however, the historic visit also marked the first and most public defection from the company, as ten leading male dancers of the troupe sought political asylum on the day of the closing night gala that was to be attended by President Georges Pompidou.

The actual defection was not planned in advance. It was simply a matter of an opportunity emerging as a reality. They were in Paris and they improvised. One of the ten dancers was Laura Alonso's second husband, Lorenzo Monreal, the father of Alicia's only grandson, Iván Monreal. Laura's first husband, Ricky, lest we forget, had been murdered by the Castro regime. In France, where they could speak freely for the first time, the gang of ten dancers wasted no time in telling stories of terror and persecution that did much to

damage the reputation of the Cuban Revolution in the eyes of European sympathizers. Monreal, interviewed by French television, spoke with typical discretion when asked why he chose to seek asylum. "There are many things in Cuba," he hesitated. "For example, art is rather compromised, and we cannot express ourselves the way we want, only the way we must."

"What do you think of Fidel Castro?" the journalist asked.

"I don't agree with his ideas."[2]

His circumstances, captured in Néstor Almendros and Orlando Jiménez-Leal's poignant film, *Improper Conduct*, was only part of the story of the Cuban reality in the 1960s. But it was true. The outtakes for the film, transcribed and included as supplements in the published version of the script, are even more revealing.[3] Julio Medina tells how Alicia Alonso herself had sprung him from jail once, but also how he was not sure he would be that lucky the next time. Besides, the friends alongside whom he was arrested never returned from the UMAP concentration camps. Bernard Minoret told Almendros how the dancers all "had immense respect for Alicia Alonso. We didn't want to hurt her. That is why we all decided to leave the company on the last day of the tour."

Jorge Riverón, a dancer who stayed with the company in 1966, recalled how he suspected many dancers would want to leave because so many had had close calls and had been saved only by Alicia's intervention. The night of the gala, Riverón ended up dancing three different parts, as ballerinas offstage began to cry upon realizing how many colleagues had left. "It was very sad, but at the same time very joyful," said Riverón in an interview that did not make it to the final cut of *Improper Conduct*. "Joyful because I knew my friends were free. It was difficult to accept that I would be separated from so many friends I loved so much."

Riverón eventually left, too. He was part of the Mariel Exodus of 1980, the mass departure

of more than 125,000 Cubans from Mariel Harbor. This event followed the unprecedented and heroic move by a handful of dissidents to crash a bus through the gates of the Peruvian Embassy in the Havana suburb of Miramar. Although the Castro regime attempted to categorize those who left in the boat lift between April and October, 1980, as *lumpen, escoria*, undesirable human garbage floating into Florida in shrimp boats— and although the arrival of that many refugees in Miami at once severely tested the local economy of South Florida—the Mariel generation in fact contributed much to the Cuban diaspora. Reinaldo Arenas, the greatest Cuban writer of the revolutionary era, left Cuba this way after years of humiliation, imprisonment, and torture. The Pulitzer Prize winner Mirta Ojito, the MTV *Real World* star Pedro Zamora, the Cuban-American soap-opera heartthrob David Fumero, the AFCA football coach Mark Bauer, the opera singer Elizabeth Caballero, and the founder and director of the Cuban Classical Ballet of Miami, Pedro Pablo Peña, all were *Marielitos*. The Hialeah Campus of Miami Dade College, the largest institution of higher learning in the United States with 160,000

students, was established initially to teach *Marielitos* English.

Many have left since, of course. Still, it was the 1966 Paris defections that changed the character of the Ballet Nacional de Cuba just as its international prestige as one of the world's leading companies was continuing to grow. These changes would remain in place for decades and continue to influence the subsequent defections to this day. There were more KGB agents in the company than Alicia even cared to think about. There were firm recommendations from the feared Comité de Defensa de la Revolución dictating who could dance abroad and who could not—and dancers started "volunteering" dutifully for afternoon Marxism-Leninism seminars that cut into their company class. The Paris incident had been an international embarrassment for Castro's government, as socialist and moderate intellectuals began to see that Cuba was not the workers' paradise they had envisioned. By 1966, the Cuban government's occasional strategy of persecution had become a habit of terror. In particular, the violent homophobia of the regime grew as party hacks understood what a convenient accusation it was to hurl at any dissident; it seemed

ABOVE LEFT: Alicia Alonso and Fernando Alonso with Chairman Mao Tse Tung in Beijing, 1961. Courtesy of the Ballet Nacional de Cuba.

ABOVE RIGHT: Alicia Alonso with President Ho Chi Minh in Hanoi, 1965. Courtesy of the Ballet Nacional de Cuba.

that most human rights organizations who pestered the revolution did not consider gays human. Occasionally some real homosexuals had to be found and punished, and the ballet was an easy target. Police raids at the Gran Teatro García Lorca stage door were less common than the frequent raids at Parque Coppélia, the Cinemathèque, all along La Rampa Avenue to the sea, at the Carmelo restaurant across the street from the ballet school, or in the Hotel Capri bar. These raids were greeted by organized crowds shouting, "Shoot them! Burn them!" But the theatre raids happened too. And Alicia could only show up so many times at the police stations shouting, "My public must be respected!" in the hope of springing dancers and balletomanes out of jail.

Alicia and Fernando realized that their influence was powerful but only within a small circle, and they would seldom presume to extend it further. That circle, the Ballet Nacional de Cuba, became Alicia's only concern. She did manage to have the Ballet Nacional de Cuba declared a Comité de Defensa de la Revolución unto itself, with Alicia Alonso as director. This bureaucratic maneuver allowed the dancers to escape the more brutal rituals of accusation and confession that were being dutifully performed everywhere else in Cuba. As long as the dancers behaved and were discreet, all was fine; all dancers over the age of twenty-five were encouraged to marry. During the worst of the food shortages, the dancers always ate well. The unofficial exclusion of Jews, Jehovah's Witnesses, and devout Roman Catholics—a directive from the Ministry of the Interior to discourage ideological deviationism—was taken care of at the early levels of the national ballet schools, so the question simply did not come up with adult dancers. An exception worth noting is that of Pedro Pablo Peña, Lupe Calzadilla's frequent dance partner, whose uncompromising religious convictions would cut short a promising career as a danseur noble in Cuba in the 1970s. Even when token dismissals from the Ballet Nacional de Cuba were in order after the 1966 defections, these only meant transfers to the Danza Nacional, a fine company in its own right. A few very young students of the Escuela Nacional de Ballet were dismissed—a wise move given that any child over the age of twelve was treated legally as an adult by the revolutionary government and several children were sent to the firing squad. At least out of the limelight of the ballet school these few children might hope to be ignored by the authorities.

By all accounts, Alicia Alonso did much to help the victims of each wave of political oppression that followed, but her public stance remained—had to remain—staunchly on the side of the revolution. Pedro Simón, who was not yet married to Alicia in 1966, downplayed the many apocryphal tales of Alicia's running into the police station shouting that her public and her dancers must be respected. "It was seldom that melodramatic," he told me, "just a matter of making a few phone calls." Perhaps she could have done more. But she, too, had to improvise. She really thought that everyone who was going to leave had left already and that she must build her company with the dancers who stayed, making sure that what she built stayed in place. She kept going, and her Ballet Nacional de Cuba kept going. The names of the defectors were expunged from all company records and photos, just as her own sister's had been only a few years before. She went along with portraying the defectors as greedy deviates in search of bilk and money. She knew that was not true.

That was the situation as the Ballet Nacional de Cuba entered the 1970s in all its artistic glory.

Giselle's ethereal first appearance in Act Two, from the Paris production of *Giselle*. Courtesy of the Ballet Nacional de Cuba.

Interlude

Alicia Alonso, Dancemaker

> The beauty of art is higher than nature.
> The beauty of art is born of
> the spirit and born again.
>
> —G. W. F. Hegel, *Aesthetics*

Since the dawn of the twenty-first century there have been pointed criticisms of Alicia Alonso's ability to run her company the way she used to, and there have been especially cruel ones about her not being able to see what is happening on stage. The very idea that this blind woman could choreograph a new ballet would seem a publicity hoax, or at the very least a touch of magical realism. I prefer the latter, and I will not be the first to suggest that in many ways there is nothing outlandish or imagined about what many people call "magical realism." That may well be the way reality impossibly emerges in Latin America; and so too with Alonso. Yes, she is blind and, yes, she choreographs.

Ballet Nacional de Cuba company class. Courtesy of the Ballet Nacional de Cuba.

Alicia relaxing in the Bosque de a Habana during the ICAIC filming of *Swan Lake*. Courtesy of the Ballet Nacional de Cuba.

OPPOSITE: *Giselle*, without doubt, is Alonso's greatest choreographic contribution and the one closest to her heart. Courtesy of the Ballet Nacional de Cuba, photo by Frank Alvarez.

~Interlude~

Alicia Alonso, Dancemaker

Laura Hormigón and Oscar Torrado, Spaniards who dance with a Cuban accent, rehearsing in the Ballet Nacional Cuba studio, 2002. Courtesy of David R. Garten.

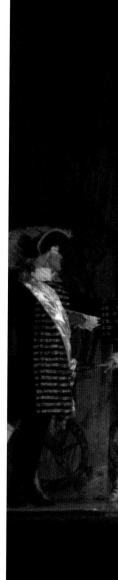

I remember getting an excited phone call in 2005 from Alicia about a new idea she had for a ballet that she was going to base on new Cuban paintings, set to Ravel's orchestration of Mussorgsky's *Pictures at an Exhibition*, freely inspired by Viktor Hartmann's original pictures. I had to smile. I quickly thought, "She'll do it, too!" She did. The following season she also choreographed the breathtaking *Love's Naked Light* as a present to her

friend Carla Fracci, set to Chausson and meant to evoke a lifetime's worth of loves remembered by a woman no longer young. La Fracci, gorgeous as she waved her fan or felt a sudden breeze, remembered and brought to life her old lovers at various ages— ranging at the premiere from the teenage Taras Domitro (at sixteen, surely Fracci's youngest partner), followed by the increasingly older Javier Torres and Victor Gilí, Alicia's inspiring muse in recent years. It is a truly lovely ballet. "Lots of arms, lots of pantomime," Domitro recalled, "but a beautiful gift for Carla."

History will be forgiven for perhaps not celebrating Alicia Alonso as a choreographer, given there is much else to praise. Certainly the best of her dancemaking has been the careful reconstructions and transformations of the works of the canon beginning with *Giselle*. Her *Coppélia*, the version that so impressed a twelve-year-old Mikhail Baryshnikov, is at least as sensitively rendered as her *Giselle*. George Balanchine once declared *Giselle* to be ballet's greatest tragedy and *Coppélia* its greatest comedy. Alicia Alonso has spent a lifetime refining both to perfection, and the Cuban people's love of the two ballets runs deep. It is worth remembering that Alicia Alonso's involvement with *Coppélia* precedes her life with *Giselle*. She first danced the role of Swanilda in 1935 in Nikolai Yavorsky's Pro-Arte production when she was only fifteen. She collaborated with Leon Fokine, whom she and Fernando Alonso brought to Havana to teach at the Alicia Alonso Academy, on

Alonso's staging of *The Sleeping Beauty* for the Ballet Nacional de Cuba. Courtesy of Museo National de la Danza.

Interlude

Alicia Alonso, Dancemaker

her own first production of *Coppélia* in 1948. Igor Yousekevitch was her Franz, setting the tone and revealing possibilities for that role for future generations of Cuban danseurs, from Jorge Esquivel through Victor Gilí, Osmay Molina, and Joel Carreño. Andre Eglevsky was Franz in Alonso's historic *Coppélia* at the Greek Theatre in Los Angeles in 1957, and this deliciously witty staging became the blueprint for her definitive 1968 choreography for the Ballet Nacional de Cuba.

happy ending of this romantic tragedy. Her *Sleeping Beauty*, however, is something else. A happy commission from the Paris Opéra Ballet in 1974, followed almost immediately by the Ballet Nacional de Cuba's own production the same year, and then by a lavish staging at La Scala in 1983, Alicia Alonso's *Sleeping Beauty* was the product of the full flowering of Cuba's ballerinas in the 1970s. This was the time of Cuba's Four Jewels and the Three Graces. The depth of casting possibilities given Alonso's pick among the young veterans Loipa Araújo, Aurora Bosch, Josefina Méndez,

BELOW: The Ballet Nacional de Cuba's corps de ballet in Alonso's *Swan Lake*, Act Two at the Sala García Lorca, Gran Teatro de La Habana, 2004. Courtesy of David R. Garten.

Like her 1972 *Giselle* for the Paris Opera Ballet and the Ballet Nacional de Cuba, the Alonso *Coppélia* is the standard by which other choreographic versions must be judged.

Her uncharacteristically slightly abbreviated *Swan Lake*, which has been transformed for the better over the years, is thrilling and remains the best argument to be made for the misguided Soviet-style

and Mirta Plá, as well as the younger still Amparo Brito, Ofelia González, and Rosario Suárez fired Alicia's imagination and led to the careful reconstruction of individual variations for all the Fairies and their Cavaliers as well as to the restoration of much else in Tchaikovsky's score.

Mastering Petipa, with the examples of both Tudor and Balanchine absorbed deep in her soul but also with the very practical example of Alberto Méndez as her resident choreographer in

OPPOSITE: Sadaise Arencibía performing as the Snow Queen in Alonso's version of *The Nutcracker* at the García Lorca in Havana. Courtesy Museo National de la Danza.

Alicia Alonso, Dancemaker

Viengsay Valdés as Kitri in *Don Quixote.* Courtesy of The Washington Ballet, photo by Carol Pratt.

reconstructing other nineteenth century treasures, Alicia became more audacious in her own dancemaking. Her 2008 version of *The Nutcracker* succeeds in revitalizing all the Act Two divertissements she remembered well from her Ballets Russes days. In Alicia's 1988 version of *Don Quixote*, which was showered with honors particularly in Spain during the 2005 *Don Quixote* anniversary celebrations, she corrected the use of folk dances such as the jota and the sevillana that Petipa had glossed over in his original divertissements—knowing that, for example, Petipa never would have mixed up a czarda and a polonaise and that he in fact did not know much about Spanish dances. The Cuban *Don Quixote*, if only for that reason, remains the truest both to the spirit of Petipa and to that of the land of Cervantes.

But the truth is that Alicia Alonso has always made original dances, beginning with *La Condesita* and the poignant *El Pillete* more than sixty years ago and ranging wildly from a Béjartian science fiction spectacle set to Luigi Nono called *Génesis* to recent ballets including *Shakespeare y sus máscaras*, another Gilí vehicle, set to a Gounod pastiche; and *The Magic Flute*, a tribute to Lev Ivanov, set to a long-lost score by Riccardo Drigo that Alicia found with Richard Bonynge's guidance. In 2008 she created *Serenata Goyesca*, to the music of Joaquín Rodrigo. In 2009 she set a García Lorca poem to dance, *Preciosa y el aire*, for the Huella de España festival in Havana.

Alicia works out the dances, old or new, alone in the darkness in her mind; she then dictates the ideas to her maîtres, and together they create the mechanics of rehearsal, the actual steps, and the spatial relations. Nelson Madrigal has a point in saying "that Alicia simply can't see what goes on up on that stage," and there is also some truth to the claim that, especially in recent years, even her maîtres are not the same. "I can tell you that, since the death of Josefina Méndez in particular, the company has declined—it has declined a lot," said Taras Domitro, who, like Madrigal, has had more than a little experience making dances with Alicia. "Alicia today can see nothing. She has a million people to see for her, but that's not the same."

True. Then again, the blind Borges could bring to life an indefinite, infinite library purely from his imagination. The deaf Beethoven could create a vast and heartbreaking aural universe in his last quartets, a universe he would never hear. The blind Alonso can create ravishing, human dances. Quite literally, she feels them. These dances she has been making since she herself

Interlude

Alicia Alonso, Dancemaker

Alicia Alonso in *El Pillete*, one of the first dances she choreographed, filmed in the Plaza de la Catedral de la Habana. Courtesy of the Alicia Alonso Collection.

OPPOSITE: Alicia's 1980 science fiction ballet, *Misión Korad*, honored the first Cuban cosmonaut opening night of the VII International Ballet Festival. Courtesy of the Ballet Nacional de Cuba.

stopped dancing come from the soul and are born again on stage. Her choreography, now as before, is conservative, anchored in classical syntax in the shadow of both Balanchine and Tudor. Most of these recent ballets are not seen outside of Cuba, and not only because foreign impresarios want to see the Ballet Nacional de Cuba in *Giselle* and *Swan Lake*. It is also because of their innocence of so much of what has gone on in dance in the last five decades. Some of these pieces—even some of the ensembles in *Shakespeare*—can fall somewhere between Susan Sontag's camp and Milan Kundera's kitsch. Yet at its best, as in the Victor Gilí role in *Shakespeare y sus máscaras*, Alonso's choreography can bring to mind Christopher Wheeldon in his storytelling mode. And

as in Wheeldon, though never as effectively, the quicksilver timing of the classical combinations dazzle precisely because of how little new ground is broken. Unlike Wheeldon, whose surprising ballets always ring true, Alicia's often feel like translations. It is here that her recent detractors may have their strongest arguments. Her sight is the worst it has been, and her most trusted collaborators are dead. At her considerable best, however, Alonso taps into the timelessness of classical ballet. That she happens to be blind while making ballets is not always the point—she has been blind a long time. As Cervantes noted in *Don Quixote*, the proof of the pudding is in the eating. *Shakespeare y sus máscaras* is one tasty dance.

Lorena, Lorna, and the Feijóo Effect

I want to dance for our people again, for an audience that knows us a little better. And I am optimistic. I want our Cuban people someday to have the art they deserve, without the all the hardships and oppression they have suffered. Someday we will have that.

—Lorena Feijóo

We are everywhere, and we learn a lot from everywhere. But the Cuban style is inside us all, inside every Cuban dancer no matter where. It is alive as long as we dance.

—Lorna Feijóo

Lorena and Lorna Feijóo. Courtesy Greg Gorman.

Little Lorena, one of those children who simply could not sit still. Courtesy of the Feijóo Family Collection.

We can never predict where life will take us, and I know I have hardly been the first Cuban to wonder what I was doing in San Francisco. Not long ago, as she prepared to coach a City Ballet School student production of *The Nutcracker* at Fort Mason in the city by the bay, Lupe Calzadilla was far from another city by another bay, where she was born. She was far from the Havana where she and the handsome actor José Lorenzo Feijóo Menéndez grew up, married, and raised two beautiful daughters; the Havana where they learned to dance. Lupe's daughter Lorena Feijóo was across town at the War Memorial Opera House in San Francisco Ballet's *Nutcracker*. Across the country in Boston, her other daughter, Lorna Feijóo, and her son-in-law Nelson Madrigal were on stage with the Boston Ballet. Fast approaching the age of seventy and looking every inch the ageless ballerina, Lupe Calzadilla teaches ballet, something she has done since almost as long as she has danced. Her husband died June 20, 2007. She has every right to be at least as surprised as her daughters by the turns her world has taken.

Lupe Calzadilla was born September 25, 1944. She studied at the Escuela Nacional de Ballet and was quickly chosen for the Ballet Nacional de Cuba, where she would dance for a dozen years. She stopped dancing briefly after the birth of Lorena, October 13, 1970, and after the birth of Lorna, May 6, 1974. It took no great seer to predict that Lupe and Jose Lorenzo's daughters would go far in dance someday, even if that was the last thing on the couple's mind as they raised their family during some of the Cuban Revolution's most difficult years, years that also coincided with some of the most beautiful for Cuban ballet. Lupe studied with Alicia Alonso and Fernando Alonso, as well as with Ana Leontieva, José Parés, and other luminaries who had flocked to the Alonsos' school in El Vedado in those heady days. Ballet was indeed a world apart, and the dancers were kept busy. Baby Lorena, like baby Lorna after her, was watched over by stagehands and costume assistants offstage as their mother danced. Soon, as she realized her calling as a dance teacher, Lupe spread her wings and helped found the Ballet del Teatro Lírico de La Habana, the troupe that performed with the opera and also explored crossover Cuban dances following the trailblazing steps of Alberto Alonso. Her dance partner at the Lírico was a religious young man named Pedro Pablo Peña, whose life in exile years later would again intersect with the Feijóos.

The Feijóo-Calzadilla family lived in La Víbora, a Southern working-class suburb of Havana, where the future actor and filmmaker Andy García also was raised. Their house on 555 Calle Saco, between Acosta and O'Farrill, was roomy, and its patio an ideal playground for the girls — though their evenings were often spent backstage. Dressing up and dancing was second nature to the girls, who after all saw their parents wearing stage make-up more often that not. It came as no surprise when the toddler Lorena, one of those children who simply could not sit still, announced that she would be a ballerina. Lupe would become her first teacher.

She was tough on her daughter. She still is. Lupe learned the habit of perfection from Fernando Alonso, and by the time Lorena entered the company school, Lupe was known as one of its most demanding teachers. Laura Alonso, a few years older than Lupe and by this time also easing her way into teaching, years later would be fond of this joke. Question: "What is the difference between a terrorist and a ballet mâitre?" Answer: "You can negotiate with a terrorist." That sums up the uncompromising side of Cuban ballet teachers all over the world, and Lupe carried it to the point where, in school competitions, other jury members would insist she raise Lorena's scores. She was hardest on her daughter, because she knew how good she could be. When Lorna, too, announced she wanted to be a ballerina, Lupe tried to steer her away — she was afraid the sisters would compete too much with each other. She sang the praises of Cuba's budding modern dance scene, and she suggested acting — after all, it was her husband's calling. But Lorna, always quieter than her sister but no less determined, simply sneaked off on her own, auditioned, and earned a place in the Escuela Nacional de Ballet. Lorena won her first ballet competition at the age of thirteen, and later Lorna would do the same. "Mami never wanted to take sides," Lorna told me. "She didn't want us to compete." Lupe needn't have worried. The sisters loved and love each other at least as much as they love to dance. "My sister is one of my models," Lorna has said more than once. "She is my inspiration, along with Alicia." Both were accepted into the ranks of the Ballet Nacional de Cuba and both precociously took on leading roles in their teens. It is worth remembering that these were children who spent their days not only in ballet, but also in a folk dance class, in acting and history lessons, and in music and mime workshops — a curriculum that prepares a complete dancer. Complete Cuban dancers are what they became.

The Feijóo Calzadilla family at home in La Víbora. Courtesy of the Feijóo Family Collection.

Always the shy one, Lorna nevertheless managed to go around her mother and audition. Courtesy of the Feijóo Family Collection.

Yet there was a glut of dancers at this time in Cuba. Miraculously, Alicia Alonso was still dancing, and the younger generation of ballerinas—everything is relative—consisted of forty-something stars including Aurora Bosch, Loipa Araújo, Mirta Plá, María Elena Lorente, and Josefina Méndez, all of them gorgeous and very much still active. It would take a lot for an actual youngster to land a plum role. The example of Amparo Brito was a living warning. Brito, the wife of Jorge Esquivel, was an exquisite young ballerina and was the youngest and best Myrtha in the company. She had to be content watching her husband partner Alicia Alonso in *Giselle*, but she herself was never given the same chance. As Lorna joked years later, about her own rise to the role of the Wilis Moina and Zulma but never Giselle in Cuba, "I think you had to be at least thirty-nine to be Giselle then. That was the minimum age requirement." It was hardest of all for Lorena, who decided to leave Cuba in 1990 while Lorna was still a student. At this time Lorena was a favorite of Fernando Alonso, who nicknamed her his "Tropical Beauty," and a budding ballerina of choice for Alicia Alonso's own future plans, even if those plans didn't yet include the role of Giselle. Alicia was not pleased by Lorena's departure. While she allowed other dancers who left Cuba, including José Manuel Carreño and Carlos Acosta, both the freedom to return and an open invitation to dance with their home company, Lorena would never again be asked to dance with the Ballet Nacional de Cuba.

It wouldn't matter. Lorena carried her Cuban style to the Ballet de Monterrey and to the Royal Ballet of Flanders. She went to California in 1995, under contract with the Los Angeles Ballet—which went bankrupt and disbanded before Lorena stepped on stage. The Joffrey Ballet offered her a ballerina spot, and she stayed in Chicago four years, until "I got restless, repeating the same repertory," she told me. "It was just time to move on." She did that in 1999, landing as a principal with San Francisco Ballet, the oldest ballet company in the United States. Her career, there and beyond, has been nothing short of miraculous.

In 2000, she famously danced a historic *Giselle* in a Helgi Tomasson San Francisco Ballet production that managed to be even more musically complete than Alonso's own, partnered by the elegant Roman Rykine. Also in 2000, coached by Natalia Makarova, Lorena danced a staging of *La Bayadère*, partnered by her fellow Cuban exile Joan Boada, that let both explore and nurture the Cuban way with the Russian classic. I will never forget a rehearsal for *La Bayadère* in the San Francisco Ballet where Makarova was stopped short by Lorena's speed; the Cuban ballerina simply did not mark the transition between steps and—this, incidentally, is part of what makes Cubans such natural Balanchine dancers—seemed to finish her duet with Boada in triumph with no visible preparation or break anywhere in her long phrases. "That is a little too patriotic, dear," Makarova told Feijóo. "Too communist."[1] For Makarova's style, a dancer's preparation is a moment of freedom to be savored by herself and her audience, a break from classical strictures. Lorena gave the Russian a withering look, but she took the note to heart and softened the phrasing even more. She never did show her preparation, though, and neither did her partner. In performance, Feijóo and Boada created a vision of what classical ballet might have been like before the Soviets. "Lorena has soul," Makarova told me, won over. Once, in one-on-one *La Bayadère* rehearsal, Natasha announced, "Lorenishka, let's do something else—already I am bored with *Bayadère*. Let's do *Giselle*—show me." Makarova sang to Feijóo a passage from Act One, and the two ballerinas then worked on scenes from *Giselle* together.

The Kingdom of the Shades scene in *La Bayadère* brings such classical purity that it is easy, when the piece is danced well, to look simply

ABOVE AND RIGHT: Lorna's extension and sexy épaule-ment were there from the start. Courtesy of the Feijóo Family Collection.

BELOW LEFT: José Manuel Carreño, a stalwart of the American Ballet Theatre. Courtesy of Fabrizio Ferri.

BELOW RIGHT: Carlos Acosta, leading dancer of the Royal Ballet, Covent Garden. These two are among Cuba's most impressive dance exports, male division. Courtesy of Illume productions/Candela, photo by Cynthia Newport.

at the sublime symmetries and forget the very human dancers creating them. With Joan Boada as her ideal partner, however, Lorena Feijóo made sure the humanity of the dance was as inescapable as their virtuosity was thrilling. "Dancers with this much panache are rare," I reported in the *San Francisco Chronicle*.

Feijóo is a prima ballerina of the old school. Her musicality is sensual, her upper body expressive and her footwork fresh. It is frankly tough sometimes for Nikiya's role to stand out well amid the kaleidoscope of twenty-seven

FAR RIGHT: The sisters in exile, Lorna and Lorena Feijóo. Courtesy Robb Aaron Gordon.

other women who represent her image in Solor's mind. It was impossible not to notice Feijóo. If the Shades represent the aspects of perfection, Feijóo was perfection itself in all its innocence. As for Boada, the daring pyrotechnics and gentle landings, the superhuman jumps and tender partnering added up to dancing that drew the matinee audience to frenzy. Makarova originally set *La Bayadère* in 1980 for herself and Anthony Dowell, a performance

I will always treasure. I expect that years from now Feijóo and Boada will be remembered with no less affection and wonder.[2]

After Lorena's *Giselle* and *Bayadère*, she made her debut in a *Don Quixote* opposite Joan Boada that set a new company standard and etched their names alongside Baryshnikov and Kirkland and Dowell and Makarova as the great Basils and Kitris of our time.

> Feijóo was in her element as Kitri, sublime in her musicality, breathtaking in her footwork and impossibly sexy in her upper body's every gesture. She flirted with her fan, paused and teased with endless balances, and tossed triple turns in fouettés with an aplomb Alicia Alonso would have recognized. Boada, returning from a serious knee injury and surgery, was miraculous. The pyrotechnics of old are there, and the virtuosity of the Act Three grand pas was ravishing. But a new authority informed his dancing, from his quicksilver phrasing and gentle landings to his tender partnering of Feijóo. Here was a couple the likes of which few dance companies in the world can boast.[3]

It has been a pity that San Francisco Ballet is not the kind of company that lets partnerships such as this bloom—Feijóo and Boada have been paired beautifully and variedly with other company dancers, but after *Don Quixote* they have not been paired up again in their home company.

Val Caniparoli, an underrated American choreographer who knows how to bring out the unexpected in his dancers, gave Lorena—and also later Lorna—one of her most enjoyable roles in his exhilarating *Lambarena*, a ballerina role originally made for San Francisco's own Evelyn Cisneros. In *Damned*, Yuri Possokhov's rethinking of the Medea myth set to Ravel's Piano Concerto

for the Left Hand, his classically spare and specific choreography let Lorena tap into her vast dramatic forces and create a monumental character not unlike what Alicia Alonso brought forth in Jorge Lefebvre's *Oedipus Rex* a generation earlier. Lorena was monumentally tragic, her supple line distorted by her character's desire for vengeance. Her Medea was a trapped animal, surprised to find her children in the same cage. Possokhov's *Study in Motion*, this one created for Lorena, pushed the frontiers of dancer and dancemaker alike—both in sympathy with the natural dialectic of tradition and radical change in dance. Lorena Feijóo has excelled in the Balanchine and Robbins repertory that is vital to the San Francisco Ballet, albeit in a style that tells of her Cuban roots. Certainly her intense way with *Symphony in Three Movements*, *Emeralds*, and even *Serenade* is miles away from what the naughty French once derided as Balanchine's "style frigidaire." In Tudor's *Gala Performance*, Lorena seemed to have a ball in a role Alonso herself famously enjoyed. "This is one wild woman," the *San Francisco Chronicle* review ran, "and her turn at Tudor's take-no-prisoners Russian ballerina is a comic creation ranking with Barbara Streisand's Swan Queen in *Funny Girl* or Carol Burnett's bonkers Norma Desmond."[4] In Miami, for Pedro Pablo Peña's Cuban Classical Ballet of Miami in 2009, Lorena took on a ballet that was beyond her reach in Cuba, Alberto Alonso's *Carmen*, coached by Alberto's widow Sonia Calero. It was a resounding success, not least for the ways in which it departed from Alicia Alonso's iconic model.

Never shy with the press, Lorena gave *The Miami Herald*'s Lydia Martin some especially choice observations at the time of her Miami *Carmen*. "In Cuba, we were never taught that everybody is entitled to a difference of opinion. . . . To this day," Feijóo continued, "my main discussion with every Cuban I know is that you don't have to win every argument. You can have

OPPOSITE: Lorena Feijóo as the fiery Kitri in *Don Quixote*. Courtesy R. J. Muna.

The Cuban premiere of Alberto Alonso's *Carmen* with Alicia Alonso and Azari Plisetsky in Havana. Courtesy of the Alicia Alonso Collection.

OPPOSITE: Lorena Feijóo in what she calls her "Audrey Hepburn pose." Courtesy David Martinez.

an interesting discussion without anyone being right. You can play a song more than one way. You can dance a ballet more than one way. And as an audience, you can be open to receive what each artist has to offer and not expect them to be copycats of one another."[5]

Carmen is telling. The ballet is something that Cubans tend to feel proprietary about, even if it was created by Alberto Alonso for the Bolshoi. It is also, like Roland Petit's more interesting version, a ballet that gives critics license to sharpen their banderillas. *Carmen* is delicious to dance and audiences respond to the dancer's delight. That it was forbidden fruit as long as Alonso danced it only adds to its worth among Cuban ballerinas. In Lorena Feijóo's Miami *Carmen*, the striking grands battements devant recalled Alonso's saucy virtuosity in the first variation; but Feijóo's way of almost laughing as she struck a balance en pointe and grabbed her ankles with both hands was a teasing moment very much her own. Lorena told Olga Connor of *The Miami Herald*, "When

I left Cuba, *Carmen* was not open to the public yet."[6] And it is true that the role was, as Connor put it, forbidden territory, because Lorena could not dance it as long as Alicia Alonso and Maya Plisetskaya were the only women alive allowed to take the role.

By the time Lorna joined the Ballet Nacional de Cuba after Lorena left, Alicia herself had stopped dancing it and other women were given the chance. Lorna took it. She took, in fact, every leading role in the Cuban repertory and, along with her husband Nelson Madrigal, was showered with honors in Cuba. This was the 1990s, a time when defections increased, and the company briefly tried a more relaxed attitude in the hopes both of keeping its dancers and also earning hard currency from some of their jobs abroad. "I was so sad when Lorena left," Lorna recalled, "but it was also a better time for dancing, a time of more opportunities for me and Nelson."

Lorna and Nelson were friends in ballet school and, before they became a couple, it was Nelson

Lorna Feijóo and Nelson Madrigal on the roof of the Gran Teatro de La Havana, 2001, shortly before becoming exiles. Courtesy David R. Garten.

who first got a taste of dancing outside Cuba. Carla Fracci spotted him in Havana and took him along with another youngster, José Manuel Carreño, to La Scala as guest dancers for a new production of Rossini's epic opera *William Tell*, choreographed by Heinz Spoerli. "I think the public liked us better than they liked the singers," recalled Madrigal, who was eighteen when he danced in the opera. Spoerli offered him a contract on the spot with the Dusseldorf Ballet, which he directed at the time. "I didn't want to be classified as a defector, and I still had to finish my obligatory social service," said Madrigal, "so I decided to go back to Cuba then." Spoerli confided in the young dancer that he would be in charge of the adventurous Zurich Opera Ballet in two years and would welcome him there when he was ready. On his return, Nelson fell in love with his school friend Lorna Feijóo and the couple moved in together. A critic sent word of Lorna to Spoerli—by this time Lorna was very much on the rise in the company—and the couple jointly was offered a guest contract in Zurich. To their surprise, Alicia let them go.

"I was beginning to get tired of doing only the classical roles, always the same roles in Cuba," said Madrigal, "*Giselle* and *Swan Lake*, then *Giselle* and *Swan Lake*, again and again." He continued,

Cuba doesn't have the good fortune of having new choreographers in the company. Of course Alicia makes her own choreography, but her idea of movement stayed fixed in her time dancing forty years ago, when she could see. Now she makes the steps, but it is one thing what she imagines and another what happens on stage. Another choreographer, a mâitre, sees for her and changes her steps depending on what happens in the studio. Alicia can't change them as she makes the dance because she can't see. Imagine trying to write a book and not be able to read what you write.

148

LORENA, LORNA, AND THE FEIJÓO EFFECT

LORENA, LORNA, AND THE FEIJÓO EFFECT

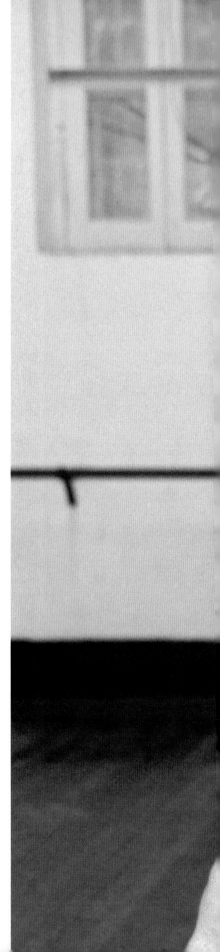

"Heinz Spoerli was different, and Zurich gave us the chance to do a lot of neoclassical and modern works, to try new things. We had a wonderful time." When it was time for them to return to Havana, the seed of freedom had been planted, and this time Lorena would help Lorna and Nelson make a more decisive move.

In a sweet aside that reminds us what a small world ballet is, Nelson remembered that the driver who came to the airport in Zurich to pick him up with Lorna and take them to their Swiss home was an affable, instantly likable dancer master named Mikko Nissinen, who at the time was exploring the surprises of retirement from a stellar dancing career with San Francisco Ballet. That Nissinen one day would give the exiled Lorna and Nelson an American home in Boston was not something any of them could imagine. The couple returned to Havana and they were named principals of the Ballet Nacional de Cuba. They usually did not dance with each other in the company, but often partnered instead with the members of another charismatic married couple, Laura Hormigón and Oscar Torrado. The entire repertory open to Cubans was theirs for the taking, and both especially enjoyed the Ballet Nacional de Cuba's Balanchine as much as the definitive Alonso *Giselle* and other standards of the canon.

Merrill Ashley would end up coaching both Lorena Feijóo and Lorna Feijóo in *Ballo della Regina*, teaching one sister in Havana in 2000, the other in San Francisco in 2002. "Their Cuban training was a fantastic foundation," Ashley told Suki Johns for *The New York Times*. Balanchine's all-American muse added about Lorna that "I've watched her transform from *Ballo* to *Giselle*, Ms. Alonso's signature role and the litmus test for a Cuban ballerina. Lorna looked like she didn't have a bone in her body, so ultra stylized." Ashley continued, "If I was reduced to one ballerina in the world, Lorna would be the one I'd want to see in anything."[7]

Reviewing Lorna in Balanchine's *Ballo*, which she danced opposite Gonzalo García at the New York State Theatre, Anna Kisselgoff in *The New York Times* was straightforward; "Like her sister, Lorna is an astonishingly strong dancer. Her air turns, landing on toe in fifth position, were only some of the marvels on view, not to speak of the forceful fouettés. In her hand-to-hip solo she evoked a leisurely folk dancer, but when it came to hard-core Balanchine speed she was able to shoot her leg out in arabesque after every piqué turn well within the musical phrasing provided by Hugh Fiorato."[8]

Victoria Morgan, artistic director of Cincinnati Ballet, saw Lorna and Nelson in Cuba when she joined Washington Ballet's Septime Webre in a trip to the island that was caught in the documentary

Merrill Ashley teaching
Lorna Feijóo at the Ballet
Nacional de Cuba studio,
2000. "If I was reduced to
one ballerina in the world,"
said Ashley, "Lorna would
be the one I'd want to see
in anything." Courtesy
David R. Garten.

Dance Cuba: Dreams of Flight. "It began with that trip," said Morgan. "I was so inspired by the whole company, by company class, by everything, and Nelson, who's gotten even better—what a lovely, caring partner that man is. But Lorna! I saw her in *Ballo della Regina* and in *Swan Lake*. I had never seen anyone with her speed, with her artistry. I had never seen faster piqué turns in my life. I knew her sister Lorena, of course, and I had seen her dance with Boada—he is amazing. But the idea that Lorna and Nelson might dance in the United States began that trip." By this time, the Cincinnati Ballet had become the American version of Great Britain's English National Ballet, a company that under both Ivan Nagy and Peter Schaufuss facilitated visas or work permits and secured jobs for more than a few Cuban dancers in exile. Morgan suspected that Nelson and Lorna would not remain long in Cincinnati,

but that didn't matter. It doesn't matter whether her current crop of Cuban exiles remains in Cincinnati either. At this writing, the extraordinary Camagüeyan Cervilio Amador, as well as Adiarys Almeida and Gema Díaz—all Cuban exiles more recent than Lorna Feijóo and Nelson Madrigal—bring a touch of Cuban *sabor* to the Cincinnati dance banquet. They do feel at home in the American company, and "I am thrilled to have held onto them," says Morgan. Still, she adds, "of course I wish they all could stay, and I know some of them move on. It is a delicate balancing act for an artistic director; it's not always about grooming and growing, it's also about what's on stage tonight." A good artistic director is ever conscious of variety and balance in her troupe, and Morgan is very good at her job.

On a 2001 Ballet Nacional de Cuba United States tour, Lorna and Nelson made their decision

Lorna midflight, in Act Two of *Swan Lake* in Havana. Courtesy of Illume productions/Candela, image from *Dance Cuba*.

ABOVE: The Swan Queen, Lorna Feijóo's last role in Havana before joining her sister in exile. Courtesy of Illume productions/ Candela, image from *Dance Cuba*.

OPPOSITE: Boston Ballet's Lorna Feijóo and Nelson Madrigal performing at the Citi Performing Arts Center (SM) Wang Theatre. Courtesy of Boston Ballet, photo by Marty Sohl.

and were ready to join Lorna' sister in exile. I first heard about the Cincinnati offer a few days after I reviewed Lorna's *Giselle* in Berkeley, and the Cold War cloak-and-dagger details of the defection seem to matter a lot less now than the fact that both Feijóo sisters have left, and that they have become a fascinating living chapter in the annals of both Cuban and American ballet.

That chapter is still being written, and many dances are still to be danced. It was an accident that Cynthia Newport's documentary *Dance Cuba* happened to catch Cuba's leading ballerina as she became Cuba's latest dance exile during the film's production. "We didn't choose Lorna, she just happened to be dancing when we were there. We have a lot of footage of Lorna and also of Alihaydée Carreño," said the filmmaker. Carreño would leave Cuba in 2009, but Feijóo's defection in 2001 certainly made for high drama as the film was in production. "Lorna was very brave to be as forthright as she was on camera," said Newport. "We were fortunate to have filmed

Lorna in *Swan Lake* in Cuba, but we had a character with no voice. When Lorna and Nelson came to Boston—and I also have a lot of footage of Nelson that didn't make it to the film—she was brave and gracious. What she had to say in those interviews, what impressed me most powerfully, was the deep sense of longing. That was there for each and every one of those people, even those who are still there in Cuba." Newport's gem of a dance film revealed something real, and it emerges as a poignant snapshot of a culture. They shot in Havana with five cameras, and the results are spectacular. But the most dramatic scenes in *Dance Cuba* were filmed in Boston, where none of the principals had expected to be. The director herself was deeply moved by "the human story, by how much these Cubans love Cuba. I don't mean politically, I mean Cuba the country, how much all these dancers love it. What Lorna misses the most is the sea."

One of *Dance Cuba*'s loveliest and most devastating images is of Lorna and Nelson in a snowy

Swan Lake—the hunter and his enchanted prey. Courtesy of Illume productions/Candela, image from *Dance Cuba*.

Lorena Feijóo, beautiful even while stretching. Courtesy of David Martínez.

The incomparable Lorena
Feijóo. Courtesy R. J.
Muna.

Boston park in 2003, far from home but happy, together through everything, dancing whatever they want to dance. We really can never predict where life will take us. For these dancers, the opportunities and surprises have not stopped. Lorna and Nelson's spectacular success in Cincinnati with their debut there in Balanchine's *Tchaikovsky Pas de Deux* surprised only those who did not remember that the couple had been raised on the piece since ballet school in Cuba. Lorna made her Royal Ballet, Covent Garden debut in Anthony Dowell's *Swan Lake* opposite her compatriot Carlos Acosta, a dancer who has made history of his own in London. It was a lovely experience to be sure, and it was followed by several invitations to join that company. But having left the Ballet Nacional de Cuba for Cincinnati Ballet, and having left that company together for Boston Ballet in 2003, the prospect of being separated, even only for a promised season or two until two contracts turn up at the same time, was not for Lorna and Nelson.

Besides, their art is being lovingly nourished in Boston Ballet, and the Cubans have especially enjoyed dancing together in Val Caniparoli's intense *Lady of the Camellias* and Peter Martins' eerie neoclassical *Distant Light*. Boston Ballet's 2009–2010 Opening Night Gala unveiled an insouciantly sexy Lorna in *The Afternoon of a Faun*. Lorna and Nelson both continue to grow in Nissinen's own *Swan Lake*, "a very different production from Alicia's," Lorna said, though happy to be keeping at least one Cuban touch: the serene double ronds-de-jambes in the Act Two solo variation, something so difficult virtually no ballerinas outside Cuba dance it these days. "Mikko lets me keep them," said Lorna. "He gives his dancers a lot of freedom." In San Francisco, Lorena also keeps that detail in Tomasson's 2009 version of *Swan Lake*. Coast to coast, each sister's arabesques a cambré in *Swan Lake* are akin to sighs. For both sisters, each simple attitude held is formed from

a right angle in relation to the line etched by the foot and bended knee, unlike the Soviet fashion that still influences performance practice in many companies. Such details matter, and in this case they are one more indication of how the Cuban School is influencing American ballet. That is but one example of the Feijóo effect. On a wider scale, it is exhilarating to notice how two of the finest Cuban ballerinas before the public today, neither any longer anywhere near the Ballet Nacional de Cuba, are revitalizing and changing the way American ballet is danced.

Lorena, a single woman but seldom alone, remains a principal in her prime with San Francisco Ballet. Like Lorna, Lorena loves to cook

and is wonderfully at home in a Cuban kitchen. There are worse places to live than San Francisco, and when Lorena's love life coincides with her dance, the results have been fascinating; her long affair with the danseur noble Roman Rykine, with whom she bought a house in Twin Peaks, resulted in a dance partnership that brought out the best in both in *Giselle* and challenged Lorena to sensual heights that later would served her well in *Don Quixote* and *Carmen*. "We learn to bring out the best in each partner," said Lorena, echoing Alicia Alonso's teachings. And the dance world keeps getting smaller. After his breakup with Lorena, Rykine—a young veteran not only of San Francisco Ballet but also of the English

National Ballet, with an enthusiastic following in both companies—joined the Boston Ballet at the invitation of Mikko Nissinen.

For Lorena and Lorna, moonlighting together has been rewarding, as the unique sister act has come to the attention of the press. Magazine covers and two guest appearances on *Sesame Street*, where the pair genuinely had a giddy good time dancing with Muppets, represent a publicity blitz dancers haven't experienced since the heyday of Russian defectors. In one of many firsts, the two starred in *Swan Lake* in Boston, with Nelson partnering both sisters who took turns as Odile and Odette. Lorena and Lorna, as well as Nelson, have heavy touring schedules, and the chance to dance

LORENA, LORNA, AND THE FEIJÓO EFFECT

alongside other Cubans is seldom passed up. Both return to Miami, to their Cuban public, as often as they can.

Lorena had a featured role in Andy García's 2006 *The Lost City*, a melancholy love letter of a film co-written with García by Guillermo Cabrera Infante, in what would be the great Cuban writer's posthumous work. The filmmaker, it is worth remembering, grew up in the same working-class Havana neighborhood as Lorena and Lorna Feijóo. The motion picture is an ineffably sad look back at Cuba's tragic history, and in particular at Havana. Lorena plays a dancer called Leonela (very much an inside joke on the part of Cabrera Infante), and her sensual dances recalling the glory days of Havana's Cabaret Tropicana were choreographed by Lupe Calzadilla. An especially lovely solo, and this is no accident, is danced to Ernesto Lecuona and carries echoes of Alberto Méndez's unmistakably Cuban ballet *Tarde en la siesta*. Almost no one commented on how Lorena held her own in the dramatic scenes, in a cast that included Garcia, Dustin Hoffman, and Robert Duvall. "Lorena is a born actress," said García. Of course she is as good an actress as she is a dancer—it seems only natural.

"Lorena reminds me a lot of her mother Lupe," said Pedro Pablo Peña. "My first performances in Havana were with Lupe, you know. She wasn't as technically great as Lorena, but she was illuminated, she had this brilliance and light the moment she came on stage. Lorena is luminous like that. She has this light from within, and she is very strong—a lot like Alicia that way too. . . . I am a *fanático* of Lorena," confessed Peña. "She has such abundant energy, such spontaneous talent, musicality—but also this peace. And she has an audacity very few ballerinas can match.

I think her sister Lorna is easy to underestimate, she is more measured, more probing than Lorena. But I tell you she may be even better, frankly. I think she is the more natural Giselle, for

Lorena Feijóo with Andy García in his melancholy love letter of a film, *The Lost City*. Courtesy Andy García, photo by Fernando Calzada.

Lorena Feijóo and Rolando Sarabia in *Don Quixote*. Courtesy of the Cuban Classical Ballet of Miami.

OPPOSITE: Lorna Feijóo on the roof of the Gran Teatro de La Habana, 2001. Courtesy David R. Garten.

example. But in truth Lorna and Lorena are more alike than they are different."

They are probably most alike in Miami, both nervous before their public but expecting that public to welcome them home. Lorena has nerves of steel, at least on the surface, and she never experiences stage fright—except in Miami. "I broke the ice," she remembers of her first appearance with the Cuban Classical Ballet of Miami, opposite an incandescent Rolando Sarabia in *Don Quixote*. "People in Miami will judge you, Sarabia warned

me, because they know ballet. He and I rehearsed in San Francisco, and then we flew to Miami. Lorna tells me she herself, too, gets nervous in Miami—and my sister is never nervous. I think part of the nerves is how they will see it in Cuba." It is true that dancing with the exile troupe carries a definite stigma with the communist intelligentsia inside Cuba. Lorna and Nelson, who have not given up hope of dancing with the Ballet Nacional de Cuba again some day, have limited their Miami appearances to guest spots in the Miami

Lorena Feijóo. Courtesy
R. J. Muna.

162

International Ballet Festival that is produced and presented in Miami Beach by the Cuban Classical Ballet of Miami but is not part of its season. Lorena, exiled earlier than her sister, throws that caution to the wind. "I left for freedom, and I am free. I know things like this, and like being in Andy García's movie, matter in Cuba. I know they will make it more difficult not just to dance again in Cuba but even just to go there and see my family. I know these things." But she is a dancer, and she dances wherever she wants. Besides, there is something about Miami.

"I feel Cuban in San Francisco, and I feel Cuban in Miami," said Lorena, who enjoys considerable critical acclaim not only with San Francisco Ballet but also, like her sister, around the world. "There is no difference. I feel the warmth of the public in San Francisco, and I feel it in Miami—but that is different. So many people who see me in Miami saw me when I was in school, remember my debuts, they tell me things about my career that I'd forgotten. I feel a little bit like I am back home in Cuba when I dance in Miami."

Still, Lorena knows, "I want to dance for our people again, for an audience that knows us a little better. And I am optimistic. I want our Cuban people someday to have the art they deserve, without all the hardships and oppression they have suffered. Someday we will have that." Lorna, embracing a global perspective, points out, "We are everywhere, and we learn a lot from everywhere. But the Cuban style is inside us all, inside every Cuban dancer no matter where. It is alive as long as we dance."

The Feijóos are both Cuban to a fault, and both boast the elegant épaulement, sensual back, disconcertingly slow turns and endless balances that are their birthright. Both own a mercurial classical technique, perfect passés and entrechats, and crystalline-clear articulation with their feet. And it is true that in many significant ways Lorena Feijóo is, like Alicia Alonso before her, a perfect classical

Lorna Feijóo. Courtesy David R. Garten.

ballerina who has willed herself into the romantic mold. Romance, the soft lines and ethereal phrasing at the heart of, say, Act Two of *Giselle*, seem to come more easily to Lorna Feijóo, whose upper body seems of a piece with an evanescent romantic line. Both Lorena and Lorna make *Giselle* their own, one most often in Helgi Tomasson's staging, the other in Maina Gielgud's. Both make *Giselle* seem Cuban.

That, too, seems just right somehow.

Interlude

Four Jewels, Three Graces, and a Rebel

There is no great artistic age save through cross-breeding, between a reclaimed time and a new horizon, between a newly discovered world and a reconstituted past, between cultures and techniques that seem antagonistic but are in fact complementary.

—**Maurice Béjart,** *Lettres a un jeune danseur*

For a time, all too brief, they were all there. Some had been formed artistically before 1959 and had grown alongside Alicia Alonso through the heyday of Ballet Pro-Arte, Ballet Alicia Alonso, and the Ballet de Cuba.

The younger among them became ballerinas after the revolution, but took company class at the barre alongside their older colleagues in the vast second floor studio of the Ballet Nacional de Cuba's home in Havana's El Vedado, where the Cuban School of Ballet was lovingly nurtured and sent out to the world. All but one of them chose to stay, and the rebel who left did so only after a spectacularly distinctive career in the bosom of the Cuban tradition. Some of them are no longer with us, but all are assured a place in Cuban history.

Loipa Araújo, Aurora Bosch, Josefina Méndez, and Mirta Plá were dubbed the Four Jewels of Cuban Ballet by an admiring Arnold Haskell in the 1960s, and the veteran British critic was able to marvel at their successors as well. "I have seen three generations of Cuban dancers," Haskell wrote in a special 1973 festival edition of *Cuba en el ballet*. "The tradition is not only maintained intact, but enlarged."[1] In the 1970s, Cuban ballet was enriched by the "Three Graces," idols of the younger balletomanes, Amparo Brito, Ofelia González, and Rosario Suárez—the dance hurricane affectionately known as Charín. Other names hovered in this stratosphere. Certainly there was Marta García, the "Fifth Jewel," who along with her husband, Orlando Salgado, and the heartbreaking soubrette, María Elena Llorente, became principals in the Ballet Nacional de Cuba. That was no small achievement; rising through the ranks could and did take sometimes decades in a company that was embarrassingly top-heavy with ballerinas. Amparo Brito, a Varna Competition gold medal winner at age eighteen, had to wait until her fortieth birthday to be made a principal. The rest remained soloists, clearly capable of dancing the principal roles that were hopelessly kept away from them, in part, by Alicia Alonso's superhuman stage longevity. All garnered highest honors in Varna

Aurora Bosch, Alicia Alonso, Mirta Plá, and Loipa Araújo in Alonso's witty, pitch-perfect staging of the *Grand Pas de Quatre*. Courtesy of Museo National de la Danza.

Poster for the Ballet
Nacional de Cuba's United
States debut at the John
F. Kennedy Center for the
Performing Arts. The image
is from Brian Macdonald's
Remembranza. Courtesy
of the Alicia Alonso
Collection.

and Moscow and earned lavish reviews in New
York, Paris, and Milan, but only a select few were
allowed to dance the role of Giselle.

The Four Jewels were unique. All four benefited from taking class at Pro-Arte as well as in
the forerunners of the Ballet Nacional de Cuba
with teachers that included not only the Alonsos,
Joaquín Banegas, Jose Parés, and Anna Leontieva,
but also an impressive teaching staff recruited for
the newly reorganized post-revolutionary company
that included Leon Fokine and Alexandra Fedorova. Like the later Three Graces, they enjoyed
the first full flowering of the Ballet Nacional de
Cuba and were allowed a luxury later generations would not have: that of creating dances with
great Cuban choreographers in their prime such
as Alberto Alonso, Alberto Méndez, Iván Tenorio,
and Gustavo Herrera as well as the Chilean Hilda

LEFT: The Ballet Nacio-
nal de Cuba at the Paris
Opéra. Alicia Alonso, Azari
Plisetsky, and the corps
de ballet in *Swan Lake,*
1966. Courtesy of the Ballet
Nacional de Cuba.

Interlude

Four Jewels, Three Graces, and a Rebel

Passing the torch—Loipa
Araújo teaching at the
Ballet Nacional de Cuba
studio, 2004. Courtesy
David R. Garten.

Riveros, in addition to the Spaniard Antonio Gades and the Canadian Brian Macdonald. Although the Cuban troupe boasted its share of thrilling male dancers, and certainly Jorge Esquivel inaugurated a new age of ballet for Cuban men, it is easy to understand Esquivel's own recollection that "it was the women, always the women, the women, the women," with Cuban ballet. This golden age for the Ballet Nacional de Cuba was defined by its Four Jewels and Three Graces, and by a corps de ballet that promised a future that would never end. That the Three Graces would never be promoted to principal status was but a mere suspicion at first.

For a time, I will never forget, they were all on stage. The 1978 United States debut of the Ballet Nacional de Cuba at the John F. Kennedy Center for the Performing Arts in Washington, as well as the longer 1979 tour that followed on its heels, boasted not only the dawning of Alicia Alonso's miraculous Indian summer, but also the riches of Charín and Loipa Araújo in Alberto Méndez's *Rara Avis*, of Charín, María Elena Llorente, Ofelia

González, and Josefina Méndez in *Les Sylphides*, and of the alternating casts of Mendez's Tudor-esque masterpiece *Tarde en la siesta* that boasted Mirta Plá, Marta García, Loipa Araújo, María Elena Llorente, Aurora Bosch, and Amparo Brito. Marta García and Mirta Plá danced as impossibly youthful Swanildas in *Coppélia* with Amparo Brito as Dusk and Charín as Dawn. Loipa Araújo performed an almost supernatural Odile-Odette, and audiences enjoyed the perfect cast of *Grand Pas de Quatre* with Alicia Alonso as Mme. Taglioni, Loipa Araújo as Mlle. Grisi, Mirta Plá as Mlle. Cerrito, and Josefina Méndez as Mlle. Grahn. All Four Jewels took on the role of Giselle and all held up to comparisons to the obvious—particularly in exposing an originality that made each unique as well as a fidelity that branded them as part of a glorious living tradition. Depth of casting such as this is a historical fluke that few companies ever enjoy.

All these women had heartbreaking moments in their dancing careers, each in a different way. For some of them the usual, cruel natural life of a dancer simply took its course. Mirta Plá—the

María Elena Llorente, Loipa Araújo, Alicia Alonso, and Mirta Plá in Alonso's *Grand Pas de Quatre.* Courtesy of Museo National de la Danza.

Four Jewels, Three Graces and a Rebel

ABOVE AND OPPOSITE: Shades of Pavlova—Rosario "Charín" Suarez in *The Dying Swan*. Courtesy of Pedro Portal.

sweetest of them all, was a dancer whose spirit seems to shine these days whenever Lorna Feijóo takes the stage—began as a trusted right hand to Alicia and Fernando and scoured the countryside for young male students; her search yielded the Carreño family, among others. She became a great teacher well before she stopped dancing. Her death in Barcelona in 2003 left a void in Cuban ballet but also a loving legacy. Loipa Araújo, a Varna gold-medalist who became a favorite of Maurice Béjart and Roland Petit (and of her first husband Azari Plisetsky, whom she met while winning the gold in the Moscow competition) was allowed to travel more than most. She created the leading role in Petit's Proustian meditation *Les intermittences du coeur*, and her high opinion of Petit's *Carmen*

made her controversial in the Alonso household. In a rare private moment of cattiness I will never forget, Alicia Alonso once gave me her opinion of Loipa's *Giselle*: "She has beautiful hair, doesn't she?" Loipa Araújo was always the most cosmopolitan of her class, yet she remained the closest to the Cuban tradition, her example still very much alive for a new generation of Cuban ballerinas. Answering the difficult question of who should be in charge of the Ballet Nacional de Cuba after the Alonso era, Joel Carreño—José Manuel Carreño's younger brother—courageously told *The New York Times* in 2005 in Havana, "My opinion is that it should be Loipa—and not when Alicia is gone. It should be her right now."[2] Aurora Bosch, the most severe of the Four Jewels but also the most crystalline technician, eased into teaching with surprising warmth and style in Laura Alonso's mold. Josefina Méndez, the most like Alonso of them all, was fiery on stage but disarmingly humble in private life. Often without credit, it was she who executed Alicia Alonso's choreographic designs in new ballets, she who watched carefully over the company style, she who gave the most unforgettable classes along with Fernando Alonso, and she who effectively ran the company. Her son Victor Gilí, a brilliant Cuban dancer who only recently left Cuba following his mother's death in 2007, may be the most touching living proof of her example. These women raised before the revolution, made their own revolution in dance.

The Three Graces were all kept from the summit in the Ballet Nacional de Cuba. Amparo Brito, the finest Myrtha in my experience, had to be content with watching her husband Jorge Esquivel partner a Giselle three decades their senior. Still, she had access to other roles, and visiting choreographers made the most of her talents. Brian Macdonald created the role of Desdemona for her in his ravishing *Prologue for a Tragedy*, and I remember thinking at the time that if there was such a thing as a Cuban Gelsey Kirkland, Amparo Brito was it. Alicia Alonso, more than a tad jealous of the way *Prologue* was turning out in the studio, convinced Macdonald to "make me a little something for me and Jorge." The resulting *Remembranza*, a serene whirl for a blind ballerina following a path of light at the end, carried, as the choreographer's own program note said, what proved to be a visionary epigraph by Rabindranath Tagore:

Interlude

Four Jewels, Three Graces, and a Rebel

I'm going. I leave you the grass I rested
On and the shade of your garden's farthest tree,
    my refuge.
Close your door, the sun recedes.
I continue my journey . . . The day is dead.

The approaching dusk was suspected by only a few. But it became increasingly clear that even the women—not just the men, as had been the rule at first—would have reason to leave Cuba. Frustration, artistic as well as political, grew up and down the ranks. Charín stayed longer than most, perhaps in the hopes that her artistic closeness to Fernando and Alicia Alonso might give her hope. She was technically fearless, her pyrotechnics outrageous yet never empty, her serenity in adagios marking her as a worthy successor to Alicia Alonso herself. Her claque at the Gran Teatro García Lorca in Havana was known to riot at the slightest provocation, and they would be only a bit more subdued years later at the Jackie Gleason Theatre in Miami Beach. Charín defected to Madrid in 1994, then moved to Miami in 1995, where she staged a memorable version of *Cecilia Valdés* that gathered as its cast a troupe of exiled Ballet Nacional de Cuba alumni.

She founded the Ballet Rosario Suárez, without which there would have been no Cuban Classical Ballet of Miami. In her own repertory, well into the twenty-first century, Charín has kept *The Dying Swan*, a ballet she learned from Alonso, who learned it from Fokine. A role Alicia Alonso had given up for deeply personal reasons became one Charín could not give up for reasons at once personal and patriotic. She founded the Rosario Suárez Dance Academy, and I'll never forget seeing her students at a school recital at the Manuel

LEFT: Lorena Feijóo. Courtesy of R.J. Muna.

OPPOSITE: Lorna Feijóo. Courtesy of Robb Aaron Gordon.

Interlude

Four Jewels, Three Graces, and a Rebel

Artime Theatre in Little Havana, dancing a cobbled-together *Pas de Vivandière* that made me cry; the perfect épaulement, careful carriage and carefree phrasing, the sexy upper body lines from the neck to the curve of the lower spine, the subtly forward romantic presentation of the torso, the jumps into perfect fifths, and the grace. These young girls were not copies of Charín, they were living proof of a vibrant style, a style that by the late 1990s was in danger of becoming dangerously ossified inside Cuba as more and more dancers defected in search of the artistic freedom Alicia Alonso herself once enjoyed.

By leaving Cuba in 1994, Charín narrowly missed out on the Alberto Méndez 1995 miracle *In the Middle of the Sunset*, set to Ernesto Lecuona's historic recordings of several of his own piano scores. I loved the piece and was especially touched by the fact that three or four generations of Cuban ballerinas were on stage in such a thoroughly Cuban ballet, though I confess I also noticed its air of melancholy resignation.[3] I was moved by seeing Alicia Alonso, who at this time already had trouble walking, holding hands with Alihaydée Carreño, María Elena Llorente, Loipa Araújo, Marta García, and Aydmara Cabrera, each woman a shining star and each part of a dazzling constellation. Anna Kisselgoff in *The New York Times* frankly had a more objective view than mine.

Alberto Méndez, in his premiere, *In the Middle of the Sunset*, has astutely created a little ballet with the resonance of a bittersweet farewell. The party is over in Cuba. *In the Middle of the Sunset* offers only a subtext of this idea, but any ballet that looks nostalgically at a family gathering is looking back at better times. The work, by extension, could also be seen as an allegory about the National Ballet itself . . . When Miss Alonso opened her arms in a fleeting, poignant moment at the end, the future appeared to be a question mark.[4]

That question was answered, and continues to be answered, by the growing diaspora of Cuban dancers. That question was answered by Lorena Feijóo, another favorite of Fernando Alonso who felt she had to leave if she was to grow as an artist. It was answered by Lorna Feijóo, who followed her sister's footsteps and also entered the pages of Cuban ballet history.

"If you look carefully," Lorena Feijóo told me, "the style inside Cuba has become démodé, the women's port de bras too round, too academic. Alicia wasn't like that, and I remember seeing her and María Elena Llorente in class and learning that. But today what you get there too often is a timid copy of what Alicia's style must have been. The Cuban School needs some of its old freshness back."

History needs the clash of cultural forces, the dialectic of opposing impulses, the freshness of new voices in any art that is precisely what is being stamped out by the sameness of life under a dying communist regime. The Cuban School of Ballet was born of free artists dancing abroad and returning home with news of a beautiful new frontier. It was born in freedom. The Cuban School of Ballet was born not out of homogeneity but its opposite, from Cuban, Italian, Russian, English, and American antecedents in living, crossbreeding exuberance. That exuberance lives, against all odds, in exile. The line from The Four Jewels and the Three Graces, from Charín the Rebel to the sisters Feijóo is nothing less than one more surprising turn in the story of dance in our time. The story, of course, continues.

174 FOUR JEWELS, THREE GRACES, AND A REBEL

A very young Mirta Plá and Alicia Alonso giving class at the Escuela de Ballet de Cubanacán, formerly the Havana Country Club, in 1960. Courtesy of the Ballet Nacional de Cuba.

All Those Cuban Men

Women, women, women, always the women in Cuba—
I think we were pretty good too.

—Jorge Esquivel

We dance in New York, in Paris, in Havana. It is not about
politics, and it is not even about being thought of as good or
even great. It is about going to bed at the end of the day and
being able to look back and think to myself, what an incredibly
wonderful time I have had. There is no bigger joy.

—Victor Gilí

One of the giddy shocks of seeing the Ballet Nacional de Cuba's *Giselle* for the first time is the pas de dix in Act One, set to the interpolated Burgmüller music for the customary peasant pas de deux, when the sheer power of those men—no matter what cast happens to be dancing—inevitably makes the audience gasp. The huge elevation out of nowhere and the almost surrealistic ballon that follows, the result not just of raw athleticism but also of a perfect demi-plié, can simply be taken for granted in all those Cuban men. They defy gravity, these muscular Cubans, and they seem to fly.

The matrix for the male Cuban style remains Esquivel, but the roots go a little deeper. "Jorge was our first experiment," Alicia told me, "with a little bit of Yousekevitch, and a little bit of me." She should have said "and also a little bit of Fernando," actually, since it was her first husband who set the tone for the company and decidedly set the pattern for the classes at the Escuela Nacional de Ballet as well as for the Ballet Nacional de Cuba. These roots go back to the Alonsos' New York days, to their lessons with Fokine and Tudor, and to the beginnings of both the American Ballet Theatre and the Ballet Nacional de Cuba. It is the approach to Fokine's *Les Sylphides*, in fact, that best suggests the origins of the Cuban male style.

OPPOSITE: Alicia Alonso and Jorge Esquivel in Jorge Lefebre's *Salomé*, 1975, set to a Richard Strauss score with designs by René Portocarrero. Courtesy of the Alicia Alonso Collection.

"I remember Antony Tudor asking me once if I thought of anything while dancing the male part in *Les Sylphides*," Yousekevitch wrote in 1969.

I told him I always thought of something and explained the approach that, I felt, helped me interpret this role. Fokine used to say that in this romantic ballet the male dancer represents Chopin himself. I took my impulse from the great choreographer. Of course, merely thinking of Chopin could not do me any good, so I was pretending to compose the music, bar by bar, as I danced. In the solo variation, for example, while reaching forward in an arabesque, I would say to myself, 'I am reaching out to write a bar of music on imaginary notepaper.' Jumping up and stepping back in attitude, I would pretend doubts and dissatisfaction with what I had composed. Besides, I was trying to maintain an overall feeling of a dream in which the Sylphides were just images created by the composition. Of course this approach necessarily produced a certain romantic feeling, inasmuch as the movements become conveyers of expression rather than goals in themselves.[1]

The Poet in *Les Sylphides* would, after Yousekevitch, become emblematic of the Cuban style; and it is in that ballet as much as in *Giselle* or *Theme and Variations* that the essence of Cuban male dancing in opposition to its Soviet counterpart is most pronounced. "Never, ever confuse the Soviet style with the true Russian style," Yousekevitch once told me after yet another benighted critic had commented on the supposed Soviet influence in Cuban ballet. The ease with which Cuban dancers take to both Fokine and Balanchine as well as to the nineteenth century canon has to do with that distinction; the exaggerated Soviet preparations made into events, the flashy tricks and frank athleticism are all admittedly thrilling, but,

Yousekevitch was not alone in noting, they have no place in either Fokine or Balanchine though they might be the key to mastering Yuri Grigorovich's *Spartacus* or Oleg Vinogradov's *The Knight in the Tiger's Skin*. Even in some of these testosterone-filled Soviet ballets, it is fascinating to witness what a male dancer exposed to something other than Soviet training can do with them.

Irek Mukhamedov, by far the most exciting Russian male dancer since Vladimir Vasiliev, grew immensely as Spartacus at the Bolshoi after joining Anthony Dowell's Royal Ballet, Covent Garden. The Cuban Carlos Acosta, also from the Royal Ballet, took his unmistakably Cuban style to the Grigorovich role and made it his own, also at the Bolshoi Theatre itself. The old Russian

ABOVE: The prototype for the Alonso-Esquivel partnership—Alicia Alonso and Igor Yousekevitch in *Coppélia*. Courtesy of the Alicia Alonso Collection.

OPPOSITE: Alicia Alonso and Jorge Esquivel in *Nos veremos ayer noche, Margarita*, choreographed by Alberto Mendez in 1971 to a score by Henri Sauguet, with sets and costumes by Salvador Fernández. Courtesy of the Ballet Nacional de Cuba.

style in the late twentieth and early twenty-first centuries has been best served not inside Russia but rather in companies such as the Royal Ballet, the American Ballet Theatre, and the Ballet Nacional de Cuba (the Paris Opéra, as in so much else, is its own rule).That is one reason that even now a Russian production of *Chopiniana* seems less true than *Les Sylphides* in those three companies and especially in Alonso's Cuban production. One detail among many will suffice here to suggest the Cubans' understanding of Fokine as well as Fokine's importance to the Cuban School of Ballet. "In *Les Sylphides*," Alicia Alonso said, "Fokine always emphasized his differences with the traditional romantic style. Before Fokine, in the pas de bourrée, for example, the body followed the feet. But in *Les Sylphides* it is the torso that is presented and advances first, with the feet following the body. This means a very specific inclination of the torso, of the line of the neck, the position of the arms and especially the port de bras. And there is also his use of breathing as an

expressive device. In *Les Sylphides*, Fokine aimed for an ethereal projection of dance; he didn't mean for us ever merely to jump, but rather to levitate. His is a poetic vision." That vision is central to the birth of the Cuban School. Understanding Fokine's innovations, as well as understanding the old Russian style, was something Yousekevitch and the Alonsos shared.

Les Sylphides in Fokine's own staging was in the repertory of both the American Ballet Theatre and the Ballet Nacional de Cuba since the infancy of the two companies, with Alonso and Yousekevitch in the first casts. Fernando Alonso also danced it memorably in those days, and he taught it to generations of students in Cuba. His approach, also harking to Fokine, is telling. "A lot of dancers ask me about the lifts of the women, how high it should be, how it fits in the musical phrase." The veteran teacher was and is conscious of the Fokine style, with its short arcs, clean steps, and languid phrasing. He is keenly aware of the Soviet influence on that style and for decades has fought it in Cuba. "I tell them it is not a matter of lifting anybody—it is a more a matter of holding on to the sylph so she won't fly away. That is what Fokine taught me."

That is the way Cubans dance. Esquivel, who took class not only from Fernando but also from Laura Alonso, partnered Alicia Alonso and learned much from her about partnering. His tale is positively Dickensian. He was born in Havana on December 5, 1950, raised in an orphanage, plucked by the Alonsos along with a few mates, and placed in "this big rich person's house in Miramar," as he remembers it, "that we pretty much destroyed. A nice lady took care of us, made sure we went to bed early and all that, and every morning we'd take a little bus to ballet class. I was not the best in the group, you know, I was just one of the *mejorcitos*." His first ballet, as a corps de ballet member, was *Giselle*, with Alicia and Rodolfo Rodríguez. Azari Plisetsky arrived

Alicia Alonso and Jorge Esquivel in Alberto Méndez's *Lucrecia Borgia* set
to Bela Bartok, 1981. Courtesy of the Alicia Alonso Collection.

Alicia Alonso as Cleopatra and Jorge Esquivel as Antony in *La Muerte de Cleopatra* choreographed by Vittorio Biagi and set to the music of Berlioz, Havana, 1979. Courtesy of the Ballet Nacional de Cuba.

ALL THOSE CUBAN MEN

in 1962, and his extraordinary choreography in *Canto Vital* at once embodied and signaled the path for Cuban male dancing. Jorge Esquivel, Orlando Salgado and Francisco Salgado, Lázaro Carreño (not one of the orphans, but a country boy Mirta Plá found while on tour of the island soon after the revolution), Andrés Williams, Raúl Barroso, Pablo Moret, and others would get their trial by fire in *Canto Vital* and show their stuff as Cuban dancers. It became for the Ballet Nacional de Cuba what Anton Dolin's exhilarating 1957 divertissement *Variations for Four* long was for ABT, a calling card and a test for the company's rising male stars.

This was Esquivel's generation, the new generation of male Cuban dancers who came of age artistically surrounded by the wildly popular Four Jewels and Three Graces who, following Alonso's example, sometimes treated male dancers as so many plinths on whom idols rested. These were athletic men who seemed capable of flight, but also they were poets who, with Fernando Alonso, knew how to treat any magical creature in their grasp. Their partnering was selfless, caring, and sublime. These are the men who led Mikhail Baryshnikov to say, "It is impossible not to notice a Cuban dancer the moment he walks into the studio."

Alonso and Esquivel—the resplendent models for all Cuban dance couples, in Cuba as well as in the diaspora. Courtesy of the Alicia Alonso Collection.

José Manuel Carreño dressed for *Le Corsaire*, American Ballet Theatre, 2006. Courtesy of Fabrizio Ferri.

One reason there has never been any doubt that Jorge Esquivel was the finest Cuban male dancer of his generation is that his one contemporary rival for that spot happened to be American: Fernando Bujones. Semantics and geography are at play here, but Bujones was hailed by Anna Kisselgoff and others as "the greatest American male dancer of his generation." There was no reason to argue. Born in Miami of Cuban parents on March 9, 1955, Bujones began his studies in Havana and took classes alongside Esquivel. An early role for both was a school production of *The Pied Piper of Hamelin*, where Esquivel and Bujones were the two leading little mice. Bujones returned to the United States and in 1966, at the age of eleven, got a scholarship to the School of American Ballet. His potential was obvious. "He was like this puppy who we all knew would grow into this amazing dancer," recalled Edward Villella of the precocious student.[2] Bujones passed on the chance to join New York City Ballet and

instead joined the American Ballet Theatre at the age of seventeen. The Cuban-American prodigy, sponsored by ABT and Lucia Chase, went on to become the first American male dancer to win the gold in the International Ballet Competition in Varna. Yuri Grigorovich was president of an illustrious jury that also included Alicia Alonso and Anton Dolin. "The real sensation was Fernando Bujones, born in the USA of Cuban parents," Alicia Alonso's first Albrecht wrote in his diary. "There is only one word—perfect. Bujones is everything [Clive] Barnes told me he is; extraordinary presence, intelligent, and simplicity of showmanship. One must hope and pray he won't be spoilt, for there is no doubt he is the public's favorite."[3]

Bujones was not spoiled and he did become the public's favorite as well as the youngest principal in the American Ballet Theatre's history. An exemplary artist who seemed to combine the virtues of Erik Bruhn and Ivan Nagy, Bujones in the subsequent seasons would partner a glorious constellation of ballerinas including Cynthia Gregory, Eleanor D'Antuono, Gelsey Kirkland, Margot Fonteyn, Antoinette Sibley, Natalia Makarova, Marcia Haydée, and more. He never failed to make them all shine. When ABT, in 1980, celebrated its fortieth anniversary with a now legendary gala at the Metropolitan Opera House, a breathtakingly simple, perfect performance of Balanchine's *Tchaikovsky Pas de Deux* by Bujones and Yoko Morishita acted as a prelude to Alonso and Yousekevitch's emotional homecoming in a pas de deux from *Giselle*. Bujones' bitter, well-publicized rivalry with Mikhail Baryshnikov can in retrospect be seen as a sign of what an extraordinary age it was that boasted both of them. The twenty-minute ovation Bujones received at his ABT farewell performance in 1995 was proof that his public would never leave him. After semi-retirement, Bujones became director of the Orlando Ballet. He was diagnosed with cancer in

Lorena Feijóo and Joan Boada far from home, yet somehow at home with the San Francisco Ballet. Courtesy of R. J. Muna.

2005, fought the one battle he could not win, and tragically died at the age of fifty. In 2009, Zeida Cecilia Méndez—the Cuban ballet teacher and spiritual guide who lovingly saw to Bujones's impeccable training all the way from Varna to his glorious American career and beyond—finished and published Bujones' autobiography.[4]

After Esquivel and Bujones, the spectacle of all those Cuban men has been dazzling. Consider José Manuel Carreño, Lázaro Carreño's nephew. He, too, rose early, the "most distinguished graduate" of the Escuela Nacional de Ballet in 1986, when he also won the USA International Ballet Competition in Jackson, Mississippi. He was a soloist with the Ballet Nacional de Cuba in 1989, a principal within two years, and a star of the American Ballet Theatre soon after that. He is the envy of his most brilliant colleagues and he is an inspiration and a model for Nelson Madrigal and Taras Domitro. "José Manuel is masculine on stage, so elegant and strong," said his fellow ABT star Angel Corella.[5] Carreño himself counts among his "most beautiful experiences" being coached by Yousekevitch in New York, a rare meeting of generations; and, like the Alonsos before him, he has benefited from many teachers and has known how to keep his Cuban accent.

"The tree can't move far from the roots," he told me. "My roots are in Cuba." His repertory is wide, but his favorite role, not surprisingly, is Albrecht. He spends most of his time abroad and is a staple of the American Ballet Theatre's New York season, but he always returns to dance in Cuba. "It is like an insulin injection. It is hard to explain. My mother asks me why I get up so early when I am in Havana, only in Havana. It's because I need all the time there, there is so much to take in, so much I miss." In 2004, José Manuel Carreño received the *Dance Magazine* Award for significant contributions to dance, the first Cuban dancer to receive the honor since Alicia Alonso. Among his trade secrets, he confesses, is one that

makes dancing Balanchine seem easy for Cuban men. "I think we are always slightly ahead of the beat," said Carreño. "We don't wait for the music then move. We Cubans move as it happens."

Joan Boada is in some ways the finest male dancer Cuba has produced since Esquivel and, despite a cruel string of injuries and knee surgeries, is also one of the most emotionally devastating and discreet dancing actors before the public. Boada was handpicked by Alicia Alonso from the Escuela Nacional de Ballet, made a principal of the Ballet Nacional de Cuba at sixteen, and was immediately entrusted with the role of Franz in her *Coppélia*. He defected in 1995, joining the touring Jeune Ballet de France, and in Paris and elsewhere he was soon compared to Rudolf Nureyev in his youth and Mikhail Baryshnikov in his prime. He is like neither, and that of course is part of the excitement he brings. Boada's uniquely Cuban mix of bravura and vulnerability, of classical elegance and Latin sensuality, add up to one of Cuba's most generous gifts to the dance world. It's not about the double air tours into assemblé, about the exuberant phrasing, or about the insouciant, perfect landings that led to the easy comparisons to Nureyev early on—it's about not being able to look anywhere else when this Cuban dancer is on stage. Boada danced principal roles in his teens, in quick succession, with Roland Petit's Ballet National de Marseille, the Royal Ballet of Flanders, and the Australian Ballet, where Maina Gielgud pronounced him "perhaps the most exciting young dancer in the world today."[6]

At San Francisco Ballet, his artistic home since he turned twenty-one, Boada has been the model of the Cuban School of Ballet in everything from *Giselle*, *La Bayadère*, and *Don Quixote* to Balanchine's *Prodigal Son*, *Theme and Variations*, *Rubies*, and *Symphony in Three Movements*, Robbins' *Other Dances*, Mark Morris' *Sylvia*, Yuri Possokhov's *Magrittomania*, William Forsythe's

OPPOSITE: Rolando Sarabia, perhaps the most exciting of the latest wave of Cuban men, at the Sala García Lorca, Gran Teatro de La Habana, 2003. Courtesy of David R. Garten.

Artefact, and Christopher Wheeldon's *Within the Golden Hour*. Tellingly, he became only the second dancer allowed to take on Roman Jacobson's explosive *Vestris*, a whimsical hurricane of a solo originally created for Baryshnikov in 1969, coached by the choreographer's widow Irina Jacobson in 1997.

"I owe everything, everything to Cuba," Boada told me in exile in San Francisco. "Joan," said Esquivel, "what a Cuban talent, what a partner, and a marvelous *muchacho* with real genius but also with a great heart. I admire him so much." Boada's partnership with Lorena Feijóo in Helgi Tomasson and Yuri Possokhov's *Don Quixote*—a production that, truth be told, works better than any current American, Russian, or Cuban version—not only made San Francisco Ballet history but marked a high point in the Cuban diaspora's growing influence on American ballet.

Then there is Rolando Sarabia, known as Sarabita, the beloved Cuban Nijinsky, whose 2003 defection to Mexico broke more hearts in Havana than any other dancer's since Charín's. His asking for political asylum was international news: "The 'Cuban Nijinsky' Seeks Asylum and Stardom," announced *The New York Times* in an article that showed the young dancer to be very clear about his motives.[7] Sarabita first joined Stanton Welch's Houston Ballet. He then joined his brother Daniel, who defected in 2004, at the Boston Ballet—the company where Rolando had first been offered a contract that Cuban authorities prevented him from accepting in 2003. The brothers made their way to Miami City Ballet and soon also became regulars at the International Ballet Festival in Miami and guest dancers with the Cuban Classical Ballet of Miami. To witness this Cuban dancer in action in the heart of Edward Villella's decidedly Balanchinean American company is a thrill and a guilty pleasure; Sarabita makes it look so easy, his speed is so natural, his landings so soft, and his phrasing so clear that it comes as a

refreshing shock to be reminded that Balanchine also calls for more—an eloquent upper body, emotional commitment, and heart. Watching him in *Symphony in Three Movements* in Miami, much like watching Lorena Feijóo in the same ballet in San Francisco or José Manuel Carreño in *Theme and Variations* in New York is like seeing those familiar Balanchine masterpieces for the first time. Rolando Sarabia has everything.

Osmay Molina with his luminous serenity is a perfect prince, and in so many ways the sort of selfless partner Esquivel perfected. Like his frequent partner in Havana and more recently in exile, the beautiful Alihaydée Carreño, Molina walked away quietly and without political fanfare from the principal ranks in Cuba in 2009, and has been turning up as a principal with the Cuban Classical Ballet of Miami. His contemporary Victor Gilí, Alicia Alonso's muse in her most recent choreographies, is the son of the great Josefina Méndez and, like her, is possessed of an innate theatricality that informs every otherwise abstract step. Since joining the Ballet Nacional de Cuba, Gilí zigzags between principal and character roles, enjoying playing the Dance Master in Pedro Consuegra's *Cinderella* as much as playing the Prince. His Mercutio in Alonso's *Shakespeare y sus máscaras*, a tour de force by any standards, is only the most recent example of this dancer's wicked wit and easy phrasing. "I first wanted to be an actor," he said, "and I still love playing a character. That is what dancing is to me." There's something else he once told me, over drinks after a wildly successful *Cinderella* in Los Angeles, that I found both telling and moving.

We are probably the most disciplined company in the world, and that discipline comes from Alicia right through the youngest students in our school. But that is not what it is all about. We have shortages, bad shortages. Our production materials are not always right. We don't

ABOVE: Rolando Sarabia
rehearsing *Le Corsaire*.
Courtesy of the Cuban
Classical Ballet of Miami.

OPPOSITE: Victor Gilí in
Alonso's *Swan Lake* at the
Sala Garcia Lorca, Gran
Teatro de La Habana,
2004. Courtesy of David
R. Garten.

have everything we need and we have to put
up with a lot. That, too, is not all it is about.
It is about having the privilege of doing something like this tonight. It is about dancing.

We dance in New York, in Paris, in Havana.
It is not about politics, and it is not even about
being thought of as good or even great. It is
about going to bed at the end of the day and
being able to look back and think to myself—
what an incredibly wonderful time I have had.
There is no bigger joy.[8]

Carlos Acosta must count as among the most artistically voracious of all these Cuban men. He has
conquered the classics of the canon within a company, the Royal Ballet, Covent Garden, that certainly boasts its own proud tradition. He has been

The indomitable Carlos Acosta, alone on stage (above) and with his father Carlos Acosta, Sr. in Havana (right). Courtesy of Illume productions/Candela, image (above) from *Dance Cuba,* and photo (right) by Boris Crespo.

OPPOSITE: Miguelángel Blanco taking class in the Ballet Nacional de Cuba studio in Havana, 2004. He later joined Joffrey Ballet Chicago. Courtesy of David R. Garten.

expanding his horizons with breathtaking ease, creating crossover popular dance entertainments from Havana to London in the manner of Alberto Alonso's old Ballet Nacional. He has, perhaps most surprisingly, taken on *Spartacus,* injecting new vitality—and not a little Cuban accent—to that epitome of Soviet ballets. "Thank God I did *Spartacus,*" Acosta told *The London Daily Mail* in 2009.[9] It was at this time that he announced he would be slowing down after dancing his classic roles one more time. "After that, no more *Corsaire,* no more *Don Quixote,* no more *Swan Lake.* I have danced everything. I feel fulfilled as a dancer,"

added Acosta as he contemplated his fortieth birthday just a few years away. "I want to have children, dogs, rabbits, I want to have everything. And I will go back to Cuba. It's where I belong."[10]

Among the fresh arrivals to the diaspora, there is the modest, noble Miguelángel Blanco, who just joined Joffrey Ballet Chicago in 2009 after making a splash with American audiences in the Cuban Classical Ballet of Miami's *Le Corsaire.* There is the impulsive Cervilio Amador in Cincinnati Ballet, so different from his fellow defectors yet unmistakably Cuban from the first step. Then there is Miami City Ballet's Cuban All-Star

Balanchine line-up of the stolid and charismatic Carlos Miguel Guerra, the precociously assured Carlos Quenedit, and the exuberantly sweet Daniel Sarabia—certainly not leaving out Sarabita himself. In Boston, Nelson Madrigal is carefully and lovingly keeping the Cuban style alive, enriching the American style in the process

There is more: Yosvani Ramos at the English National Ballet, Rudy Candía in San Jose Silicon Valley Ballet, Octavio Martín in Cincinnati Ballet, Julio Arozarena in the Ballet de Nice, Lienz Chang freelancing in Spain, and there is sunny Joel Carreño, the latest addition to the diaspora

LEFT: Cincinnati Ballet's Cervilio Amador. Courtesy of Peter Mueller.

ABOVE: Boston Ballet's Lorna Feijóo and Nelson Madrigal at the Citi Performing Arts Center (SM) Wang Theatre. Courtesy of Boston Ballet, photo by Marty Sohl.

so far and the youngest from that extraordinary dancing family. Holding the fort in Havana, the unassuming virtuoso Rómel Frómeta and the impetuous Javier Torres give notice that the current generation of male dancers at the Ballet Nacional de Cuba shows no signs of resting on yesterday's laurels—Frómeta in Cuba and throughout Europe as the Basil of choice in the BNC's *Don Quixote* and Torres breaking hearts as Romeo in Alicia Alonso's recent crowd-pleaser *Shakespeare y sus máscaras*. These are beautiful Cuban men who dance.

Consider one more, Taras Domitro, who is not yet allowed to go back to Cuba following his widely publicized 2008 defection alongside Miguelángel Blanco and Hayna Gutiérrez. In his teens, Taritas was a favorite of Alicia Alonso and was given leading roles in her *Don Quixote*, *Swan Lake*, and *Le Corsaire*, as well as the honor of creating one of the three male leads opposite Carla Fracci in Alonso's *Love's Naked Light*. Handpicked by Helgi Tomasson within hours of his defection, Taritas today dances with the San Francisco Ballet and flies to Miami as often as possible to take class with his mother, the legendary Magaly Suárez. She coached him for *Le Corsaire* with Lorena Feijóo, and she will likely coach them both in *The Sleeping Beauty* if Pedro Pablo Peña succeeds in staging that ballet in his Classical Ballet of Miami. "They all just want to take class with my mom," Taras told me.

He was born on June 16, 1986, "and when I entered the company Alicia was no longer dancing." He happens to live with Joan Boada in San Francisco, he looks up to Jorge Esquivel, and he is making the most of a varied repertory that includes plum roles like the lead in *Rubies* while "of course remaining Cuban—I don't have a choice in that." He is a Cuban dancer in everything, his gasp-inducing jumps, his multiple turns that carry Old World ballon and New World speed, and his witty, precocious aplomb.

Balanchine comes easy to him, though Miami's Peña believes, "Taras really belongs in the classics. He should be dancing Petipa." Perhaps, but Taritas himself has said that his main reason for leaving Cuba and the Ballet Nacional de Cuba was precisely to be able to dance more than the classics. "I was four years at the Ballet Nacional de Cuba, dancing the classic ballets," he told *Dance Magazine*. "Here I'm learning new movement—it's very different to the way I worked in Cuba. And that's what I wanted; I wanted to do different things."[11] The truth is that Cuban dancers never have been limited to a single style or a particular historical period. It is just that their artistic upbringing in the Cuban School of Ballet makes them feel perfectly suited for whatever ballet they happen to dance.

The Cuban style lives, always lives, wherever a Cuban dancer dances," Taras told me while visiting his mother in Miami. "It is our training, our port de bras, our masculine way of carrying ourselves on stage. It is how we move. When you see Carreño on stage, you know he is a Cuban artist. When you see Acosta, or when you see Esquivel, even doing nothing, just standing there as Drosselmeyer in *The Nutcracker*, he is a Cuban artist."

So is Taras Domitro. So is Sarabita. So is Joan Boada, and so are they all. Esquivel had every right to be a tad exasperated that journalists kept asking him about "Women, women, women, always the women in Cuba—I think we were pretty good too." They were, and they are. It never has been just the women.

OPPOSITE: Joel Carreño, the youngest arrival so far from that illustrious dancing dynasty, soaring in Alonso's *Swan Lake* at the Sala García Lorca, Gran Teatro de La Habana, 2004. Courtesy David R. Garten.

Taras Domitro and Adiarys
Almeida in exile, starring
in Pedro Pablo Peña's 2008
production of *Swan Lake*
with the Cuban Classical
Ballet of Miami. Courtesy
of Frank Díaz.

Interlude

Giselle

Romantic ballet can be conceived not only as a style from a past era, but also as a state of mind, a sensibility, an emotional necessity that can emerge—and in fact has emerged—in every era, in every place. Even as its expressions vary into infinity, the romantic era, examined historically, brought dance a series of timeless values that are inseparable from the most treasured in the culture of humanity.

—Alicia Alonso

OPPOSITE: Alicia Alonso as Giselle. Courtesy of the Alicia Alonso Collection.

Giselle is about love and loss, about forgiveness, and about hope. It is a masterpiece that speaks to us today at least as frankly and surely as sweetly as it did to its first audiences in 1841. For many, many reasons, it means more to Cubans than any other ballet. It also provides the key to understanding the Cuban School of Ballet. Alicia Alonso's Ballet Nacional de Cuba boasts one of the most extensive and varied classical repertories anywhere in the world, but it is this romantic ballet that the Cuban troupe and its alumni in the Cuban diaspora claim as their own. Alonso's *Giselle* has a place of honor in the history of dance in the Americas.

Set to a score by Adolphe Adam, *Giselle* had its world premiere at the Paris Opéra on June 28, 1841, with Carlotta Grisi in the title role, Lucien Petipa as Albrecht, and Jean Coralli as Hilarion. It did not take long for the ballet to reach Havana, where it premiered at the Teatro Tacón on February 14, 1849, with Henrietta Javelly-Wells as Cuba's first Giselle. The ballet entered the repertory of the Teatro Nacional, now the Sala García Lorca of the Gran Teatro de La Habana, on February 8, 1917, with Anna Pavlova and Alexander Volinine as Giselle and Albrecht. In 1920, three years after Pavlova's first Havana *Giselle*, Alicia Alonso was born.

In ways both ineffable and undeniable, Alonso and the Cuban School of Ballet have deepened our knowledge and appreciation of this dance tale about a love so powerful it transcends even death. That a French masterpiece based on a German poem, once best known through Russian interpretations, would be spectacularly recreated and defined by a Cuban ballerina is one of history's loveliest surprises. But it is no exaggeration to say that one can now divide the history of *Giselle* into the eras before and after Alonso.

Alicia Alonso, born in 1920, and Vladimir Vasiliev, born in 1940, as Giselle and Albrecht in a 1980 single performance that made history. After the performance, Galina Ulanova declared, "She *is* Giselle." Sir Anton Dolin, Alicia's first Albrecht, said "the performance was a miracle." Courtesy the Alicia Alonso Collection.

and Olga Spessivtseva's, which began filtering the ballet's romantic vision through a Janus vantage point of both classical and modern eyes. It was the tragic Spessivtseva's interpretation with the Ballets Russes that the young Antony Tudor learned and later taught to Alonso, Nora Kaye, and Maria Karnilova in the early days of Ballet Theatre in New York. Alonso, whose complete staging would in time transform many of the work's details for contemporary audiences, was from the start miraculously at home with the romantic impulse.

"I am often asked to justify our version of *Giselle*," said Alonso.

It remains above all a romantic ballet, the same that was inspired by a popular Central European legend that was gathered and reinterpreted by the great German lyric poet Heinrich Heine. Another famous poet, the Frenchman Théophile Gautier, appropriated the theme for a ballet that was then mounted by Coralli and Jules Perrot and premiered at the Paris Opéra. [2]

Well, it was precisely there, to the Paris Opera, that I took my choreographic version that was and is the result of our scholarship on romanticism, of the ways we conceptualize the classics—but also the result of our Latin American culture and the encounter of our national idiosyncrasies with a European work created a century and a half ago.

Alonso herself has called this turn of events "not a personal success, but rather a triumph for Latin American culture." [1] She has a point. The Paris Opera, Vienna State Opera, Teatro Colón in Buenos Aires, and other major dance centers—in addition to Havana's own Ballet Nacional de Cuba—have turned to Cuba for guidance in staging their own productions of *Giselle*. Elsewhere, often without credit, the *Giselle* tradition itself has been indelibly marked by Alonso's touch.

The first decades of the twentieth century saw interpretations of *Giselle*, including Pavlova's

The story of *Giselle* is simple, and in Alonso's version it is clearly told, with pantomime passages restored and, crucially, with emotional intensity informing every step. [3] A peasant girl falls for a boy who is really a nobleman in disguise; when his elegant fiancée turns up, Albrecht abandons Giselle with the ease of a cad who's already had his way. Giselle descends into madness and dies. We know she was sickly anyway, but she may have killed herself or perhaps she just died of love. Whatever the reason, and each ballerina has the freedom to choose one within the choreography,

Giselle's love for Albrecht transcends the grave. In Act Two, when eerie female spirits roam the night to punish men who betrayed their lovers, there are miracles afoot and Giselle's ghost dances with Albrecht until he is safely back in the sunshine of a new day. By then, of course, Albrecht has lost her forever.

The choreography, too, is in many ways simple. *Giselle* was created in 1841, when seeing women up on their toes was still a novelty and the illusion of dancers floating was a recent bit of stage magic. There were later additions by Marius Petipa to Jules Perrot and Jean Coralli's original choreography, but except for the Russian bravura of Giselle and Albrecht's solos, these have been kept to a minimum over the years. The ballet we have now is very much a product of Paris in the Romantic Era, not least in terms of choreography. Nothing in *Giselle* is merely decorative, every step and every gesture has a theatrical purpose.

There is no reason to assume that these details were any less crucial in 1841 than they might be today. In the *Giselle* tradition, particularly as transmitted through Tudor after Spessivtseva, these are not just dance parts, they are dramatic roles. Alonso took that Tudor lesson to heart, letting it inform her dancing in general but her lifelong work on *Giselle* in particular. The critics Arnold Haskell and Ann Barzel on several occasions were among the first to notice how, for example, Albrecht's fiancée Bathilde was traditionally a cipher usually danced by a corps member in every *Giselle* production until Alonso's, where Bathilde is always danced by a principal ballerina. It is telling that it is the Cubans' habit of taking seriously the dramatic motivation and the emotional truth of each step, and that it defines not only the performance practice of Alonso's *Giselle* in the Ballet Nacional de Cuba today but also the art of the Cuban diaspora as exile dancers bring their Cuban schooling to *Giselle* in productions across the world.

Let a single step provide a good example here. If the arabesque in all its forms makes up most of the choreography, it is dazzling to witness how much feeling that one step can communicate—the innocent arabesques piqués of Giselle's entrance, her playful arabesques while teasing Albrecht with her kisses, and later her desperate whirling in arabesque as she is called back from the grave. There are melancholy arabesques, swaggering arabesques for Albrecht and Hilarion, menacing arabesques for the Wilis in temps levés, and even a final arabesque of farewell that is as devastating as any of

Alicia Alonso rehearsing *Giselle* in Havana for the 1980 Havana International Ballet Festival. Galina Ulanova coached her protégé Vasiliev and Anton Dolin coached Alonso. Each dancer brought out surprising new accents in the other. Courtesy the Alicia Alonso Collection, photo by Enrique Falcón Tejada.

Giselle

the more intricate step combinations that followed in dance history.

That history is the key to the success of Alonso's *Giselle*. It is of course the human content of dance that keeps it from being just an ancillary function of the music. There are two things at work here—the inspired calculation that creates the illusion of spontaneity and the immaculate professionalism that seldom lets the effort show. The pantomime Cuban dancers learn in school is not totally traditional. Everything from Giselle's rebuffing of Hilarion to the slowly mounting inevitability of the Mad Scene is much reworked from what we know of the 1841 original choreography. There are other, telling examples.

Many details are modern and are designed for today's audience. In the original pantomime, for instance, Giselle tells Bathilde she sews for a living. In the original 1841 libretto, she mimed the action of weaving, which would be meaningless to today's audience. This is a moment among many, a change in dramatic detail that Alonso devised while working with Tudor for what was to be her unexpected debut in the role in New York in 1943. It is at once endearing and revelatory to find, in the twenty-first century, some smaller European companies such as Moscow's Stanislavsky Ballet or St. Petersburg's Maly Theatre Ballet maintaining in their repertory the "weaving" mime in Act One that virtually every other company by now has changed after Alonso's example, from Havana to Paris, from San Francisco to New York and London.

Decades after Alonso's *Giselle* debut, in her own production, class differences are more marked between Bathilde and Giselle and between the peasants and Bathilde's aristocratic entourage; the class differences are doubtless stronger in Alonso's dancers' interpretations than they needed to be in the original at a time when they were taken for granted. This does by no means betray the original text of the ballet; rather it revitalizes its message in the context of a new era. Lorena Feijóo

notes nostalgically, "This is not just in the leads; I danced in the *Giselle* corps in Cuba before I left, I danced the two Wilis, Moina and Zulma, and I can tell you that everything in the mise-en-scène was considered and studied down to the last gesture and the last emotion. We needed to know those characters; we needed to know who they were before we were allowed onstage to perform them in Havana." [4] Even those ethereal, heartbreaking spiraling renversées Zulma dances in Act Two, her sister Lorna Feijóo also reminisces, "have to tell the audience 'This is how I died, this is how I drowned myself.'" [5] The psychological as well as technical preparation of these and other details cannot help but inform performances that instantly, accessibly communicate emotional truth.

Some changes are accidental. The round dance for the villagers in Act One originally consisted of one long line, half facing one way, half the other. Alonso, with her severely damaged eyesight, could not easily negotiate the uninterrupted run from Giselle's end of the line to Albrecht's—and this with the aid of subtle finger snapping or whispering from the helpful corps. So, in the Alonso version, the line is broken into four spokes of a wheel, all facing forward, with an easier route for this blind Giselle to follow in the dark. The change has worked so well on purely aesthetic and practical terms (a four-spoke wheel of dancers takes up a smaller stage area than one large line spanning a wider circle) that several productions from New York to London now also dance it this way—even without a blind ballerina. The resulting impact on the performance practice of *Giselle* is remarkable. It is undeniable that blindness alienated Alicia Alonso from her praxis, but she resolved that alienation and its resulting limitations by absorbing those very limits into her praxis. It cannot be overstated how difficult it is to dance without sight—just trying walking and turning with one's eyes closed should suffice to demonstrate this. This theft of her praxis by material conditions in the

When Alicia had her dancer's praxis stolen by blindness, she both accepted that brutal physical condition and refused to be determined by it.

context of artistic creation on stage led, throughout her life, to an appropriation and phenomenal transformation of those conditions. In a real sense, Alicia Alonso's unique situation has taught Cuban dancers to refuse to accept the most brutal limits, to embrace a freedom defined by that refusal.

In the diaspora, the theft of a Cuban identity, indeed of a Cuban homeland, has led many dancers to a bold refusal to accept that brutal change in their own material conditions. When an artist's—or anyone's—praxis is stolen, the resulting alienation is as clear as it is cruel. It becomes impossible to ignore the material conditions in which art is created. It becomes impossible, too, not to want more than sheer resignation to these conditions. Paradoxically, to accept one's lot is also to refuse. When Alicia Alonso had her dancer's praxis stolen by blindness, she both accepted that brutal physical condition and refused to be determined by it. The rest is history. When Cuban exile dancers in the diaspora had their praxis stolen by the loss of their homeland, their refusal led and continues to lead to a dialectical acceptance of their condition that is at once a refusal to accept these limits. Jean-Paul Sartre was right in noting that freedom is what you do with what has been done to you.

These Cuban dancers, often far from their homeland and more distinctly Cuban for it, say with every step, "No, you will not take Cuba away from me." Even more than in the case of Cuba's musical or literary traditions, exile has meant a regeneration and revitalization of Cuban ballet and its rich tradition. Nowhere is that tradition more ravishingly embodied, and nowhere is the example of Alicia Alonso more telling, than in the Cuban *Giselle*.

Most of Alonso's changes to the original 1843 version of *Giselle* are of course not accidental, but rather conscious aesthetic choices. Turning the interpolated Act One peasant pas de deux into a pas de dix for the villagers—an impressive tour de force for the male dancers who must display superhuman ballon in strings of jetés—manages to preserve a beloved scene in the *Giselle* tradition going back to the original Paris production, while at the same time avoiding the dramatic awkwardness of introducing an extra principal couple without a story of their own. Alonso's solution solves that problem. Earlier in Act One, when the entire corps of villagers turns and stares over their shoulders at Hilarion, who is unmistakably identified as outside the community identity embodied in the ensemble, the clarity of dramatic detail also subtly appropriates and elevates what is elsewhere a dispensable connective musical passage. These and other musical matters, incidentally, could by no means be taken for granted before Alonso restored the *Giselle* score to its full splendor in 1972, when her productions both for the Paris Opera and the Ballet Nacional de Cuba boasted the most complete versions of Adam's score since the 1843 original.

In earlier twentieth century versions, including all Soviet stagings as well as the one Alonso learned from Tudor and also the Ballets Russes and Royal Ballet, Covent Garden versions, the music was cut—sometimes severely, as in Mikhail Baryshnikov's breezy 1980s *Giselle* for the American Ballet Theatre. That was the rule. Frederick Franklin, whose memory makes him a living encyclopedia of performance practice, once joked, "I hear the recording by Richard Bonynge and think to myself, 'What wonderful music, I wonder what it is?' We didn't dance that. In the old Ballets Russes days, people wanted three ballets a night, so we gave them just that."[6] His own undeniably attractive versions, including the celebrated Dance Theatre of Harlem's *Creole Giselle*, are musically incomplete and dramatically foreshortened.

Giselle

Alicia Alonso and Flemming Flindt rehearsing *Giselle* in Copenhagen, 1969. Courtesy of the Ballet Nacional de Cuba.

What is it about ballet, and what is it about the Cuban *Giselle*, that is so personal? The easiest way for a critic or anyone else to look at a ballet is just that. Look at it and pay attention. There are all those beautiful people, usually moving to ravishing music, using their bodies in ways athletic and sublime, telling tales in motion that reveal truths and suggest mysteries that the audience might otherwise be too shy or afraid to see. Details are everything, and they mean different personal things to different people. There is a small, emotionally shattering moment in *Giselle* when the poor peasant girl suddenly faces a rich elegant woman who is wearing what must seem like impossibly beautiful clothes. Giselle's simple pantomime—no more than a few bars of music—as she reaches and almost touches the hem of Bathilde's dress embodies innocent hope against all odds, longing for so much happiness that Giselle will never know, and ineffable sadness. The gesture was in the original Paris production, seven years before the Revolution of 1848 and well before Marxist theories of class differences. Yet there it is, in a different context today, in all its simplicity and

timeless universality. How each ballerina plays that moment can be as telling as how a Violetta in Verdi's *La Traviata* notices the ravages of a fast life staring back in the mirror in the simple line, "*O, qual pallor.*" Or it can be as devastating as how the dying Ase in Ibsen's *Peer Gynt* can suggest irony, fervor and terror all at once as she listens to her fantastical liar of a son describe the gates of heaven she will soon enter. Ballet encompasses dance, music, and drama; it takes place in lived history; it is ephemeral.[7]

A product of the artist's unique labor within specific material conditions, ballet is as unnatural as it is beautiful. Dancers, if one looks closely, also give away an almost immodest, disarmingly personal treasure of details; the sum of choices they have made throughout their lives as dancers, their unique body language and, some might say, their souls. No other artist is as naked before you as a dancer—no singer, no actor. A dancer's body is the instrument of dance, a dancer's emotions its texture. What you see really is what you get. Cuban dancers dance, of course. They also stand, fierce and exposed, in the thickets of living Cuban history.

History helps us understand ballet. The actual performance practices of major ballet companies taken together form the living, dialectically rich history of ballet from its origins in the 1760s, through the first pointe work in romantic ballets of the 1820s, to Petipa's exquisite classicism, through the end of the nineteenth century and Fokine's self-conscious apotheosis of romanticism at the start of the twentieth, on to Tudor's dark and unsettling dance dramas and Balanchine's kaleidoscopic transformation of the classical line, and to the strikingly original ballets of more recent geniuses. History sometimes informs even the endearingly parochial neoclassical patois that is the lingua franca of so many minor post-Balanchine choreographers. Where do Alicia Alonso and her Ballet Nacional de Cuba fit in that history? How will history judge her? And what of *Giselle*, her most important contribution to the canon of classical ballet?

A critic, or anyone else concerned with the aesthetics of dance, most likely works from a theoretical framework as well as from knowledge of history; good criticism should move one closer to the actual historical praxis of dance. It is bad criticism that takes us away from the experience of dance and into the realm of theory.

To a critic with a hammer, everything looks like a nail. That is the arrogant reductionism of political criticism of the arts. That is one problem with Marxist-Leninist aesthetics, for example, or with other utilitarian views of the arts that can turn critics into propagandists or censors.[8] Political criticism of Cuban ballet is facile. Talk of whether or not a dance is socially relevant or politically useful is interesting, but the real question ought to be whether a dance is good or bad. Being able to tell the difference, dance by dance, is crucial and that means separating competence from incompetence, acting from acting out, professional polish from mere good intentions, political agendas from artistic reality, art from dross or worse. It is not by

any means, at least not necessarily, a political question. Alicia Alonso is not a key figure in the theory and praxis of ballet because of or despite her politics. The truth is that her *Giselle* was not bourgeois art in the 1940s and 1950s, no more than it was communist art after 1959. That would be impossible—it is the same *Giselle*. Antony Tudor was right when he told me that she is only a ballerina, and that is all she is. That is a lot. The material conditions that have shaped her life, as well as the life project through which she shaped those conditions, are dialectically inseparable. It would be as much a mistake to judge the Ballet Nacional de Cuba and its founder solely by its political situation as it would be to judge it hermeneutically as pure movement. There is no such thing.

The phenomenal thing about ballet—in every sense of that very useful term—is that it takes two to give meaning to the phenomenon. There is no unmediated, essential truth in ballet. The truth of a ballet arises not in a vacuum but in public, in real life, in the magical moment when the audience witnesses the dancers in motion. Should ballet tell a story at all? Or is ballet at its purest simply a matter of bodies in motion with no meaning other than the movement itself? Alonso's *Giselle* raises questions about what ballet is and what it ought to be. Of course it raises questions about the role of the artist in a communist society, but here it is the ballet itself and not the society that must be the object of judgment. *Giselle* and the rest of the narrative-rich Cuban ballet repertory from 1948 to this day also raise questions about the role of George Balanchine's so-called abstract dances in today's repertory, and perhaps about the often overlooked role of the other great genius of the Balanchine generation, Antony Tudor. After Fokine, Tudor and Balanchine were defining influences in Alonso's artistic development. The conditions their teachings and choreography created for Alonso, and later for her company, remain at least as vital as any passing political situation.

Interlude

Giselle

Situating Alonso and the Cuban School of Ballet means situating the artists and their art in this context, not mainly or even necessarily in the context of the politics of their time.

Audiences everywhere seem to love story ballets, even if most American ballet critics betray an inordinate fondness for ballets devoid of dramatic content. "I always thought the very idea of an abstract ballet very foolish," asserted Tudor.[9] "People have to dance it, don't they? How abstract can the human body be? How can it not tell a story?" The world did not pay much attention when Tudor changed the face of ballet. Yet that is precisely what he did, subtly, irrevocably. He was the greatest poet of modern ballet. Tudor's genius lay in his complete absorption of classical technique into the fabric of human psychology, lessons Alonso and her Cuban dancers and choreographers have absorbed and transformed over decades. It was difficult not to be influenced by these forces as Alicia Alonso's aesthetics developed, just as Galina Ulanova absorbed the lessons of Stanislavsky's method acting in her dancing as she worked with Leonid Lavrosky in *Romeo and Juliet*. "Lavrosky would ask me how I felt when I lifted Romeo's mask and saw his face for the first time," Ulanova told me in Havana in 1980. "He insisted I remember that as he held me up. That is how we worked." I marveled at how this psychological approach to creating a dance role was remarkably similar in Soviet Russia to what was going on in Tudor's New York in the 1940s as he coached Alonso as his Juliet and taught her the role of Giselle for the American Ballet Theatre.

For both Alonso and Ulanova, dramatic, psychological insights would become the way to marry meaning and technique. In the late 1940s and 1950s, as the Ballet Alicia Alonso grew into the Ballet Nacional de Cuba, this dramatic method was simply taken for granted and was in fact the rule in Cuban theatrical circles. The first drama lessons in the Stanislavsky method

in Havana were taught by Adolfo de Luis, a Cuban disciple of Stanislavsky and Piscator, in Alonso's own Academia de Baile Alicia Alonso in Havana.[10] Method acting, in dance as in the non-musical stage, was the rule in Cuba as influential new theatre companies sprung up in Havana before the revolution, including Las Máscaras, Sala Talía, and El Sótano. This atmosphere mirrored the situation of the theatrical avant-garde in both New York and Moscow. Coincidence or *Zeitgeist*, it was very much part of the material artistic conditions of Alonso's *Giselle* initially in her two companies, the American Ballet Theatre and Ballet Nacional de Cuba. And, in her particular case, it was certainly not the politics of Cuba before or after the revolution that were telling. The key to her art is not political, no matter what political uses may be found for that art. A major element of the Alonso characterization and approach to *Giselle* and all her other roles from the 1940s onwards is the uniquely happy result of Balanchine's astringent technical demands and Tudor's psychological intensity.

Alicia Alonso recalls with fondness her work with both Tudor and Balanchine. Tudor, who was the classical ballet master of American Ballet Theatre as well as its resident choreographer, gave Alonso the choreographic foundation for *Giselle*. He also paid her the rare compliment of letting her choreograph several key moments in his *Romeo and Juliet* based on what they agreed were Juliet's feelings. He drilled her on such puzzling exercises as arabesques of joy followed by arabesques of sorrow. Not everyone took to these subtleties in what some still view as simple ballet steps, but when the dancer and choreographer breathed the same air, the results were spectacular. And the influence was not limited to Tudor's own ballets; it was Tudor who taught Alonso the role of Giselle, and it was in *Giselle* generations later that he discovered Gelsey Kirkland, the last great Tudor ballerina. The choreographer Glen Tetley was inspired to follow a life

OPPOSITE: The powerful emotional highlight of the VII International Ballet Festival, Havana, 1980—Alicia Alonso and Vladimir Vasiliev in *Giselle*. Courtesy of the Ballet Nacional de Cuba.

Giselle

Alicia Alonso as Giselle with Igor Yousekevitch as her best-loved Albrecht. Courtesy of the Ballet Nacional de Cuba.

theatre, and painting, still entrances American ballet critics and impresarios. Companies such as the Royal Ballet, Covent Garden, the Bolshoi, and the Kirov all become apologetic in the United States when they continue to use ballet to tell a story—and often they are viewed as somehow retrograde, not as advanced as whatever ossified neoclassical model passes for tradition in Manhattan. True, that the opposite has been the case in Russia and in Cuba is in part the result of fetishizing an aesthetic of socialist realism. But it is also true that, well before socialist realism was proclaimed as an artistic ideal of Marxism-Leninism, narrative ballet was the status quo; ballet told stories, period. And in Cuba, also well before the revolution, narrative ballet was the rule at Pro-Arte Musical, at Ballet Alicia Alonso, and at the Ballet Nacional de Cuba. A coincidence of aims does not by any means constitute a relation of cause and effect.

Technique matters, of course. The articulation of a cellist's phrasing, for example, the steps of a dance, the rhythmic texture of an aria, the words of a play, and the notes of a symphony all can be described objectively. A flat note is not a matter of opinion, and neither is flawed turnout or lazy épaulement. But we respond to more than these objective components of a work of art. The object of our attention transcends its material character: Suddenly, miraculously, steps are more than steps, words become theatre, and a string of notes can break your heart. That is why it is fair to call the aesthetic experience sensual. In ballet, this sensuality is undeniable.

There is no essential artistic meaning out there waiting to be discovered, and neither is there just a series of step combinations waiting to be analyzed. The fact is that a score unperformed, an aria unsung, a play unread or a dance merely intended are never the point. The experience of an actual performance is what matters. In situating the Cuban *Giselle*, what matters is the *Giselle* tradition in all its lived transformations together with the

of dance after seeing Alonso in Tudor's *Romeo and Juliet*. His memories of Alonso in the first *Theme and Variations* in 1947 also throw light on the sort of Balanchine dancing we see too seldom today. "The wonderful thing about Alicia was that when she was dancing the most abstract ballet—even with this wonderful technique she had—there was this emotional quality in the dance. That is what Tudor taught." [11]

Should abstraction be abandoned as an ideal? Ballet is unique among the arts in holding on to a quaint modernist aesthetic. That same 1950s and 1960s modernism, long abandoned in music, actual performance practice in and out of Cuba. The material conditions that are the groundwork of Alonso's work are undeniable, and they are undeniably tied to Cuban political realities. But those conditions, over the arc of a lifetime, have had a wide range. Consider that, for example, Alonso's contemporary, Maya Plisetskaya, garnered such Marxist-Leninist honors as being a People's Artist and receiving a Lenin Prize, yet history does not and will not judge her because of her associations with the Soviet government. Consider then this: Alicia Alonso received honors such as the Order de Carlos Manuel de Céspedes and was named a Dama de la República when Cuba actually was a republic before 1959; and she also has been named a Hero of Labor and was vice president of the Cuban-Soviet Friendship Association after 1959. Should we posit an "Alonso I" and "Alonso II"? Can these in any meaningful way be claimed as ways to judge her? Or her *Giselle*?

An alternative explanation is more difficult, but it also is necessary to ponder. Alicia Alonso chose to remain in Cuba after 1959. She could have had a career outside her country, as so many dancers everywhere do; she chose not to. Her choices have earned her praise, and they have earned her scorn and vilification. Reflecting on exile, soon after the fateful 1980 Mariel exodus that changed the political tenor of both her audience and her working conditions in Cuba, Alicia Alonso told me that "to emigrate, not just for political reasons but for economic reasons or even for art. . . to emigrate always means that so much is taken away from you. You live for the permanent question, What if? So much is robbed from an exile, most of all the admiration of one's possibilities."[12]

She was not about to be robbed of her own possibilities. That this involved a certain willful blindness, quite apart from her physical condition, is clear. The Alonsos kept their company insulated from much of the everyday terror of living in Castro's Cuba, but their influence of course

was limited to the company. Elsewhere, Castro's "Words to the Intellectuals" sent a chill through the arts in Cuba soon after the revolution.[13] The Heberto Padilla affair, which soured Jean-Paul Sartre, Simone de Beauvoir, and so many other European left-wing intellectuals on Castro's socialist paradise, not only sidelined that great poet simply because of his poetry but also turned him into an informant. This would become the rule, and writers suffered the worst but were by no means the only artists affected. Arturo Sandoval, a protégé of Dizzy Gillespie and one of the founders of the fusion jazz band Irakere, was monitored carefully and was told by the Minister of Culture Armando Hart Dávalos to take care that his music not sound "so American."[14] The gay German composer Hans Werner Henze was evicted from Havana, and Alonso had to abandon plans to commission a ballet set to his Cuban oratorio *El Cimarrón*, which was based on Miguel Barnet's Cuban novel. Barnet himself was subsequently reduced to writing sociology rather than fiction. Padilla in his confession to the National Union of Writers and Artists (UNEAC), a grotesque bit of Stalinist theatre, accused José Lezama Lima of antisocial tendencies, and the old gay man found all his works withdrawn and never published again in his lifetime; he died in fear in Havana in 1976.

Homosexuals and dissidents were officially classified as antisocial criminals by the National Congress on Education and Culture. Virgilio Piñera was under virtual house arrest; Guillermo Cabrera Infante was exiled; Reinaldo Arenas was jailed, tortured and eventually put on a fishing boat to Miami during the Mariel Exodus. Even as Castro himself singled out the Ballet Nacional de Cuba as heroes of labor in his speech to the First Congress of the Cuban Communist Party in 1975, there was no question that even Alicia Alonso had to be careful.[15] It would be facile at this juncture to render a severe judgment of what one might see as Alonso's cowardice in the face of these injustices.

Interlude

Giselle

It also would be pointless; if she was to remain in Cuba, what else could she do?

"Cuba is such a small country," Alicia told me in 1980 the first time I interviewed her for *The Washington Post*, "and it has suffered so much." [16] The scope of that suffering within Alonso's grasp was and is limited; what she could do artistically and practically to keep her company well and dancing was and is something else. It is worth noting that these are not small details.

Wilhelm Furtwaengler, in wartime Berlin, could do little to alleviate the madness and terror of Hitler's holocaust, but what he could do was keep German culture alive for the future by making music in the present. For decades Dmitri Shostakovich endured the uncertainty and horror of Stalin's grip, by managing to create beauty the way he could. These are considerable achievements, and it would be foolish and thankless to point out that both artists might have done better by leaving their country. For decades, Alicia Alonso has not left hers. And the ballet company she has nurtured reflects—and has thrived within—the brutal reality of those material conditions. She may be accused of becoming a silent partner in the oppression of the Cuban people, but she must be held at least as responsible for keeping her people's culture alive. Yes, narrative ballet with a message was the way to proceed under a socialist-realist agenda. Yet Alonso did so within the classical canon, not by commissioning agitprop works. This turned her Ballet Nacional de Cuba into one of the world's most aesthetically conservative companies. Cuba is not the place to discover new choreography or new music; there are dancers in that company, in 2010, who have never met a choreographer of new works and who never saw Alonso dance. Yet, within those limits, what a breathtaking achievement it is that the repertory on which her company concentrates has been extraordinarily well served. Cuba is the place to find valid, fresh dancing of the canonical nineteenth century repertory. Cuba is the home

of the truest and most moving *Giselle* staging anywhere in the world. Elsewhere, in productions as far from Cuba as San Francisco and Boston, Alicia Alonso's pupils Lorena Feijóo and Lorna Feijóo embody and expand her example and are doubtless the finest Giselles before the public today.

Political criticism is of course possible, and frequent, of Alonso's very stay in Cuba. As I write this, celebrations of her official ninetieth birthday—actually her ninety-first—are underway in her New York alma mater, the American Ballet Theatre; and a historic debut of the Ballet Nacional de Cuba in Miami in 2011 is being discussed seriously amid frank assessments of the danger and controversy of having the Cuban troupe perform for the first time in the second largest Cuban city, the capital of the Cuban diaspora.

Besides her work, Alonso herself long has been a source of political controversy—her name has the power to call up a complex maelstrom of meaning that can only be realized in its totality. This, despite the fact that the passage to political activism was much more difficult for her than for her husbands—Fernando Alonso (a member of the Communist Party since the 1930s) and even Pedro Simón (a philosopher and critic well connected to the Cuban intelligentsia and adept at survival in that environment). The shift from individual artistic discovery and personal excellence to political commitment has been at best shallow in Alicia Alonso; a case of *"cubrir la forma,"* doing enough to survive and to maintain her ability to make dances. She can be accused of never coming to grips with the tragic consequences of the political philosophy she often claims to espouse in the right interviews, just as she can be praised in practical terms for improving the artistic conditions of her dancers in Cuba as well as for more than once springing some of them out of communist jails. "She is a whore," Reinaldo Arenas once told me, far from home, in New York. "But she did get people out of jail, I can tell you that." [17]

Capturing an era and transcending it in triumph are what make Giselle *rank with* Hamlet *and* Le Cid, *with* Parsifal, *and with* Peer Gynt.

"Alicia kept a lot of them from being thrown into the UMAP camps," Arenas continued, referring to the concentration camps of the Unidades Militares de Ayuda a la Producción (UMAP). Begun by Raúl Castro in 1965, the camps interned gays as well as Jehovah's Witnesses and other non-conformists to the socialist ideal. The camps continued until 1971, when the United Nations Commission on Human Rights shamed the Cuban government into closing them as such.

Political criticism of Alonso's *Giselle*, of Alonso herself for that matter, is pointless. Ballet is not a political tool, but one reason it is in fact so important in Cuban culture is that its nuances carry political meanings that can be very subtle and never oppressive. Her life project has been impeccable, the results of her labor beautiful. She has remained an elitist in her art, surrounded by fetishized populism. Under any political conditions, and perhaps especially in a climate of oppression, beauty and goodness have to count.

"I helped my country take the first strong, certain steps towards a future of dance," Alonso told me in 1980. "I am very proud of our company. Most of all I believe in the human being, and I believe that art makes us human. I have learned to trust that, over so, so many years." [18]

Her *Giselle*, over all those years and above all her other achievements, has been a profession of that faith. Capturing an era and transcending it in triumph are what make *Giselle* rank with *Hamlet* and *Le Cid*, with *Parsifal*, and with *Peer Gynt*. Ballet has no richer masterpiece than this deceptively simple, endlessly fascinating dance about a love that overpowers death. Hegel famously observed that the owl of Minerva takes wing at dusk, that wisdom and deepest understanding arrive at the close of an epoch, at the birth of a new day. That is true of *Giselle*, at once the apotheosis of romantic ballet and the glittering model for all classical ballets to come. It is true also of Alonso's staging of this and other masterworks of the classical canon.

The text and the context of that canon have been enriched, and transformed by her labors. She chose to cut the Gordian knot of uncertainty, and perhaps some mistakes were necessary.

The twentieth century's greatest interpreter of the most beautiful of all ballets continues to revitalize and redefine this nineteenth century masterpiece for the twenty-first century. Alicia Alonso truly was born so that *Giselle* would live. Her unique *Giselle* remains a dialectical synthesis of boundless romantic passion and elegant classical rigor, of impeccably schooled respect for our cultural past and indomitable faith in our future. Alonso, born in 1920, first danced *Giselle* in 1943, and owned the role for the next fifty years. In the truest existential sense, she is what she does, and what she does above all else is this. Alicia Alonso is Giselle, in history, and forever in my memory. Today, Lorena Feijóo is Giselle, and Lorna Feijóo is Giselle. The future of Cuban ballet is limitless.

The integrity of the Cuban *Giselle* matters. So does technical virtuosity, an element of performance practice that has grown considerably since 1841. The endless secure balances of the ballerinas, the insolent extension and stratospheric jump of the men, all these and other by now necessary details make *Giselle* as accessible as it is thrilling. Alonso's ghostly Wilis, not coincidentally, are the most dramatically charged anywhere. These are not the abstract dancing patterns seen today in productions from San Francisco to St. Petersburg. These Wilis are avenging spirits, and their vengeance resounds in their moves. The Feijóos are not alone among exiled Cuban dancers outside of Cuba in longing for the communal mise-en-scène company rehearsals at their alma mater. In some of the finest American and European classical troupes,

Interlude

Giselle

Alicia Alonso and Erik Bruhn rehearsing *Giselle* at Jacob's Pillow. Courtesy of the Alicia Alonso Collection.

when the corps de ballet is not nurtured dramatically as well as technically, it shows. The sensible Marxist directive to make art clearly accessible to the people—to all of the people—has no quarrel here with Alonso's artistic integrity. The changes she has organically integrated into her reconstruction of this nineteenth century jewel only make it shine that much brighter for audiences, any audiences, in the twenty-first. These are valid changes because they remain true to the text of the original ballet and they also reflect and transform the context of that ballet today. The material conditions of the *Giselle* text are given, the transformation of those conditions within the phenomenon of performance is dialectical, and the performance in practice again and again revitalizes the artistic context itself. Here in Alonso's *Giselle* is praxis dictating theory, theory reflecting truth on stage.

In performance, the beauty of Alonso's dancers at home and abroad is that one can take so much for granted: Balances are solid and assured, the line is exquisitely uniform and historically informed, épaulement and port de bras are exquisite and subtle, the technique is superhuman but the acting is always humane. From corps dancers, coryphées, and soloists up through the splendid principals, Cuban dancers tend to dance as if their lives depend on it.

Conscious of the dialectical, transforming role she has played in the project that has defined her life, Alonso is proud of the success of her Cuban *Giselle*. She is proud that "after Paris I also later staged it for the Teatro San Carlo in Naples, the cradle of Italian ballet and, consequently, of world ballet. You can see, then, how it is possible for us to return a gift we received from Europe, revitalized and enriched, quite apart from the infinite possibilities of our own, original Latin American arts across all genres, whether the original artistic expression be from Scandinavia or from China. We, of course, are Cubans, but art is universal." [19]

Breaking barriers—Alicia Alonso and Vladilen Semyonov rehearsing *Giselle* in Moscow. It was the young Kirov dancer's Bolshoi debut, as well as Alicia's. Courtesy of the Alicia Alonso Collection.

Alonso's deeply humanistic interpretation of *Giselle* ranks as the finest in the late twentieth century as well as now. Her choreography improbably emerges as the epitome of the romantic ballet tradition. "Real tradition," Alonso has said, "living, valid, and positive tradition must be open. It must be received from all around. One has to search out tradition, study it, acquire it, and then feel free to live it freely; this way, a dance becomes a dialectical assimilation, not an imposed anachronism. This way everything depends on the creative talent that must be the starting point of any artistic endeavor." [20]

It is the exhilarating interpretive freedom possible within the boundaries of tradition in Alonso's *Giselle* that makes it particularly interesting. As Alonso said:

There are so many different ways to bring to life Giselle's character, without transgressing the style and choreography. There are different shadings possible in every scene, certain emphases that can vary while still guided by the pattern I have created that I consider appropriate for this work. Giselle can be simple or ingenuous, or perhaps something more lyrical. She can be vivacious or languid. Tragedy can strike her as a surprise, or it can be foreshadowed from the moment of her entrance, in subtle premonitions. There must be, however, certain constants in her character that conform to the theatrical logic of the ballet. She can be a simple peasant, for example, but she must also be possessed of an elevated spirituality. In the second act, my goal always has been to bring together the surreal and evanescent nature of the spirits that come alive onstage with the very real, earthly reality of human love. [21]

She knew the role well before she ever danced it. Tudor taught it to her in the classroom, alongside her fellow students Maria Karnilova and Nora Kaye—"I thought it would be useful for them to know it," Tudor told me, smiling. In Havana, while recuperating from her third eye surgery, Alicia Alonso, bedridden and blindfolded, was prescribed complete rest with her head firmly couched between sandbags so as to avoid danger of detaching her retinas again. It was here, in solitary stillness, in this kaleidoscope of darkness, that she famously went over every detail of what she had learned, seen, and absorbed about *Giselle*. She impressed her friend Agnes de Mille with the story of working out the ballet on her own lying down; she later even joked with the critic Walter Terry, "I danced it before you reviewed me." [22] By the time of her historic debut in the role—replacing Alicia Markova on very short notice—Alicia Alonso was ready. Many people would take the credit. Tudor, of course, but also her husband Fernando, and her partner Anton Dolin. When I confronted her with all these competing possibilities as to who was responsible for that November 2, 1943, *Giselle*,

Alicia Alonso's own answer was quick, "*La que lo bailó!*" ("The one who danced it!").

The history of Alonso's own version of *Giselle* is rich. She first staged it for the Sociedad Pro-Arte Musical at the Auditorium del Vedado in Havana on June 5, 1945. She danced the title role, with Fernando Alonso as Albrecht and Rosella Hightower as Myrtha, Queen of the Wilis. The following season Alonso was joined in Havana by Andre Eglevsky as Albrecht and Marjorie Tallchief as Myrtha—casting that would reappear in the American Ballet Theatre's first European tour and signal the beginning of a decade in which the Havana and New York troupes would nourish each other's casts and repertory.

Igor Yousekevitch became Alonso's ideal partner in 1946 and joined her with the American Ballet Theatre on tour in Havana for what was still billed as Anton Dolin's staging of *Giselle* at the Auditórium del Vedado. After reprising Dolin's version with the Ballets Russes de Monte Carlo in Havana in a 1948 summer season, Alonso further refined her interpretation and staged *Giselle* for her new Ballet Alicia Alonso, with John Kriza as her Albrecht. That company, today's Ballet Nacional de Cuba, made its debut on October 30, 1948. The inaugural season's *Giselle* cast included Alonso as Giselle, Yousekevitch as her Albrecht, and Barbara Fallis as Myrtha. Since 1948, *Giselle* has never left the company's repertory.

That Alonso's eyesight began failing about this time and would never fully return is only one more amazing detail in this woman's inspiring career. Like her stage longevity—and Alonso in her fifties could give even the young Gelsey Kirkland or Natalia Makarova a run for her money in exuding youth and vulnerability as Giselle—the real issues at hand have been the sheer artistic integrity and undeniable impact of Alonso's interpretation. In a feat unrivaled in the history of ballet, Alicia Alonso danced and in many ways owned the role of Giselle from 1943 to 1993.

Alonso in her fifties could give even the young Gelsey Kirkland or Natalia Makarova a run for her money in exuding youth and vulnerability as Giselle.

The Ballet Nacional de Cuba's first tour, in 1948–49, took Alonso's *Giselle* to Venezuela, Puerto Rico, Mexico, Guatemala, El Salvador, Costa Rica, Panama, Colombia, Peru, Argentina, and Uruguay. The indefatigable Alonso's Albrechts in that historic Latin American season included Yousekevitch, Nicholas Magallanes, Fernando Alonso, and Michael Maule. Alonso and Yousekevitch took *Giselle* to Paris in 1950, to Rio de Janeiro in 1951, and to Naples in 1953. Alonso's Albrecht in 1954 was Royes Fernandez, who would later call ABT his artistic home. Erik Bruhn was Alonso's Albrecht in 1955.

In 1957, at the height of the Cold War and two years before the Cuban revolution, Alonso began a series of groundbreaking performances of *Giselle* in the Soviet Union, with Vladilen Semyonov as her Albrecht in both the Bolshoi Theatre in Moscow and the Kirov Theatre in Leningrad. It is telling that detail after subtle detail of Alonso's *Giselle*, details that were unquestionably hers such as the "sewing" pantomime in Act One that she and Tudor had worked out in 1945, began turning up in Soviet and European productions of *Giselle* after these tours. In 1958, Alonso staged her *Giselle* for the Teatro Colón in Buenos Aires and the Greek Theatre in Los Angeles. She danced it for the last time with Yousekevitch in New York in 1960, to celebrate the twentieth anniversary of the American Ballet Theatre at the Metropolitan Opera House. On both sides of the Iron Curtain the Alonso *Giselle* exerted a healthy universalist influence that transcended politics.

Still, it was precisely politics that kept the ballerina away from the American public throughout the 1960s and most of the 1970s, but the Ballet Nacional de Cuba enjoyed great success with *Giselle* in Europe. One victory among many was the reception of the Cuban *Giselle* in Paris. In 1966, the Ballet Nacional de Cuba was awarded the Grand Prix de la Ville de Paris and the Prix Anna Pavlova for Giselle. Then in 1972, Alonso

was commissioned to choreograph *Giselle* at its birthplace, the Paris Opéra, and not for the first time, it was remarked that Alicia Alonso was born so that *Giselle* would live.

"She is extraordinary," said the choreographer Maurice Béjart. "Alicia is passionate, ironic, willful and tireless, possessed entirely by dance and, somehow, simply inebriated by Cuba, by her homeland. She is romantic but lucid, instinctive and intelligent, almost blind but clairvoyant. One of these days, I must make a ballet about this

Alicia Alonso and Cyril Atanassof in *Giselle* at La Opéra de Paris Ballet. Courtesy of the Alicia Alonso Collection.

Interlude

Giselle

Alicia Alonso in *Ad Libitum* with Antonio Gades, 1978. Courtesy of the Ballet Nacional de Cuba, photo by Osvaldo Salas.

extraordinary being."[23] At the onset of the most wondrous Indian summer in ballet history, Alonso in her fifties, found her most sympathetic partner since Yousekevitch in the young Jorge Esquivel. The couple first danced *Giselle* in 1972, only months before delicate eye surgery that many predicted would mark the end of her dancing career. It didn't. And her historic comeback in 1977 after five years of therapy was both a joyous dance event and a tribute to the indomitability of this ballerina. With Esquivel's support, Alonso danced *Giselle* in the United States for the first time in seventeen years at a 1977 gala tribute performance with her alma mater, the American Ballet Theatre, at the Metropolitan Opera House in New York. In May 1978, the Ballet Nacional de Cuba at last made its United States debut, with Alonso and Esquivel in *Giselle* at the John F. Kennedy Center for the Performing Arts in Washington.

The flamenco genius Antonio Gades, in a rare classical ballet appearance, danced the role of Hilarion at the Kennedy Center. He learned it on a bet, and for a lark, as at the same time he choreographed the moving, irreproducible *Ad Libitum*

218

GISELLE

for himself and Alicia. Alonso celebrated the thirty-fifth anniversary of her debut as *Giselle*, not with a nostalgic tribute, but with a performance in Havana in 1978 that by now has acquired mythic proportions in ballet lore. The long curtain call included bows not only by Esquivel but also from her first Albrecht, Anton Dolin, by Yousekevitch, and by Azari Plisetsky. That night's principal casting was duplicated in Berkeley, California, in May 1979, with Alonso and Esquivel again as the doomed lovers. Esquivel, who as a child was plucked from an orphanage by Alicia and was groomed to be the new Yousekevitch, looked back in exile thirty years later and confessed to me, "I was very lucky to partner some great, beautiful ballerinas in *Giselle*, Carla Fracci, Cynthia Gregory, Loipa Araújo, Mirta Plá—but every time I held them, and they were incredible, I felt they were not the same as Alicia. There was something spiritual dancing with Alicia that I found with no one else." The 1978–1979 Cuban *Giselle* with Alonso and Esquivel triumphed and signaled the beginning of a chapter in her story that no one expected time would allow.

The following season, at the Seventh International Ballet Festival in Havana, Alonso welcomed another great Albrecht, Vladimir Vasiliev.[24] The first and only stage collaboration of these two very different figures—with Dolin coaching Alonso and the legendary Galina Ulanova coaching her protégé Vasiliev—was a landmark in the ballet's performance history. "Her Giselle is a miracle," Ulanova told me in tears after that 1980 performance.[25]

More such miracles followed, but the 1980 Havana *Giselle* now can be seen as the last flowering of Alonso's Indian summer. Alonso traveled to Vienna that same year, staging *Giselle* for the Staatsoper and giving master classes on the romantic style in ballet in Vienna and later that season in Guanajuato's Festival Cervantino in Mexico. "Romantic ballet can be conceived not only as a style from a past era, but also as a state of mind, a sensibility, an emotional necessity that can emerge—and in fact has emerged—in every era, in every place," wrote Alicia in her notes in 1981. "Even as its expressions vary into infinity, the romantic era, examined historically, brought dance a series of timeless values that are inseparable from the most treasured in the culture of humanity."[26]

In 1983, after taking the ballet on a whirlwind international tour from Santo Domingo, Colombia, and Venezuela to Turkey and Syria, she returned to Havana to celebrate the fortieth anniversary of her debut in the role. On December 24, 1980, at the Sala García Lorca of the Gran Teatro de La Habana, she danced *Giselle* complete for the last time in Cuba. She had danced *Giselle* for half a century. Again in her hometown, on December 29, 1991, for celebrations of the one hundred fiftieth anniversary of the 1841 world premiere of *Giselle*—and this truly must be considered miraculous even by her own standards—Alonso at age seventy danced the Mad Scene, as well as the two Act Two pas de deux. She was unforgettable. Recent years have brought much change, and doubtless even more changes are in store as Alonso, no longer dancing the role and in fact leading her company from a wheelchair, keeps alive this Cuban corner of the world's *Giselle* tradition. Her Cuban dancers, her living legacy both in Havana and in the growing Cuban diaspora, today take this most beautiful element of the Cuban School of Ballet to every corner of the world. This is a sign of hope. Just as Russia's Bolshoi Ballet preceded and has outlived Soviet communism, so the Ballet Nacional de Cuba is managing to survive and even thrive through the darkest decades of Cuban history—and will likely go on dancing gloriously into the millennium after Cuba is finally free.

Dancing with a Cuban Accent

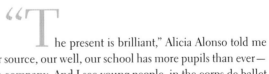

My memory prepares its own surprises.
—José Lezama Lima

"The present is brilliant," Alicia Alonso told me in 2006. "We have a tremendous force. And our source, our well, our school has more pupils than ever—just now seven of them were graduated into the company. And I see young people, in the corps de ballet who have everything. Our next generation is guaranteed."

More recently, when asked in 2009 about not only the triumphs abroad of José Manuel Carreño and Carlos Acosta but also of the sisters Lorena Feijóo and Lorna Feijóo as well as of very recent defectors such as Taras Domitro, Miguelángel Blanco, and Joel Carreño, she remained not so much stoic as serenely secure. "The tree is always here," she said. "Our fruits are our gift to the world."

What will happen after the Alicia Alonso era? Where is Cuban ballet heading once its guiding light is gone? "I am not thinking about that, and I won't," she said, again echoing a darkly funny joke she has been repeating now for a few years, "My life has been rich. My life has been intense. I have lived so many beautiful moments, and I plan to live many more. We have many more dances to do, and I plan to be here until I am at least two hundred."

She may of course mean it and, no, she is not deluded. She is a dancer, she is human, and she

OPPOSITE: Lorena Feijóo.
Courtesy of R. J. Muna.

221

Joel Carreño and Yolanda Correa in Alonso's *Swan Lake* at the Sala García Lorca, Gran Teatro de La Habana, 2004. Courtesy of David R. Garten.

is like the rest of us. The tense duality of human existence and the futile struggle to overcome harsh realities finds parallels in the life of art and in the lives of all of us. We want clarity when the world is forever opaque. We need closure but history is spectacularly open-ended. We live our own lives in a constant impossible dialectic of being thrown into material conditions that include severe limits, while simultaneously feeling and knowing ourselves to be free. Human beings are failed gods in this noble sense—and of course this includes dancers. Their situation is precisely what Camus called absurd in his *Myth of Sisyphus* and what Sartre referred to as useless passion in *Being and Nothingness*. Is Alicia Alonso's life in dance a useless project? Is her *Giselle* doomed to fail? Yes,

but only in the heroic sense that so are all human endeavors. What mark is Cuban ballet leaving on the canon of dance? The permanence of the world in itself is something the canon must see only as a challenging presence to be denied and revitalized. Dance is especially fleeting among the arts, even if, as the lovely Cuban proverb goes, "*Nadie te quita lo bailao*," "No one can take from you the dances you've danced."

Merce Cunningham was right when he famously noted, "You have to love dancing to stick to it. It gives you nothing back, no manuscripts to store away, no paintings to hang in museums, no poems to be printed and sold, nothing but that fleeting moment when you feel alive."[1] In Cuba today, the objectified reality of an aging dancer, blind and in a wheelchair, signals with cruel clarity the limitations of extreme material conditions in a starker sense than any political or aesthetic objections now or ever raised against Alonso. Her life, like all lives, will end. Her dance in time, like all dances, also will end. Yet what remains is considerable. And whatever temporal failure may loom in the horizon as dusk at last comes to her career, it is worth remembering that Alicia Alonso's life is not to be judged solely by those late moments, any more than the Cuban School of Ballet can be judged by any one moment in Cuba's tortuous political history. That would be cheating both dance and Cuban culture of one of their finest treasures.

These late moments are nevertheless significant and troubling. The severest criticism and the most significant attack on Alonso in recent times has come not from political enemies in exile or from parochial dance critics outside the tradition, but rather from her own faithful in Cuba. It began with the frank asides Fernando Alonso, her ex-husband, offered in Cynthia Newport's 2004 film *Dance Cuba* bemoaning the drain of talent to companies abroad: "Alicia doesn't seem to see what is happening," says Fernando pointedly in the film. However, he never goes so far as proposing a return to the oppressive Castro-Stalinist restrictions on dancers and their families that once were the rule.[2] Whether this is a sign of a relaxation of censorship in the island, a result of the power of the Internet, or just a historical accident, an open letter to the Ballet Nacional de Cuba signed by Mariana Sanz that appeared in www.cuba encuentro.com in early 2007 berated Alicia Alonso for not stepping down as director; then the critic, writing in Havana, said the unsayable, "Saddest of all is to pretend to ignore that those who surround her degrade her as a beacon of universal culture, since they make and destroy much, too much, in her name. There is no more ridiculous answer to a question of casting than that 'this cast stays this

way because Alicia decided it this way,' and to be expected to swallow the lie that the blind director considers a girl she has never seen better than another she will never see."[3]

Throughout her long and fruitful life, Alicia Alonso has adopted an intentional stance of political blindness towards the more brutal realities of her life. On stage, for herself and for others, she has recognized and created freedom, the freedom of her imagination as lived in her dancer's body. Dancing has been, among other things, an epiphany, a salvation, and an escape from the encroaching reality of her blindness. Her need to create herself as a dancer, with all the unreality that entails, may be the woman's most remarkable feat as well as the most indelible example for Cuban dancers now and in the future. All else, from her family life to her politics, from her estranged and difficult relation with her brilliant daughter Laura to her often ruthless decisions about other

Fernando Alonso, perhaps his ex-wife's most outspoken critic inside Cuba. Courtesy of Illume productions/Candela, image from *Dance Cuba.*

dancers in her company, came a distant second. Her refusal to be held back by actual blindness, an intermittent and growing problem for her since 1940, also can be called an intentional stance that allowed her to create art and—as Sartre noted in a different context—is as once the intention and the result of artistic creation.[4] Her consciousness of her situation is her choice. Her strengths are revealed by her limits. Her impact on the concrete existence of her chosen art has been breathtaking: Alicia Alonso taught ballet to dance with a Cuban accent. As she settles into advanced old age, however, material conditions are closing in. Even as she prepares in 2010–2011 for her company's return to the United States and perhaps even a conciliatory Ballet Nacional de Cuba debut in Miami, even as she readies to celebrate her official ninetieth birthday at the American Ballet Theatre (having already turned ninety the year before), change is in the air. That is what makes recent criticism from Cuba a melancholy affair: the end is inevitable. Yet the end is not the measure of a life. And the life of dance is endless.

The effect of history's passing on the beauty that remains behind has long been a challenge to critics and philosophers. William Wordsworth saw with unalterable wisdom in his *Intimations of Immortality* that:

> Though nothing can bring back the hour
> Of splendor in the grass, of glory in the flower;
> We will grieve not, rather find
> Strength in what remains behind.

It was in his posthumous 1835 *Aesthetics* that Hegel lamented the loss of masterworks of the canon that "have already perished in reality . . . [that] the unkindness of fate has withdrawn from our inspection."[5] Not just older dances, but ballets as recent as Tudor's *Shadow of the Wind* (made for Alonso) and Alonso's own *La Condesita* are lost to memory and to the future forever through the unkindness of fate. Dancers and dance alike rely on memory, and this woman's own memory surprises. "It is not that Alicia has good or bad memory," her husband Pedro Simón once told me in Havana. "It is different. She can reach back with the precision of a computer, but she can also erase certain things—forever."

In large part thanks to Alonso's imaginative memory, the complete *Giselle* is firmly in the canon. It is not the same as it was, and here her labor in performance practice has been decisive. The direct impact of Alonso's *Giselle* alone on that bright corner of the canon has been incalculable, as are the ways she has tried to weave the strands of the classical tradition into each other. The Cuban School of Ballet, not just in Alonso's dancers at home and not only in *Giselle*, transforms dancers and dance within and beyond the nineteenth century classical tradition, forever changing that tradition for the future. Alonso has shown that, when successful, tradition preserved is tradition transformed.

It is those transformations that appear to be at risk in Cuba. It is in those transformations that the Cuban diaspora is having its biggest impact. To see Lorena Feijóo's entrance solo in *Le Corsaire*, with her impossible balances and insolently perfect arabesques but also with her cunning precision on where to break the line to create an ineffably sensual image in slow motion is to understand the future of the Cuban School of Classical Ballet. That it may have unintended consequences is a given; Nureyev, Makarova, and Baryshnikov were living examples of the finest and most joyous possibilities of Soviet ballet, but their influence has proved most lasting well outside the former Soviet Union, in New York, in London, and in Paris. Lorena Feijóo, Lorna Feijóo, Joan Boada, José Manuel Carreño, Taras Domitro, Rolando Sarabia and others we are just beginning to know are starting to have that sort of influence well beyond their native Cuba. There is

Joel Carreño and Yolanda
Correa in full splendor
in *Swan Lake* at the Sala
García Lorca, Gran Teatro
de La Habana, 2004. Cour-
tesy of David R. Garten.

no question that Lorena Feijóo, Boada, Domitro, and certainly Jorge Esquivel are influencing the company style of San Francisco Ballet, the oldest company in the United States. There is no question either of the influence of Lorna Feijóo and Nelson Madrigal on Boston Ballet, or of Carreño particularly on male dancing at Alicia Alonso's alma mater, the American Ballet Theatre. Within Cuba, however, the situation is problematic. Immense possibilities within self-imposed limits are the very soul of artistic creation, but acceptance of fetishized material limitations is not exactly progressive.

If in fact the end is near in Cuba, in terms of Alonso's no longer being able to do what she has been doing for almost a century, reality will be made concrete soon enough. Wisdom dictates that we look beyond that end, in every direction away from the limiting present. It would be indefensible for a critic to stand outside and judge Alonso's long life from the vantage point of a moment in that life. Her goals are too vast for that, her achievements too impressive, her impact on dance too sublime. These accomplishments perforce include, though she herself claims only partial credit, the miraculous emergence of the Cuban School of Ballet as a major force in the world of dance. That was always one of her goals, and the spectacular way this woman and her dancers have reached that goal surely constitutes one of the New World's most precious gifts to the Old. A veil of respect drawn over any bittersweet late moments allows a clearer vision of lifelong accomplishments. Looking back at Alonso's goals, ahead to her growing influence, around at the epiphanies of tradition she not only maintained but recreated and transformed—these are the elements of a meaningful critique.

This critique, in a sense this living history of the artists who make Cuban dances and who make dances Cuban, allows us a glimpse of the future. Here lies the future of the classical canon in its dialectical transformations. Here lies the future of the Cuban School of Ballet. Cultural criticism becomes a necessary component of theory, but neither political nor aesthetic theory ever should fetishize itself away from actual performance practice. What counts is the dance, not the changing politics, and not the changing fashions of criticism either. This means recognizing the primacy of lived performance over any performance theory, political or otherwise. It means recognizing the artist's, or anyone's, ability to say no, to transcend, to detach, to transform reality in unreality—dance is an imaginary object, made real only within the material limitations of performance—and to refuse the most brutal limits.

Dance is freedom lived in the body. It simply is, in the same sense that for Sartre there is no difference between being and being free.[6] Can that freedom be captured by a biographer? Can it be understood by a critic? I ask these questions in humble recognition of the limits of dance criticism. Ned Rorem wittily has noted, "Critics of words use words; critics of music use words." Critics of dance are if anything farther still—in truth, the best criticism of a dance is another dance. The best criticisms of the Cuban School of Ballet may well be the actual dancing of luminaries such as Lorena Feijóo and Lorna Feijóo, José Manuel Carreño, Joan Boada, and Taras Domitro. When the Feijóos in tandem talk of blowing the cobwebs off the present Ballet Nacional de Cuba's arch elbows in the Romantic style, or when Carreño proudly calls himself an international dancer with Cuban roots, they are merely doing what Alicia Alonso herself has done throughout her long and dazzling transformations of the Cuban style. These dancers are keeping the tradition of the Cuban School of Ballet alive, precisely by not keeping it frozen in time. To see them in concentrated numbers in one of those ambitious productions Pedro Pablo Peña stages for his Cuban Classical Ballet of Miami

OPPOSITE: Rosario Suárez, the rebel Charín, dancing Fokine's *The Dying Swan.* Courtesy of Pedro Portal.

A poster advertising the Cuban Classical Ballet of Miami's production of *Swan Lake*. Courtesy of Cuban Classical Ballet of Miami.

with improbable regularity and against all financial odds is to witness Cuban dancing at its most vibrant, only miles away from Cuba. It is also to witness the newest living chapter in the exhilarating growth of the American ballet tradition.

That, incidentally, may yet prove to be the most vital cultural contribution made by the Cuban diaspora. Ballet is perhaps the most successful example of Cuban culture alive and thriving in exile even as its very existence is threatened by oppression at home. For exiles, it is not a substitute for the land we lost, but it is nevertheless a beautiful surprise to find that these labors increasingly form a part of the land we now call our own. Exiled in a country that glorifies the myth of the melting pot, Cubans honestly don't have any intention of melting. And by reaffirming our culture in exile we are also in fact adding

surprising new accents to the rhythms of American culture. When Pedro Pablo Peña and Magaly Suárez note that the Cuban School of Ballet in exile has evolved, that the most recent generation of exiles is nourishing a style that has become ossified in the Ballet Nacional de Cuba, their claim is significant both for the Cuban and the American ballet traditions. As early as 1980, when Alonso still owned the role of Giselle, Igor Yousekevitch confessed to me, "She has a tendency now to fall into the *Pas de Quatre* style," referring to the romantic jewel of a ballet that Alonso perfected after Dolin, with its exaggerated round elbows and presentational upper bodies. The piece can border on self-parody, and Alonso's finest partner saw a suggestion of that creeping into the Cuban company through its director. "She is best now in the newer pieces," he told me. "She does more.

In her old ballets she used to be more reckless—and I think blindness has taken that away a little. She is more careful now." That criticism, decades later, finds echoes in observations by Lorna and Lorena Feijóo, by Nelson Madrigal, and by Pedro Pablo Peña. "The Cuban School of Ballet grew," says Peña, "but lamentably it is now in decadence in Cuba. There is an *estancamiento*, an absence of evolution, perhaps reflecting the lack of political evolution in the country."

What Peña is doing in Miami amounts to a corrective to that absence in Cuba. The presence of the Cuban diaspora on the world stage represents a necessary growth of the Cuban style. That people like Peña feel this work to be "a sacerdotal duty, a love," only adds to its impact—and audiences from San Francisco to Boston to Miami seem to know this. Yet there may be something at least as important going on here. There is a reason all these dancers left their country, and that is not a small detail. Commenting on the 2004 defections from the Ballet Nacional de Cuba that included Cervilio Amador, Adiarys Almeida, and Gema Díaz, Miami City Ballet's Carlos Miguel Guerra told me, "I understand why these dancers left. I understand them because I remember why I left—to be able to open my mouth, to say whatever I want. That is why I left."[7]

Freedom is a potent encouragement, in art as in life. Guerra, a star of the Ballet de Camagüey at sixteen, in exile has been adding luster to the American dance scene and certainly has been influencing for the better the company style at Miami City Ballet. Across town at the Classical Ballet of Miami, that luster can be dazzling. And while keeping the Cuban School of Ballet alive and growing, a new piece is being added to the wondrous mosaic that is American dance. Like so many immigrants before them, Cuban dancers at first marginalized by mainstream culture only broaden that mainstream. Preserving one culture while assimilating into another, they contribute new colors to the dazzling work in progress that is American civilization. Poor in budget but high on hope and backed by what seems like an inexhaustible supply of Cuban exile dancers who come to Miami for a fraction of the fee they earn anywhere else, Pedro Pablo Peña, Magaly Suárez, and their Cuban Classical Ballet of Miami are both jealously guarding their Cuban heritage and, as Cuban-Americans, adding to the glories of Hispanic pride in their new country. On a larger plane, the dancers of the Cuban diaspora and their audiences are the youngest and most exciting development in American dance in decades. Choice by choice, from a Boston *Swan Lake* to a San Francisco *Don Quixote*, from *Symphony in Three Movements* and *Tchaikovsky Pas de Deux* to *Carmen*, *Le Corsaire*, and a heartbreaking Cuban *Giselle* in Miami, they are at once celebrating and making history. They are following Alicia Alonso's example.

Inside Cuba, of course, the example still shines. All dance companies have their seasons; they get better or they get worse. That is true of all the major companies being enriched by the Cuban diaspora, from San Francisco to Boston, from London to New York. In Havana, the Ballet Nacional de Cuba too has experienced some inconsistencies in the ranks, and politics may be only one among many reasons. Another might be simply that no ballet troupe ever stays the same. Even while taking seriously criticisms of today's Ballet Nacional de Cuba, it is important to remember that the company is in many ways thriving. Its place in Spain, Cuba's cultural motherland, is increasingly important, with regular tours bringing the Cuban School of Ballet everywhere from Madrid to Valencia, Barcelona to Bilbao. Laura Hormigón and Oscar Torrado, Spaniards and also products of the Cuban School, are returning the company to its cosmopolitan roots as principal dancers who are not Cuban but nevertheless are completely at home dancing with a Cuban accent.

DANCING WITH A CUBAN ACCENT

Of course many Cuban dancers have left and continue to leave Cuba. But the company still counts on about a hundred members and its tours continue unabated. A 2010 debut in London's Coliseum welcomed back Carlos Acosta and marked the first time the Royal Ballet star danced with his alma mater in his adopted British home. Even if Miami is not quite ready for reconciliation of any sort, New York is.

The American Ballet Theatre in 2010 planned a celebration of Alicia Alonso's official ninetieth birthday with an all-star performance of *Don Quixote*—though in truth the perfect gesture would have been for ABT to invite its illustrious alumna to stage *Giselle* for the company. A return of the Ballet Nacional de Cuba in 2011 to the Metropolitan Opera in New York and the Kennedy Center in Washington promise American audiences a glimpse at tomorrow's Cuban stars. It is of course difficult to keep track, but Viengsay Valdés, Rómel Frómeta, Annette Delgado, Octavio Martín, Javier Torres, and others continue to prove the impossible—Cuba's supply of great dancers seems inexhaustible. This is no slight to the Cuban diaspora and its beautiful dancers; it is a tribute to their origins. Alicia Alonso may be proved right in that Cuba's bounty of precious fruits is the small island's gift to the world, but the tree remains at home and its roots are firmly planted.

Will Alonso follow her own example? The question is not easy to answer, least of all by her. Yousekevitch was not alone in foreseeing some of the artistic and practical problems arising from this Cuban dancer's superhuman longevity. Agnes de Mille, who created *Fall River Legend* for Alicia Alonso and knew her well, noticed with a sense of wonder how the indomitable dancer kept dancing at age seventy and how she chose the brief passages from former roles that called for brilliant footwork and articulation, for ethereal balances. Yet there was more than a touch of melancholy in de Mille's

observations, as she also noted that no new major Cuban choreographers have emerged since Alberto Alonso, in part because of increasingly narrow constrictions on their creative freedom. Alberto Méndez, for example, has created a string of little jewels for the company, nineteenth-century homages all; but nothing like what his early masterpiece *Tarde en la siesta* promised—at least not until the valedictory *In the Middle of the Sunset*.

"Alicia has accomplished many great things," said de Mille in 1990:

> She has served dancing beautifully and she has served her country. Will she have the nobility of spirit to accept the fact that she is mortal? Will she be able to make the enormous gesture of yielding to history and bowing aside so that the Ballet Nacional de Cuba can develop and progress? She has done so much in her life, this fragile, nervous girl. Can she do this? To step aside requires the creative vision of a prophet, the humility of a saint. This may prove to be a crueler, more insupportable challenge than her blindness.[8]

Knowing when to bow aside and yield to history is not easy. Great dancers have dealt with it in so many different ways, and so have great company directors. Alicia Alonso stopped dancing only when she was forced into a wheelchair. She has been the director of her company since 1948, a tenure rivaled only by the late Merce Cunningham. She has kept going in difficult times, and as Heberto Padilla remarked in his brutally sardonic poem *En tiempos difíciles*, "In difficult times, *that* is the real test."[9]

What did Alicia Alonso choose to be by creating this or that dance? What does Lorna Feijóo choose to be as she steps on stage as Giselle in Maina Gielgud's affectionate staging in Boston? What does Lorena Feijóo choose to be when she takes the red-eye flight from San Francisco

OPPOSITE: *Sabor y salero*, class time at the Ballet Nacional de Cuba's studios in Old Havana. Courtesy of Illume productions/ Candela, photo by Deborah Harse.

to break up a run of *Swan Lake* there in order to dance Pedro Pablo Peña's *Le Corsaire* opposite fellow Cubans Joan Boada and Miguelángel Blanco, in sets borrowed from the Kirov Ballet in St. Petersburg for a weekend performance in Miami Beach? It was madness to debut in a ballet with such short notice, madness to close her eyes, hear the score on her iPod on the plane and trace steps on her lap with her fingers, madness to get on that stage in the capital of the Cuban diaspora. Like another Cuban woman before her who traced steps with her fingers to rehearse a role in her imagination, Lorena Feijóo succeeded. What makes these women make these choices? Who are they?

Our tale told this way has been a way to suggest the enormity of Alicia Alonso's contributions to ballet in the twentieth century as well as now in the twenty-first century, with what looks like a joyous, free army of Cuban artists who follow her example, even if that means following her example right out of their country. At least as important, the tale told this way has allowed us to understand the future of their labors. *Giselle* has survived and will survive long after the material conditions from which it arose have been consigned to the dustbin of history. Inevitability and innovation, the generosity of creation, the transcendence of cruel limitations in ecstatic temporality, the relish of a privileged Proustian moment that is simply not lived by an objective historical clock—these things pass, yet all these things also make up the phenomenological reality of dance. These are things we remember.

Alicia Alonso is one of the pillars of dance, and hers is a tale of a woman's determination and genius. But it is also a tale of revolution in a country as well as in dance, of a divided people's tragedy and hope. For me as a Cuban exile it has never been easy dispassionately to examine the material reality of her work as well as the ecstatic transcendence of her legacy, but it is easy to judge

kindly what Alicia Alonso has done, to greet with gratitude the profoundly instinctive wisdom of this modern-day Tiresias, just as it is impossible not to be moved by the success of her most perfect creation: *Giselle*.

It now has been thirty years since I last saw Alicia Alonso as Giselle. I have seen many others since then, some devastatingly beautiful: Gelsey Kirkland, Nadezhda Pavlova, Josefina Méndez, Loipa Araújo, Mirta Plá, Eva Evdokimova, Sylvie Guillem, Nina Ananiashvili, Alessandra Ferri, Viviana Durante, Alihaydée Carreño, Lucía Lacarra, Lorna Feijóo, and Lorena Feijóo. They form a Proustian panorama drenched for me in memory, carrying the perfume of Cuba whether they are Cuban dancers or not. Others will see it differently, and others of course should. For Cubans, for Cuban dancers and for the Cuban people, the subtle nuances of that ballet in particular can carry more meaning about living through a revolution, about exile, and about life, than any samizdat political treatise. Alicia Alonso is right when she writes in the foreword to this book that Cubans are a dancing people, that dancing matters to us, and it matters deeply. It matters to me. Like the first strains of Ernesto Lecuona's *La Comparsa* or the sweet smell of *sofrito* from a steaming batch of black beans, the ballet *Giselle* brings Cuba to me. José Lezama Lima, that most Cuban of modern poets was right: memory does prepare its own surprises.

Dancing through the darkness, making every gesture matter and keeping hope alive through the cruelest, most bitter ordeals; those are the devastating themes of *Giselle*. It is indeed "the most natural thing in the world," as Alicia told me, for the Cuban people to love this ballet, for Cuban dancers everywhere to mean every step they take. Alicia Alonso taught them that.

Lorena Feijóo and Taras Domitro rehearsing *The Sleeping Beauty*. Courtesy of Sasha de Almagro.

oes she fear death? She may joke, and she often says with a straight face, that she plans to live to be at least two hundred, but as a last word the formidable nonagenarian offers this sensible assessment. "I don't fear death, I don't deny death, and I don't like to think about death— why should I? It is a negation of life."

"I love life, so I only cry in the face of death," Alicia once told me, while discussing the passing of so many friends, so many times. "But tears," she added, "I have never counted. *Las lágrimas nunca las he contado.*"

This tale of dancers dancing began with a touch of madness, with a blind ballerina who chose to make us see. Alicia Alonso often has described "the need to immerse oneself in unreality" as a condition of ballet, and especially of romantic ballet,

and to this day her work as a dancemaker, as a dancer, as a Cuban artist is certainly drenched in a conscious denial of anything that might limit her possibilities. If given a choice, there is no shame in choosing joy. And we all have that choice. We have that choice at home, we have that choice in exile, and we have that choice moment by moment as we do what we have to do with what has been done to us. That is the meaning of freedom. "Reality is so rich in possibilities," Alicia told me. "Why not let it surprise us?"

Poor, blind, immensely talented, beautiful, musical, selfish, politically compromised, no longer young, growing older still—all these attributes challenge the dancer's ineffable freedom to make something out of the object she has been made into, to reinvent herself and her dance from the objectified reality into which she has been thrown. Dance is not an instrument of social change, and it is not an educational tool. Dance cannot compete with the resources of tyranny, for they are vast and life is fragile. Yet dance is subtle, it is an end in itself. It is a locus of freedom, revealed in the lived coincidence of dance, dancer, and audience. That is a dancer's concrete achievement. Because an artist is what she does, we understand this era through her deeds—this is the road to a true aesthetics of dance. This is a way of understanding Cuban ballet because few people have done so much with what has been done to them as have Cuban dancers in our time. Alicia Alonso is an exemplar of the artist's temporality that can help us assess time dialectically—its past and its future are inseparable. Her story, that of Lorena Feijóo and Lorna Feijóo, and that of all these heartbreakingly beautiful Cuban dancers I love, forms an unfinished novel that is true. Their story reveals the truth that we are alone in our own history, without excuses. Cuban dancers need no excuse. Let both memory and the future bring their own surprises.

—*La Habana, 1980–Miami Beach, 2010*

RIGHT: At the studio in Havana—a ballet barre, a window, and a young dancer looking at the future. Courtesy of Illume productions/Candela, photo by Deborah Harse.

OPPOSITE: She never officially said farewell, and she never will. But this beautiful iconic image of Alicia Alonso's curtain call is just a reminder, an ending, a bittersweet sign of time's inexorable progress. "Reality is so rich in possibilities," said Alonso. "Why not let it surprise us?" Courtesy of the Ballet Nacional de Cuba.

Endnotes

Introduction: Cuban Memories

1. Octavio Roca, "Cuba's Dancing Diplomat: Alonso at Spoleto," *The Washington Post*, June 1, 1980.
2. Octavio Roca, "Giselle Triumphs with Love: Alicia Alonso's Production puts Emotion into Every Step," *San Francisco Chronicle*, February 15, 1999.
3. Octavio Roca, "Feijóo Finds Her Calling as a Glorious Giselle," *San Francisco Chronicle*, February 28, 2000.
4. Octavio Roca, "Latin Fire Spices up the Ballet: San Francisco Ballet Dancers Full of Passion, Pride, Joy," *San Francisco Chronicle*, January 27, 2002.
5. Lynn Garafola, "Sweeping the Stage: Why Latin is the New Russian," *Dance Magazine*, September 2004.
6. Christopher Porterfield, "Psst! The Cubans Are Coming," *Time*, February 26, 2006.
7. Jennifer Dunning, "Learning Nuances of Ballet from a Master of Fusion," *The New York Times*, September 14, 2006.
8. Octavio Roca, "Dancers Fleeing Cuba Make Mark on Ballet Worldwide," *The Miami Herald*, March 2, 2004.
9. Jean-Paul Sartre, *Being and Nothingness*, trans. Hazel E. Barnes (New York: Philosophical Library, 1956), p. 420. *L'Etre et le néant* (Paris: Gallimard, 1943), 65.

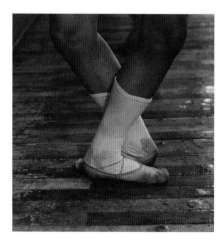

A dancer prepares—Havana, Miami, anywhere. Courtesy of Illume productions/ Candela, photo by Cynthia Newport.

10. Octavio Roca, "Latin Fire Spices up the Ballet," *San Francisco Chronicle*, January 27, 2002.

Alicia

1. The range of birthdates assigned to Alicia Alonso, née Martínez, is wide, from 1909 in Ferdinand Reynal, *Concise Encyclopedia of Ballet* (Chicago: Follett, 1967); to 1917 in Mary Clark, ed. *The Encyclopedia of Dance and Ballet* (New York: Putnam, 1977); to 1921 in Barbara Naomi Cohen-Stratyner, *Biographical Dictionary of Dance* (New York: Schirmer, 1982); and also by Walter Terry, *Alicia and her Ballet Nacional de Cuba* (New York: Doubleday, 1981) and Beatrice Siegel, *Alicia Alonso: The Story of a Ballerina* (New York: Warne, 1979). The official birthdate, accepted by most sources, is 1921; it dates from a typographical error in Alicia Alonso's 1936 passport.
2. Cristóbal Díaz Ayala, *La música en Cuba* (San Juan: Cubanacán, 1981), 118.
3. Vicente Blasco Ibáñez, "La vuelta al mundo de un novelista," *Obras Completas*, vol. III (Madrid: Aguilar, 1946), 370–371.
4. Carlos Márquez Sterling, *Historia de Cuba desde Cristóbal Colón a Fidel Castro* (Madrid: Las Américas, 1969), 426. Note that the Cuban peso was on the par with the U.S. dollar through 1959.
5. Ibid., 423.
6. The Presidential Decree No. 1963, written by Guiteras, limited the work day to eight hours; Decree No. 2142 guaranteed the independent meditation of labor disputes by the new Department of Labor (Secretaría del Trabajo); Decree No. 2605 guaranteed the right to form labor unions; Decree No. 2583, the Provisional Law for the Nationalization of Labor, protected native Cuban workers at a time when the work force was being inundated by cheap Spanish and Jamaican immigrant laborers; see Jorge Zayas, "Ramón Grau San Martín," *La enciclopedia de Cuba* (Madrid: Playor, 1975), 14: 42–92.
7. Miguel Cabrera, "Alicia Alonso: bodas de oro con la danza," *Bohemia* 74, no. 1 (January 1, 1982), 17.
8. Unsigned interview with Nikolai Yavorsky, *El Mundo* (November 26, 1932). The original is uncatalogued in archives of the Center for the Documentation and History of Dance, Havana.

9. Unpublished. Original in the collection of Laura Alonso, along with the citation and medal for the Order of Carlos Manuel de Céspedes.

Interlude: Before the Alonsos

1. Beatrice Siegel, *Alicia Alonso: The Story of a Ballerina* (New York: Warne, 1979), 14.
2. I am indebted here to the Pedro Simón, Francisco Rey Alfonso, and the Museo de la Danza in Havana for access to original archival materials on the colonial history of dance in Cuba.
3. Francisco Rey Alfonso, *Anna Pavlova en Cuba* (Havana: Ediciones Cuba en el Ballet, 1996), passim.
4. Walter Terry, *Alicia and her Ballet Nacional de Cuba* (New York: Doubleday, 1981), 5.

Ballet Nacional de Cuba: A New Company for a New World

1. Unsigned editorial, *Bohemia* (September 1956), as quoted by Lester Vila Pereira, "Un desagravio para la historia," *Cuba en el ballet*, no. 112 (September–December 2006).
2. Alicia Alonso, as quoted by Lester Vila Pereira Un desagravio para la historia," *Cuba en el ballet*, no. 112 (September – December, 2006).
3. Fernando Alonso, in Cynthia Newport, *Dance Cuba: Dreams of Flight* (New York: Illume Productions, 2004), motion picture.
4. Loinaz Dulce María, *Poemas escogidos*, ed. Pedro Simón (Madrid: Visor, 1993).
5. Octavio Roca, "Alicia's Choice," *The Miami Herald*, February 23, 2004. This interview has been reprinted widely including an electronic edition in www.alocubano.com/alicia _alonso.htm. The "Alicia Alonso Timeline" from this interview was reprinted electronically in www.latinamericanstudies.org.
6. Alicia Alonso interview with the author, partially published in Octavio Roca, "Cuba's Dancing Diplomat: Alonso at Spoleto," *The Washington Post*, June 1, 1980.
7. Alicia Alonso interview with the author, partially published in Octavio Roca, "Love Affair with Giselle: Legendary Cuban Ballerina has made it her Own," *San Francisco Chronicle*, February 7, 1999.
8. Pedro Simón, as quoted by José Luis Tapia, "Alicia Alonso con el Ballet Nacional de Cuba presentarán *Giselle* en Granada," *Granada Cultura*, September 14, 2009.

9. Octavio Roca, "Festival de Milagros," *Granma*, December 7, 1980.

10. Alicia Alonso as quoted by Octavio Roca, "Cuba's Dancing Diplomat: Alonso at Spoleto," *The Washington Post*, June 1, 1980.

11. Mariana Sanz, "Un duelo comienza," *Cubaencuentro*, February 9, 2007. This is typical of the bitter criticisms inside Cuba of Alonso's handling of the Ballet Nacional de Cuba in the waning days of Castro's regime. To view online see www.cubaencuentro.com.

Interlude: Theme and Variations

1. Alicia Alonso coaching excerpts from *Theme and Variations*, documentary film, © 1999 The George Balanchine Foundation. The film includes a lively Alicia Alonso interview with the critic Doris Hering, translated and excerpted in "Tema y Variaciones: un reto constante," *Cuba en el ballet*, January–April 2004; Alonso expanded on her original comments in her *Dialogos con la danza*, ed. Pedro Simón (Madrid: Editorial Complutense, 2000).

2. Walter Terry, "Balanchine Triumph," *New York Herald Tribune*, November 27, 1947; reprinted in Terry, *I Was There* (New York and Basel: Marcel Dekker, 1978).

3. Walter Terry, "Two Alicias and Two Dance Ways Enrich Ballet Theatre's Season," *New York Herald Tribune*, October 12, 1952; reprinted in Terry, *I Was There* (New York and Basel: Marcel Dekker, 1978).

4. Igor Yousekevitch, "The Male Image," *Dance Perspectives*, 40 (Winter, 1969).

5. Alicia Alonso, as quoted by Octavio Roca in "All the Best for ABT's Sixtieth Birthday," *San Francisco Chronicle*, May 10, 2000.

6. Octavio Roca, "Keepers of the Balanchine Flame," *San Francisco Chronicle*, November 3, 1996.

Cuca's Story and the Paris Incident

1. Fidel Castro, "Palabras a los intelectuales," in *Revolución, letras, arte* (Havana: Editorial Letras Cubanas, 1980). This unashamedly Stalinist speech, June 30, 1961, Fidel Castro gave before an invited audience of the Cuban intelligentsia across the arts and humanities in the Biblioteca Nacional José Martí effectively announced the end of the brief liberal period for the revolutionary Cuban Left and signaled the coming

suppression of any art that did not support the revolution and the punishment of any artist who did not fall in with the communist party line.

2. Lorenzo Monreal, as interviewed by Néstor Almendros and Orlando Jiménez-Leal, *Conducta Impropia* (Antenne 2-Films du Losange, 1984), motion picture. Script, outtakes, and supplementary materials reproduced in Néstor Almendros and Orlando Jiménez-Leal, *Conducta Impropia* (Madrid: Biblioteca Cubana Contemporanea, 1984), 121–131.

3. Ibid.

Lorena, Lorna, and the Feijóo Effect

1. Natalia Makarova, as quoted by Octavio Roca, "Russian Spirit Infuses La Bayadère," *San Francisco Chronicle*, March 5, 2000.

2. Octavio Roca, "Feijóo, Boada, Make Bayadère Even Better," *San Francisco Chronicle*, March 13, 2000.

3. Octavio Roca, "A Bittersweet *Don Quixote*: S.F. Ballet's Joyous Spectacle Overshadowed by Boada's Firing," *San Francisco Chronicle*, March 17, 2003.

4. Octavio Roca, "Dances That Have Aged Well," *San Francisco Chronicle*, February 5, 2000.

5. Lydia Martin, "Dancing Out from Under Alonso's Shadow," *The Miami Herald*, April 5, 2009.

6. Olga Connor, "Cuban Dancer Returns to 'Forbidden Territory,'" *The Miami Herald*, March 27, 2009.

7. Merrill Ashley as quoted by Suki John, "On Separate Coasts, a Sisterly Pas de Deux," *The New York Times*, October 9, 2005.

8. Anna Kisselgoff, "Two Guests Uncover a Different Side of Balanchine," *The New York Times*, May 15, 2004.

Interlude: Four Jewels, Three Graces, and a Rebel

1. Arnold Haskell, *Cuba en el Ballet*, festival issue, 1973.

2. Joel Carreño, as quoted by Erika Kinetz, "Alicia Alonso and the Ballet Nacional de Cuba," *The New York Times*, February 6, 2005.

3. Octavio Roca, "Alicia Alonso—Mesmerizing at 76," *San Francisco Chronicle*, May 13, 1995.

4. Anna Kisselgoff, "A Festival Presents a Legend," *The New York Times*, May 15, 1995.

All Those Cuban Men

1. Igor Yousekevitch, "The Male Image," *Dance Perspectives* 40 (Winter 1969).

2. Edward Villella, as quoted by Jordan Levin, "Ballet Star Dies—'Opened Doors' for a Generation" *The Miami Herald*, November 11, 2005.

3. Sir Anton Dolin, "Varna Diary," *Dance and Dancers* (September 1974).

4. Fernando Bujones and Zeida Cecilia Méndez, *Fernando Bujones: An Autobiography* (Doral: Higher Education Consultants, 2009).

5. Angel Corella, as quoted by Octavio Roca, "Angel Corella: American Ballet's New Star," *San Francisco Chronicle*, September 19, 2001.

6. Maina Gielgud, as quoted by Octavio Roca, "Exiled in Paradise: Young Cuban has dance world at his feet," *San Francisco Chronicle*, March 16, 1997.

7. Erika Kinetz, "The 'Cuban Nijinsky' Seeks Asylum and Stardom," *The New York Times*, August 31, 2005.

8. Victor Gilí, as quoted by Octavio Roca, "The World's a Stage for Cuban Ballet," *San Francisco Chronicle*, February 1, 1998.

9. Carlos Acosta, as quoted by Mary Greene, "In a taxi with Carlos Acosta," www.dailymail.co.uk, October 31, 2009.

10. Ibid.

11. Mary Ellen Hunt, "Latest Cuban Dancers to Defect: Update on Taras Domitro, Hayna Gutiérrez, Miguel Angel Blanco," *Dance Magazine*, January 2009.

Interlude: Giselle

1. Octavio Roca, "Love Affair With Giselle: Legendary Cuban Ballerina has Made it Her Own," *San Francisco Chronicle*, February 7, 1999.

2. Ibid.

3. Octavio Roca, "Giselle Triumphs with Love: Alicia Alonso's Production," *San Francisco Chronicle*, February 15, 1999. The article has a shorter version of this analysis of *Giselle*; for historic details of the *Giselle* tradition in Cuba before Alonso, see Francisco Rey Alfonso, *Anna Pavlova en Cuba* (Havana: Ediciones Cuba en el Ballet, 1996); and his *Grandes momentos del ballet romántico en Cuba* (Havana: Editorial Letras Cubanas, 2002); Rey and Pedro Simón, *Alicia Alonso: órbita de una leyenda* (Madrid: Sociedad

General de Autores y Editores, 1993), as well as Simón's own annotated pictorial document, *Alicia Alonso, Vladimir Vasiliev, and Giselle* (Havana: Editorial Arte y Literatura, 1981), which provides telling details of Alonso's mature *Giselle* production and performance practices.

4. Lorena Feijóo, interview with the author, 2009.

5. Lorna Feijóo, interview with the author, 2009.

6. Frederic Franklin, as quoted by Octavio Roca, "Frederic Franklin—Memory Does Serve Ballet Master," *San Francisco Chronicle*, August 26, 1998.

7. Octavio Roca, "Love at First Sight: Ballet Speaks to Each Audience Member," Deconstructing Criticism series, *San Francisco Chronicle*, August 26, 1998.

8. Ibid.

9. Antony Tudor, interview with the author, New York, 1980; quoted in part in "In Defense of Story Ballets," *San Francisco Chronicle*, March 12, 1995.

10. Matías Montes-Huidobro, *El teatro cubano en el vórtice del compromiso, 1959–1961* (Miami: Ediciones Universal, 2002); also see his *El teatro cubano durante la república: Cuba detras del telón* (Boulder: University of Colorado Society of Spanish and Spanish-American Studies, 2004). An invaluable piece of research by one of Cuba's foremost exiled theater artists that, along with its coda about theater in Havana during the early days of the Cuban Revolution, drawing a vivid portrait of the cultural context in which not only Cuban theater but, by extension, Cuban ballet arose. The book includes a useful chronology of Cuban theater in the twentieth century.

11. Glen Tetley, interview with the author, 1982.

12. Alicia Alonso, as quoted by Octavio Roca, "Cuba's Dancing Diplomat: Alonso at Spoleto," *The Washington Post*, June 1, 1980.

13. Fidel Castro, *La Revolución Cubana* (Mexico: Ediciones Era, 1972), a key collection of Castro's speeches and articles 1953–1962, including the infamous "*Palabras a los intelectuales.*"

14. Arturo Sandoval, interview with the author, Washington, 1991.

15. Fidel Castro, *Informe Central, Primer Congreso del Partido Comunista de Cuba* (Havana: Departamento de Orientación Revolucionaria, 1975), 125–126.

16. Alicia Alonso, as quoted by Octavio Roca, "Cuba's Dancing Diplomat: Alonso at Spoleto," *The Washington Post*, June 1, 1980.

17. Reinaldo Arenas, interview with the author, 1989. For a concise account of the UMAP concentration camps see Tomas Fernández Robaina, "Los homosexuales y la Revolución," Encuentro, no. 37–38 (Summer/Fall 2005), 286–292.

18. Alicia Alonso, as quoted by Octavio Roca, "Cuba's Dancing Diplomat: Alonso at Spoleto," *The Washington Post*, June 1, 1980.

19. Octavio Roca, "Love Affair with Giselle," *San Francisco Chronicle*, February 7, 1999.

20. Ibid.

21. Ibid. Alonso expanded on her own comments in *Diálogos con la danza* ed. Pedro Simón. (Madrid: Editorial Complutense, 1993).

22. Walter Terry confirmed this story with the author, and commented on it in his *Alicia and her Ballet Nacional de Cuba* (New York: Doubleday Anchor Original, 1980). Sir Anton Dolin claimed he taught Alonso the role in two days before the unexpected debut, while admitting that Tudor's coaching had prepared her; he also confirmed that Alicia Markova tried to sabotage Alonso's performance by giving her a headdress to wear in the beginning of Act Two with protruding pins that would have caused her to fall back when it was whisked off at Giselle's grave (it was Alicia Alonso's mother Ernestina, always watchful, who kept her daughter from wearing the gift). Dolin confirmed this story in an interview with the author in Havana, 1980. Alonso herself took the credit for her *Giselle* creation in interviews with the author in Havana, 1980, and subsequently.

23. Maurice Béjart, undated 1970 letter to Alicia Alonso, now in the collection of the Museo Nacional de la Danza, Havana. Béjart disarmingly goes on to say, "I am not a critic and much less a writer . . . Why could I not create a ballet to translate these powerful emotions her *Giselle* awakened in me? The ballerina is extraordinary, the character nothing less. Tonight *Giselle*, tomorrow *Carmen*, the day after tomorrow . . . dancing the Cuban Revolution."

24. Pedro Simón, *Alicia Alonso, Vladimir Vasiliev, and Giselle* (Havana: Editorial Arte y Literatura, 1981) with minimal commentary, provides a detailed photographic record of the historic occasion; *Giselle: la leyenda* (Madrid: Factoria DVD) documents the key scenes in the Alonso-Vasiliev partnership in Havana. Also see Octavio Roca, "Festival de Milagros," *Granma*, December 7, 1980.

25. Roca, "Festival de Milagros" *Granma*.

26. Alicia Alonso, "El ballet romántico," in *La era romántica* (Barcelona and Mexico: Ediciones Festival Internacional Cervantino-Salvat, 1981).

Dancing with a Cuban Accent

1. Merce Cunningham, as quoted by Judith Mackrell, "Who Will Protect the Legacies of Pina Bausch and Merce Cunningham?", *The Guardian*, August 5, 2009.

2. Cynthia Newport, *Dance Cuba: Dreams of Flight* (New York: Illume Productions, 2004), motion picture.

3. Mariana Sanz, "*Un duelo comienza,*" Asociación Encuentro de la Cultura Cubana, www.cubancuentro.com, Havana, February 9, 2007.

4. Jean-Paul Sartre, *L'Être et le néant*, (Paris: Gallimard, 1943), 65.

5. G. F. W. Hegel, *Aesthetics: Lectures on Fine Art* (Oxford: Oxford University Press, 1988), 1: 14.

6. Sartre, *L'Être et le néant*, (Paris: Gallimard, 1943), 61.

7. Octavio Roca, "Dancers Fleeing Cuba Make Mark on Ballet Worldwide," *The Seattle Times*, March 2, 2004.

8. Agnes de Mille, *Gallery Portraits* (Boston: Houghton Mifflin, 1990), 91.

9. Heberto Padilla, "En tiempos difíciles," in José Lezama Lima's *Antología de la poesía cubana*, vol. 4, ed. Angel Esteban and Alvaro Salvador (Madrid: Verbum Mayor, 2002), 206–207.